MOSTLY
SHAKER

from
The New Yankee
Workshop

Norm Abram
with David Sloan

MOSTLY SHAKER

from

The New Yankee Workshop

Little, Brown and Company

Boston   Toronto   London

To the Shaker craftsmen of the past, who left behind a woodworking tradition that I aspire to, and to all those who are dedicated to preserving and displaying their masterpieces to inspire and appreciate.

Copyright © 1992 by WGBH Educational Foundation, Norm Abram, and Russell Morash

FIRST EDITION

Illustrations: John Murphy
Photographs: Richard Howard

LIBRARY OF CONGRESS CATALOGING-IN-PUBLICATION DATA

Abram, Norm.
    Mostly shaker from the New Yankee workshop / Norm Abram with David Sloan.
        p.   cm.
    Includes index.
    ISBN 0-316-00473-1.—ISBN 0-316-00475-8 (pbk.)
    1. Furniture making. I. Sloan, David. II. Title.
TT197.A26   1992
684.1′04—dc20   91-39604

10 9 8 7 6 5 4 3 2 1

RRD-OH

Published simultaneously in Canada by Little, Brown & Company (Canada) Limited

PRINTED IN THE UNITED STATES OF AMERICA

Contents

Acknowledgments

THIS book is the result of the combined efforts of many people, and I want to express my sincere appreciation to everyone who's had a hand in the undertaking. Russell Morash's ingenuity and vision conceived *The New Yankee Workshop* and continue to move it forward. The support of David Liroff, station manager at WGBH Educational Foundation, has made it a reality. Coordinating producer Nina Sing Fialkow provided invaluable help with the research of the projects and kept the show's production on schedule.

Working from the project videos, illustrations, photographs, and our telephone conversations, David Sloan transformed each woodworking project into sensible prose. Photographer Richard Howard provided crystal clear photographs of the woodworking techniques used to construct each piece and, with the help of Derek Diggins, provided beautiful chapter openers illustrating the end results. John Murphy rendered the fine drawings from my crude sketches showing the details of each project. David Dann produced the drawings for the Corner Cupboard's construction details. Marian Morash kept the finances in proper order and our attitude positive. At Little, Brown and Company, William D. Phillips has believed in our projects and stood by us every step of the way. Christina Ward kept all the elements and participants on the right track. David Coen's assiduous eye for detail, Mary Reilly's and Barbara Werden's design sense, and the formidable efforts of Ellen Bedell and Donna Peterson have shaped both the process and the end result of the book's editing and production. Our literary agent, Don Cutler, has bolstered the spirit and substance of the endeavor from first to last.

Abiding thanks go to our series underwriters, the Parks Corporation, Vermont American Tool Company, and Ace Hardware Corporation. Their financial support continues to make the series possible.

Finally, *The New Yankee Workshop* owes its very inspiration to the dedicated craftsmen of the past whose work stands as a testament to their designs and techniques. Special thanks go to the helpful curators, directors, and staffs of Fruitlands Museums, Harvard, Massachusetts, whose beautifully preserved buildings and pristine landscape provide the backdrop for the fabulous chapter openers; Hancock Shaker Village, Pittsfield, Massachusetts; The Shaker Museum, Old Chatham, New York; The Shaker Village of Pleasant Hill, Harrodsburg, Kentucky; Antiques Orchard, Westford, Massachusetts; Wirthmore Antiques, New Orleans, Louisiana; Old Sturbridge Village in Sturbridge, Massachusetts; and to Susan and David Fine, for their private collection of antiques.

MOSTLY SHAKER

from
The New Yankee
Workshop

Introduction

Do all your work as if you were going to die tomorrow . . . and yet as though you were to live for a hundred years.

MOTHER ANN,
founder of the Shakers

THIS is a book about building practical furniture — Shaker furniture, mostly, plus a few other pieces in the Shaker tradition. Some woodworkers like to build high-style furniture. I'm not one of them. While I certainly enjoy looking at the great designs of cabinetmakers like Chippendale, Hepplewhite, Duncan Phyfe, and others, fancy furniture isn't my style. I prefer to build furniture I can really *use* in my home — pieces that are attractive and functional for the way I live. Shaker furniture fits right in.

Spirit, Function, and Form

" 'Tis a gift to be simple," go the lyrics of an old Shaker hymn. Of all the words you could come up with to describe the furniture built by the Shakers, perhaps "simple" comes closest to capturing the spirit in which it was made. "Simple" was the Shaker way. "Simple" was how they would think of their work.

The golden age of Shaker furniture lasted roughly fifty years, from the 1820s to the 1870s, although Shakers were making furniture both before and after that period. Shakers at New Lebanon, New York (known today as Mount Lebanon), were making chairs as early as 1789 and as late as the 1930s. But the best of Shaker furniture — the pieces we consider classics today — were built in the decades before the Civil War.

What is it about this plain, practical furniture that makes it so popular today? What drives collectors to pay more than $150,000 for a tall chest of drawers? What's so special about Shaker?

Shaker furniture embodies the values of the craftsmen who made it — spiritual people who saw work as an aspect of worship. They put a little bit of their soul into everything they made. Even utilitarian wooden objects like shovels, spoons, and boxes have a subtle,

PLAY IT SAFE

Woodworking is inherently dangerous. Failure to follow commonsense safety procedures can result in serious injury. Here are some simple, but important, rules for safe and sensible woodworking.

- Read, understand, and follow all the safety instructions that come with the tools you buy.

- Be alert and aware. Stop working if you're fatigued or distracted, and *never* use alcohol or other mind-altering substances when working in the shop.

- Protect your eyes and ears. Always wear safety glasses or goggles. Wear earmuffs or earplugs to protect your hearing from permanent damage by loud machinery.

- Secure your clothing. Roll up your sleeves, remove any jewelry, and make sure your shoelaces are securely tied.

- Use a push stick when feeding small pieces of stock through a table saw, jointer, or other machine.

- Keep dust levels under control by using dust-collection bags on tools and periodically cleaning your workshop. Wear a dust mask when doing extended sanding.

- Light your work area well. Good lighting is essential to safe work. Lights and power tools should run on separate circuits so a blown fuse won't leave you in the dark with a still-spinning power tool.

- Keep your shop clean. Always clean the shop at the end of the day so that you'll return to a clean workshop.

- Normalize the work area after each step of the project is completed. Clean up the clutter and put away everything that isn't needed for the next step of the project.

- Put power tools away correctly. Unplug the cord and wind it carefully.

- Never use a tool station, such as a table saw, as a workbench or a piece of furniture.

- Clamp or secure the piece you're working on. Don't take shortcuts.

- Don't make a tool do a job it's not meant to do.

- Keep your tools sharp. A sharp tool will prevent you from "forcing" the tool to do the work.

- Ventilate your finishing area. Solvent fumes are toxic and flammable. Ensure adequate ventilation and wear a respirator mask if you spray on your finishes.

- Eliminate fire hazards. Don't use or store flammable solvents around pilot lights, heaters, or any other source of a spark or flame that could ignite the vapors. Remove oily finishing rags from the shop immediately after use — they can ignite by spontaneous combustion.

quiet beauty about them — a beauty that is rooted in the function of the piece. Jennie Wells, a Shaker Sister interviewed in 1947, said it better than I ever could. "We're always being told how beautiful our things are. I don't say they aren't, but that isn't what they were meant to be. . . . All our furniture was ever meant to be was strong, light, and, above all, practical."

Whether it was meant to be beautiful or not, there's no denying that Shaker furniture is handsome. The craftsmen who built it had a knack for making things look just right. The proportions are perfect. Alter one or two dimensions and it changes the feel of a piece. Shaker furniture-makers also knew how to get maximum strength from a minimum amount of materials — a Shaker rocker is an engineering marvel.

Traditional Designs, Modern Technology

While the furniture designs in this book are traditional, many of the tools, techniques, and materials that I use are not. Craftsmen have always worked with the best technology of their day, mothballing old-fashioned tools when a better, faster method came along. Today, we're lucky enough to have power tools that allow us to machine wood without breaking a sweat. It would take me an entire week to accomplish with hand tools the work I can do in a single day with power tools. In fact, if routers, biscuit joiners, and random orbit sanders had appeared magically in the mid-1800s, I'll bet the Shaker furniture-makers would have welcomed them.

The Shakers were great technical innovators. They invented all sorts of labor-saving devices to make backbreaking chores a little more pleasant. They designed wooden washing machines to handle the mountains of laundry they faced every week. Shaker inventors also designed and patented several woodworking machines, including a thickness planer. Even the circular saw blade — a tool that revolutionized woodworking — is said to have been invented by a Shaker Sister in the early 1800s.

Plywood revolutionized woodworking in much the same way that power tools did. Old-time furniture-makers often used a secondary grade of pine or poplar to make cabinet backs, chest bottoms, and other furniture parts that wouldn't show. These "secondary woods" were less expensive than the high-grade hardwood from which the rest of a piece was made.

Today, any wood is a precious resource, and even low-grade pine and poplar are expensive. Instead of using solid wood, I often choose plywood as a secondary wood in my furniture. Plywood is a convenient, ecologically responsible, and dimensionally stable material. I use it mostly for making drawer bottoms, cabinet backs, interior shelves, and the like. For me, a plywood back on a solid-wood cabinet doesn't take away from the beauty of the piece. In fact, it ties in with the New Yankee Workshop philosophy of building things in the most practical, cost-effective way.

A Springboard for Ideas

Woodworking magazines and books aren't the only source of furniture-project ideas. There's a lot to be learned from just looking at furniture anyplace you can find it. Ideas can come from just walking around a museum or antique store. In fact, that's how I get most of my project ideas for the New Yankee Workshop.

Studying, measuring, and building the best furniture of the past has taught me a lot. I have a better eye for proportion, a better knowledge of joinery, a better feel for the way a piece goes together. It's made me a better craftsman and helped me in all my work.

I hope that you'll enjoy building the furniture projects in this book. But more than that, I hope that these projects will inspire you to do a little exploring on your own.

ONE

Shaker Step Stools

T HESE step stools are inspired by original stools that I found at Hancock Shaker Village, in western Massachusetts. The Shakers, firm believers in the virtues of neatness and order, stored many of their belongings in built-in storage units. Some of the units were very tall, and the Shakers relied on step stools like these to gain access to the highest drawers and cupboards. Step stools were common in every Shaker community and they were made in many different sizes and styles.

The pair of step stools I built are similar in size but they differ in design. The 3-step stool (*drawing 1-A*) is the easier of the stools to build. It's made of pine, as were many of the original step stools I examined, and the treads are simply nailed across the 2 sidepieces. The 3 front crosspieces, one under each tread, are joined to the sidepieces with half-dovetails that are very simple to cut. There are 2 additional crosspieces in the back of the stool. One crosspiece fits in 2 dadoes near the bottom of the stool. The other fits into rabbets cut at the top of each side.

The 2-step stool is made of cherry and modeled after an original in the "waiting room," or "gathering room," at Hancock Shaker Village. It's a little more complicated to make because the treads are joined to the sides with through dovetails instead of nails. The Shakers cut their dovetails by hand. You can still cut them by hand today if you like, but I prefer the speed and the accuracy of a dovetailing jig and a router. The 2-step version has 2 front crosspieces in front of the treads and a single back crosspiece that connects the 2 sidepieces near the bottom.

The procedure for making each stool is a little different, so I'll deal with them separately, one at a time. Let's start with the 3-step stool.

3-STEP STOOL
Time: 2 days
Special hardware and tools: None
Wood: (1) 14-ft 1 × 8 select pine
Cut two 26-in. lengths and two 18-in. lengths and edge glue one long and one short piece to make each side panel.

Cut remaining wood into 4 pieces 19 in. long. Rip two 19-in. pieces into one piece 4½ in. × 19 in. and one piece 1⅝ in. × 19 in. for 2 bottom treads and 2 crosspieces.

Rip one 19-in. piece into one piece 5⅜ in. × 19 in. and one piece 1⅝ in. × 19 in. for top tread and crosspiece.

Rip and joint remaining 19-in. piece into 2 pieces 1½ in. × 19 in. for rear crosspieces.

2-STEP STOOL
Time: 2 days
Special hardware and tools: Dovetailing jig capable of cutting through dovetails
Wood: (1) 12-ft 1 × 8 cherry
Cut two 26-in. lengths. Rip and joint 5⅝ in. wide for rear sidepieces.

Cut two 14-in. lengths. Rip and joint 6 in. wide for front sidepieces.

Cut one 17-in. length. Rip and joint 5¼ in. wide for top step.

Cut one 17-in. length. Rip and joint 6⅛ in. wide for lower step.

Cut one 17-in. length. Rip and joint into 3 pieces 1¾ in. wide for crosspieces. Rip 2 of the 3 pieces 3/8 in. thick for front crosspieces.

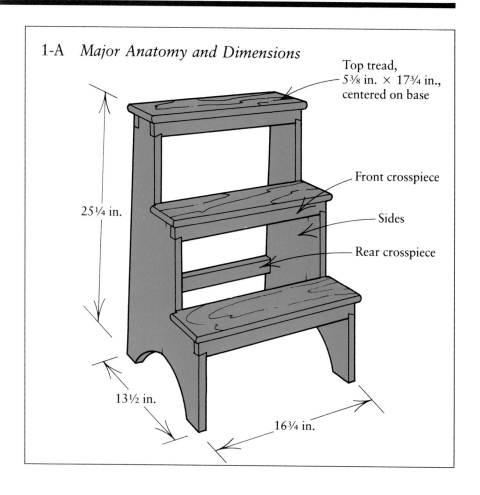

1-A *Major Anatomy and Dimensions*

Top tread,
5⅜ in. × 17¾ in.,
centered on base

Front crosspiece

Sides

Rear crosspiece

25¼ in.

13½ in.

16¾ in.

1-1   After gluing up the side panel, I joint the long edge straight and square.

MAKING THE 3-STEP STOOL

Gluing Up the Sides

The first step is to glue up the 2 side panels. From a 14-ft 1 × 8 I cut 2 pieces 26 in. long and 2 pieces 18 in. long to make the side panels (see Project Planner). I edge glue one 26-in. piece and one 18-in. piece together to make each side panel, holding the ends even at the bottom of the panel. To reinforce the joint, and to keep the boards from shifting when I put on the clamps, I cut slots with my biscuit joiner and glue in three #20 biscuits along the joint as shown in drawing 1-B. The biscuits are optional. An edge joint like this one, long grain glued to long grain, is strong enough without the biscuits.

Later on, after the glue is dry, I remove the clamps and scrape off the dried glue with a scraper. If the boards have shifted slightly, leaving a "step" at the joint, the scraper can true up any misalignment in the joint. I flatten and smooth the panels with a belt sander after scraping and give both sides of each panel a finish sanding with my random orbit sander.

When the panels are flat and smooth, I joint the long edge of each panel on the jointer (*photo 1-1*). Once this edge is straight and square, I square up the bottom of each side panel by trimming it on

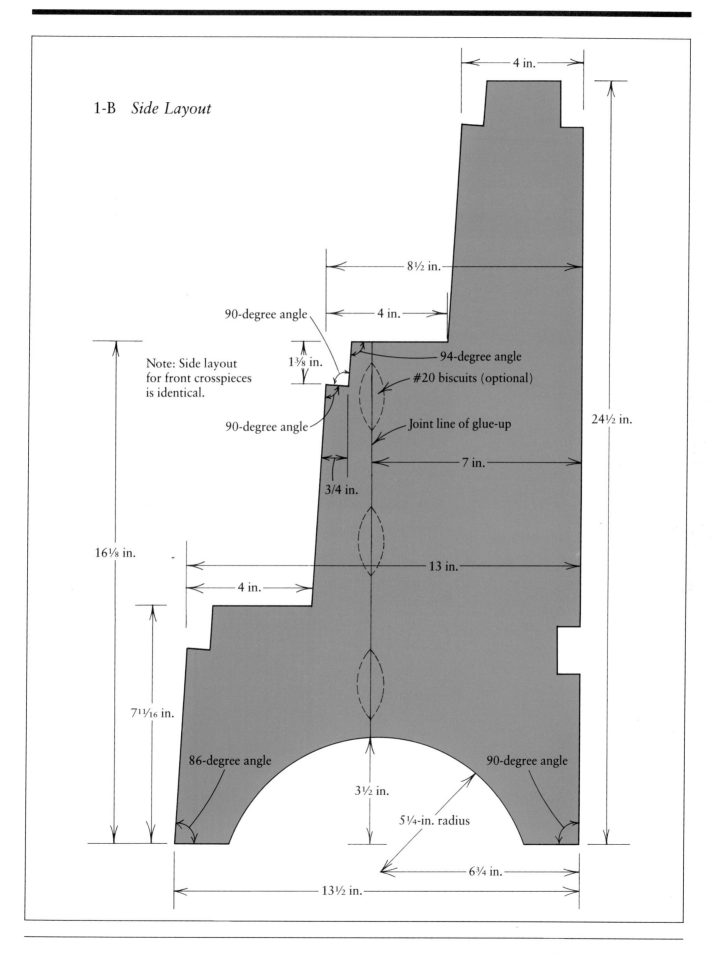

1-B *Side Layout*

4 in.

8½ in.

4 in.

90-degree angle

Note: Side layout
for front crosspieces
is identical.

1⅜ in.

94-degree angle

#20 biscuits (optional)

90-degree angle

Joint line of glue-up

24½ in.

7 in.

3/4 in.

16⅛ in.

13 in.

4 in.

7¹¹⁄₁₆ in.

86-degree angle

90-degree angle

3½ in.

5¼-in. radius

6¾ in.

13½ in.

1-2 I make a wooden gauge block as wide as the distance from the blade to the edge of the saw base.

1-3 To position the straightedge clamp, I place the gauge block on the layout line, slide the clamp up against the block, and tighten the clamp.

1-4 To make the cut, I guide the saw base against the clamp. The blade cuts right on the line. The cut stops at the riser line.

the table saw with my homemade panel cutter, making sure to keep the jointed edge against the panel cutter's fence.

Next, I measure 24½ in. up from the bottom of the panel to mark the finished height of the sidepiece and cut off the excess with the panel cutter and table saw (*drawing 1-B*). Both side panels get the same treatment.

Laying Out the Tread Cuts and Riser Cuts

As shown in drawing 1-B, the risers of the step stool are not equal in height. The distance from the floor to the first step is less than the distance between the first and second and the second and third steps to account for the thickness of the treads. The risers tilt backward slightly, making the step stool a little more comfortable to climb.

I find that it's easiest to lay out the tread cuts first. I measure up 7¹¹⁄₁₆ in. from the bottom and use my square and a pencil to draw a line across the width of the panel. Then I measure 16⅛ in. up from the bottom to mark the second tread cut. When marking these lines, I position the square against the long back edge of the panel — the edge that I jointed earlier.

To lay out the risers I measure from the back edge of the panel across the width of the stock to mark off the points where each riser and tread meet. Then I draw in the risers by connecting these points with a straightedge. The other side panel gets the same treatment but the layout lines are a mirror image of the first side panel. Finally, I lay out the rabbets and dadoes for the crosspieces. At this point I have the 2 side blanks with all the layout lines drawn in.

If you're really good with a handsaw it's possible to make the tread cuts by hand, but I like the accuracy of my circular saw and a straightedge clamp. I clamp the straightedge clamp across the work and guide the base of the saw against it to make a clean, straight cut.

The clamp must be offset from the cutline by a distance equal to the distance measured from the side of the blade to the edge of the saw's base. I could measure and mark this distance for each cut, but because I use this technique frequently, I've made a wooden gauge block that's as wide as the distance from the blade to the edge of the saw base (*photo 1-2*).

I take the gauge block, place it on the layout line, slide the clamp up against the block, and tighten the clamp (*photo 1-3*). Now I make the cut, guiding the saw base against the clamp and stopping the cut at the riser line (*photo 1-4*). The blade cuts right on the line. I repeat this procedure for the other tread cuts. To make the tread cuts on the other side of the stool I had to make a narrower gauge block to accommodate the narrow side of the saw base (*photo 1-5*).

To make the rip cuts for the risers, I use the same gauge blocks, straightedge clamp, and my circular saw (*photo 1-6*). My 10-point crosscut saw does a good job of finishing up the corners where the tread and riser cuts meet.

Notching for the Crosspieces

As I mentioned before, the front crosspieces join the sides with half-dovetails that fit into dovetailed rabbets. First, I make the rip cuts, for the thickness of the crosspieces, with my jigsaw. For a nice, straight cut, I hold the base of the saw between my thumb and the knuckle of my index finger and run my knuckle up against the edge of the stock to guide the blade (*photo 1-7*).

To lay out the angled crosscut that locks in the dovetail, I set my sliding bevel to 10 degrees and draw a pencil line as shown in drawing 1-C. I use my dovetailing saw to make the cut. I clamp the side-piece horizontally in a vise and hold my thumb against the saw to guide it as I cut straight down (*photo 1-8*).

1-5 To make the tread cuts on the opposite side of the stool, I guide the narrow side of the saw base against the clamp. I made a narrower gauge block to position the clamp.

1-6 I make the rip cuts for the risers with the same gauge blocks and straightedge clamp. The clamp must be angled to cut the risers.

1-7 I start the crosspiece rabbets with a jigsaw. For a straight cut, I like to hold the base between my thumb and knuckle and run my knuckle against the side of the stock to guide the blade.

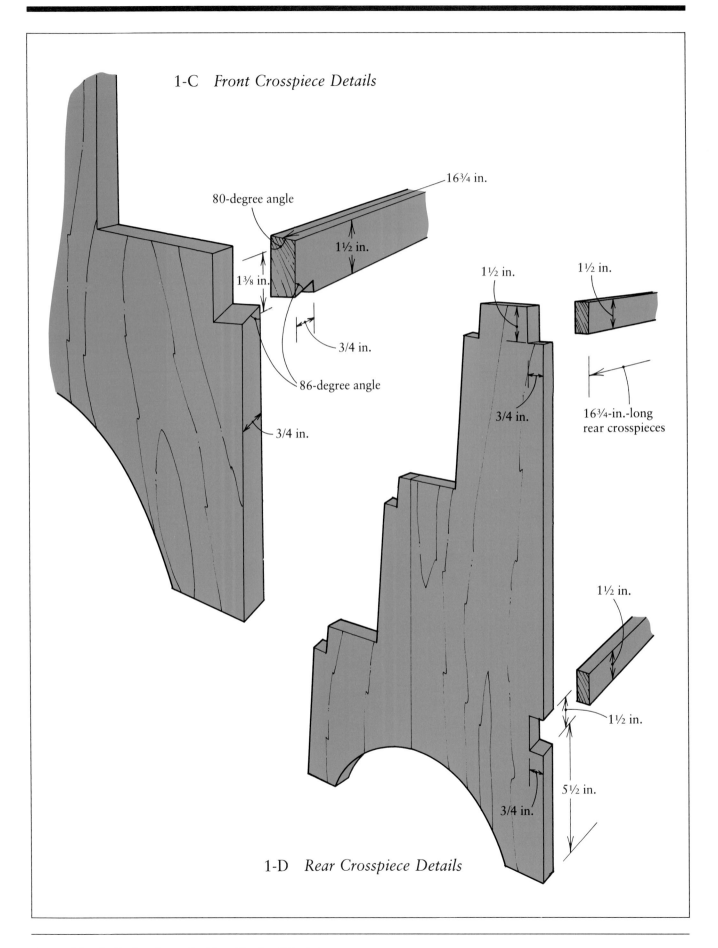

1-C *Front Crosspiece Details*

16¾ in.

80-degree angle

1½ in.

1⅜ in.

3/4 in.

86-degree angle

3/4 in.

1½ in.

1½ in.

3/4 in.

16¾-in.-long
rear crosspieces

1½ in.

1½ in.

5½ in.

3/4 in.

1-D *Rear Crosspiece Details*

The bottom back crosspiece sits in dadoes cut in the sides (*drawing 1-D*). I run the base of my jigsaw against a square to make the 2 crosscuts for each dado (*photo 1-9*). Then I cut out the waste in between. The top crosspiece fits in the rabbets, and I cut these with the jigsaw as well.

Cutting the Arch

The sides of the stool have a cutout so the stool can sit on an uneven floor more easily. The height at the top of the arch is 3½ in., but the radius of the arch is 5¼ in. (*drawing 1-B*). First I lay out a centerline on the bottom of each side. Then I set my compass to 5¼ in. and butt the 2 sides bottom to bottom so I have a pivot point to place my compass. I lay out the arch on one side, then reverse the compass to lay out the arch on the other side (*photo 1-10*). I cut out the arches with my jigsaw and sand the cut smooth with a drum sander on my drill press (*photo 1-11*).

1-8 I use my dovetailing saw to cut the angled crosscut that locks in the crosspiece dovetail.

1-9 To cut straight sides for the crosspiece dadoes, I guide my jigsaw against a square

1-10 To lay out the arches at the bottom of the stool, I butt the stool sides together and pivot the compass on one side as I lay out the arch on the other piece. I simply reverse the compass to draw the arch on the other sidepiece.

1-11 To sand the arches smooth I use a drum sander on my drill press. So the entire edge can be sanded, I put a board under the workpiece to raise it off the drill-press table.

Roughing Out the Treads and Crosspieces

Now that I've finished the sides of the stool, I'm ready to make the 5 crosspieces. I crosscut the remainder of the 14-ft 1 × 8 into 4 pieces 19 in. long. I rip those 19-in. lengths as specified in the Project Planner, to rough cut the 3 treads and 5 crosspieces.

Finishing and Fitting the Crosspieces

I set my jointer for a very light cut and joint one edge of each crosspiece. Now I can square up one end of each crosspiece with my miter box. Measuring from the squared end, I mark off 16¾ in. and cut the 5 crosspieces to length. It's important to get all 5 crosspieces exactly the same length.

Now I'm ready to do the final fitting of the crosspieces. I use a square, a pencil, and a sliding bevel to lay out the half-dovetails on the ends of the front crosspieces (*drawing 1-C*). First, I measure 3/4 in. in from the end of the crosspiece and, with my square, draw a line on the front, back, and bottom of the crosspiece. I set my sliding bevel to 80 degrees and lay out the angle of the tail. Then I square a line across the end.

To cut the half-dovetails, I clamp all 3 front crosspieces vertically in the vise. I make the angled cut with my dovetailing saw, being careful not to cut below the shoulder line I marked on the front and back of the crosspiece (*photo 1-12*). After this I flip the crosspieces end for end and make the angled cuts on the other ends. The next step is to clamp each crosspiece horizontally in the vise and make the shoulder cut to finish the joint (*photo 1-13*).

Now it's time for a little assembly. I put the 2 back crosspieces on first, starting with the one at the bottom. With a brush, I put a little glue in the dadoes, line up the ends of the crosspieces flush with the sides, and fasten each crosspiece with two 4d finish nails. Now I do the same thing for the top crosspiece.

1-12 I lay out the angled tails for the crosspiece dovetails with my bevel gauge and make the cuts with a dovetailing saw. It's important not to cut below the shoulder line.

1-13 I finish the tails by making the shoulder cut, taking care not to cut below the layout lines on front and back.

Because of the backward slant of the risers, the top edges of the 3 front crosspieces need to be angled slightly so the treads can sit flush on the crosspieces. To cut this angle, I tilt the fence on my jointer about 4 degrees and joint the top edge of each crosspiece, keeping the front face against the fence (*photo 1-14*). To test that I have the angle correct, and that the crosspiece is flush with the tread cut, I place the crosspiece in position and lay the blade of a square across the tread and the crosspiece.

When everything fits, it's time for some glue and nails. I brush a little glue on the dovetails and position the crosspieces in place. Two 4d finish nails in each end puts things together for keeps. When the glue is dry, I finish sand the sides and crosspieces with my random orbit sander.

Completing the Treads

After cutting the tread pieces to a finished length of 17¾ in., I round over the edges on the router table (*photo 1-15*). On the bottom treads, only the front edge and the ends are rounded. All 4 edges are rounded on the top tread.

To safely support the stock during the end-grain cuts, I've mounted an auxiliary fence to the regular fence of my router table. This fence is simply a sheet of 3/4-in. plywood with an opening just slightly larger than the diameter of the router bit. I leave this plywood fence on my router table most of the time.

For rounding the treads, I use a 1/2-in. roundover bit in my router table. I adjust the bit to extend about 3/8 in. above the table surface so it cuts a bullnose profile (*drawing 1-E*). I cut a few test pieces and raise or lower the bit until I get the profile I want.

To minimize tearout at the corners, I rout the end grain first, then round over the long edges. As always, it's important to feed the stock from right to left, against the rotation of the bit. Both the top and

1-14 The top edges of the front crosspieces must be angled for the treads to fit. To cut this angle, I tilt the jointer fence 4 degrees and joint the crosspiece. The top edge goes down on the table and the front face of the crosspiece faces the fence.

1-15 With a 1/2-in. roundover bit, I round over the edges of the treads on the router table. I always feed the stock from right to left, against the rotation of the bit.

1-E *Middle and Lower Tread End Detail*

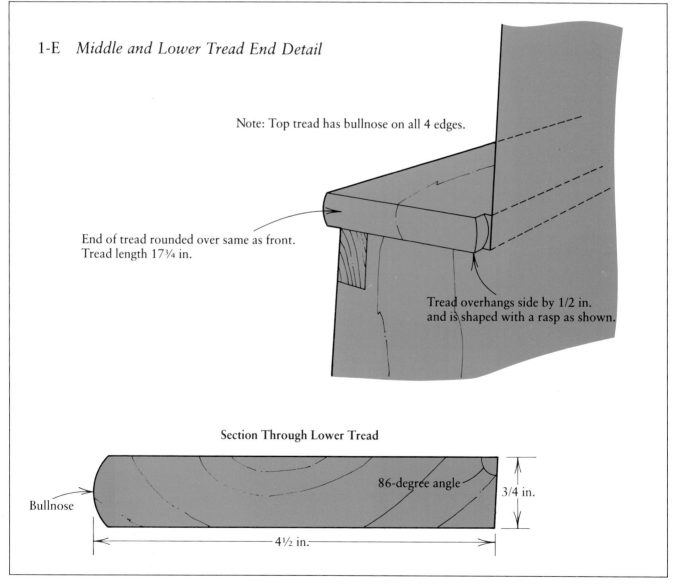

Note: Top tread has bullnose on all 4 edges.

End of tread rounded over same as front.
Tread length 17¾ in.

Tread overhangs side by 1/2 in.
and is shaped with a rasp as shown.

Section Through Lower Tread

Bullnose

86-degree angle

3/4 in.

4½ in.

1-16 I tilt the jointer fence 4 degrees and bevel the back edges of the 2 lower treads to fit against the angled risers.

1-17 To give the treads a neater look, I round over the back corners of the lower treads with a rasp.

bottom edges get rounded, and I smooth up the edges with a pad sander after routing.

Before I can install the 2 bottom treads, I have to bevel the back edges so they fit flush against the risers (*drawing 1-E*). For this, I use the jointer again, with the fence set to give me a 4-degree angle (*photo 1-16*).

I clean up the sides of the step stool with my random orbit sander. It's also easier to sand the treads before they're installed. When everything's smooth, I fasten the treads with 4d finish nails and glue.

The last detail is to round over the back corners of the 2 bottom treads with a rasp (*drawing 1-E, photo 1-17*). A final inspection, some touch-up sanding, and the step stool is ready for paint.

Painting and Puttying

The step stool in the photo is painted brick red. First, I apply a coat of latex primer. When the primer is dry, I sand the piece lightly with 220-grit sandpaper and fill the nail holes with a bit of glazing compound. Glazing compound is great for this use because it won't dry up and fall out of the hole. Two coats of acrylic latex paint, with a light sanding between coats, and the step stool is finished.

THE 2-STEP STOOL

I made the 2-step stool from 3/4-in.-thick cherry. At my hardwood outlet, I bought one 12-ft length of 1×8 cherry.

The treads of the stool are joined to the sides with through dovetails that I cut with a router and a dovetailing jig. Only a few dovetailing jigs are capable of cutting through dovetails. Most jigs cut only half-blind dovetails — the kind you find on the sides of

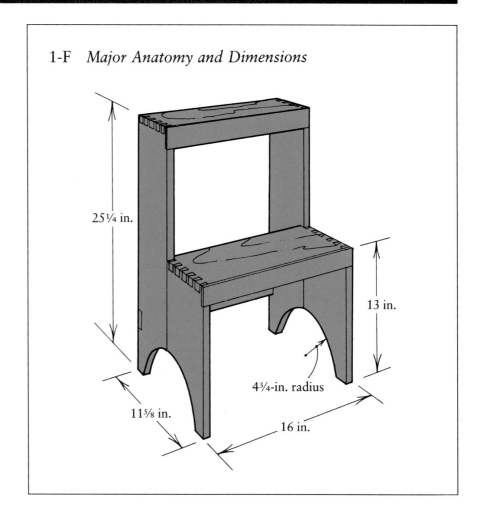

1-F Major Anatomy and Dimensions

25¼ in.

13 in.

4¾-in. radius

11⅝ in.

16 in.

drawers. My jig cuts through dovetails as well as half-blind dovetails, and allows me to vary the spacing of the pins and the tails.

Each side of the step stool is glued up from 2 boards, as shown in drawings 1-F and 1-G, with the joint line right at the riser. If I were cutting the dovetails by hand, I'd glue up the panels first and cut the dovetails afterward. But the design of my dovetailing jig requires me to cut the dovetails on each board separately before I glue the sides together.

Preparing the Stock

I start by dimensioning the stock for the sides, treads, and cross-pieces. After cutting the pieces to rough length, I rip and joint both edges to the dimensions shown in the Project Planner. Next, I square one end of each piece and cut it to final length as shown in drawings 1-F and 1-G.

Milling the Dovetails

Drawing 1-G shows the dimensions I used for the dovetail pins and tails. The pins are the same size on both steps, but the pins are spaced closer together for the top step. Note that the tails on the bot-

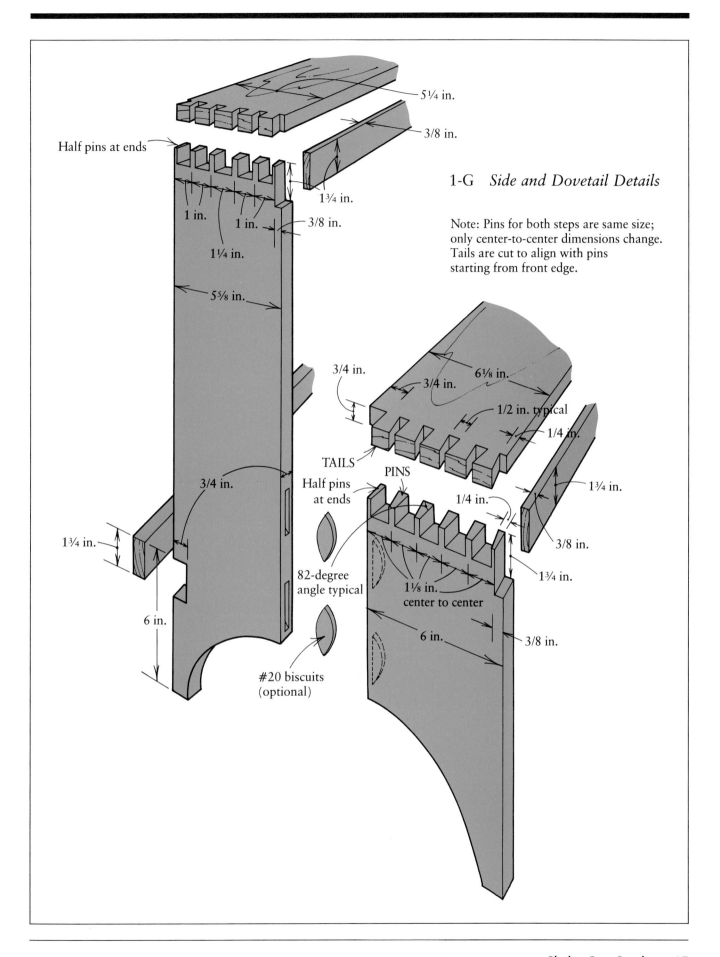

5¼ in.

3/8 in.

Half pins at ends

1 in. 1 in. 3/8 in.

1¾ in.

1¼ in.

5⅝ in.

3/4 in.

1¾ in.

6 in.

82-degree angle typical

#20 biscuits (optional)

1-G *Side and Dovetail Details*

Note: Pins for both steps are same size; only center-to-center dimensions change. Tails are cut to align with pins starting from front edge.

3/4 in.

3/4 in. 6⅛ in.

1/2 in. typical

1/4 in.

TAILS

PINS

Half pins at ends

1/4 in.

1¾ in.

3/8 in.

1¾ in.

1⅛ in. center to center

6 in.

3/8 in.

1-18 The through dovetails for the cherry step stool are easy to cut with a dovetailing jig and router. The tails on the treads are offset to the front. This offset (at right corner here) forms a rabbet at the back corner of the tread.

1-19 I switch to a straight bit to cut the matching pins in the sides of the stool.

tom tread are offset toward the front. When the joint is assembled, this offset creates a 1/2-in. rabbet at each back corner of the tread so the tread can fit between the 2 sidepieces (*drawing 1-G*).

Every manufacturer's dovetailing jig is different, so I won't go into detail about how I set up and adjust my jig, but I set up the jig to cut the tails on the bottom tread first, with a dovetail bit in my router (*photo 1-18*). Then I switch to a straight bit and cut the matching pins on the short sidepieces (*photo 1-19*). Next, I readjust the jig to get a narrower pin spacing. Then I reinsert the dovetail bit and cut the tails on the ends of the top tread. A quick switch to a straight bit, and I finish up by cutting the pins on the long sidepieces.

Notching for the Crosspieces

With the dovetails out of the way, there are a couple more cuts I have to make — the dadoes for the back crosspiece and the rabbets for the front crosspieces (*drawing 1-G*). I do this on the table saw with a regular saw blade. A dado head would be quicker, but it would take time to set up. Since there are only a few cuts, the saw blade works just as well.

First I lay out the dadoes and rabbets with a square. Then, to cut the rabbets in the front of the stool, I raise the blade height to 3/8 in., making some test cuts in scrap to get the height correct. With the sidepiece on edge, supported firmly against the head of the miter gauge, I make a series of crosscuts to complete the rabbet (*photo 1-20*). I raise the blade height to 3/4 in. and cut the 2 dadoes in the same way (*photo 1-21*).

Gluing Up the Sides

Now I'm ready to glue up the sides. With my biscuit joiner I cut some slots for two #20 biscuits (optional), taking care not to cut slots near the bottom where the arch cutout will be. With the biscuits in their slots, I brush on some glue and clamp the pieces together (*photo 1-22*). I repeat the process for the other side of the stool.

The boards were so even when I glued up the sides on this stool that I was able to continue assembly while the sides were still in the clamps. I gave the inside surfaces a finish sanding with my random orbit sander. Then I sanded the inside surfaces of the treads and crosspieces.

Assembling the Stool

With a small brush, I spread glue in the dadoes for the back crosspiece. I put the crosspiece in place and use a couple of 4d finish nails to secure it to the sides.

Next, I brush glue on all the surfaces of the dovetail pins and tails. I do one tread at a time, and try to spread the glue on quickly. If I take too long, the glue starts to set up and makes the joint hard to assemble. A couple of taps with a mallet and the joint goes together nicely (*photo 1-23*). I repeat the process on the top set of dovetails and clamp the joints together with a few clamps as necessary. While the glue is drying, I tack on the 2 front crosspieces with a few 1-in. brads (*photo 1-24*).

1-20 To cut the crosspiece rabbets, I raise the blade to 3/8 in. and make a series of crosscuts, supporting the stock against the miter gauge.

1-21 To cut the dado for the rear crosspiece, I raise the blade to 3/4 in. and make a series of cuts, again supporting the stock against the miter gauge.

1-22 I glue the 2 pieces of the step stool sides together after cutting the dovetails. The glue line is located right at the riser.

Cutting the Arches

After the glue is dry and the clamps have been removed I can cut the arches. The arches on the 2-step stool have a 4¾-in. radius with the center point located at the bottom edge of the sidepiece (*drawing 1-F*). I lay out a centerline, set my compass to a 4¾-in. radius, and draw the arch on each sidepiece. I cut out the arch with my jigsaw, then sand the curve smooth with a drum sander on my drill press.

Now it's just a matter of sanding everything smooth and flush. A belt sander works well for smoothing up the dovetails. I finish up with my random orbit sander for a nice, smooth finish ready for stain.

1-23 I brush a little glue on the pins and tails and assemble the joint. A couple of taps with a mallet brings the joint together.

Staining and Finishing

To darken the cherry a little, I brush on a coat of water-soluble stain with a foam brush. Before the stain gets any drier, I take a clean rag and rub the stain in with a circular motion. Then I wipe off the excess stain with the rag, rubbing with the grain.

When the stain is dry, I use a foam brush to apply the first of three coats of water-soluble gloss polyurethane. When it's dry, I sand lightly with 220-grit paper, remove the dust with a tack cloth, then fill the nail holes with a colored putty stick that matches the stain. Two more coats of polyurethane, with a light sanding between coats, and the step stool's ready to use.

1-24 A few 1-in. brads tack the front crosspieces in place.

TWO

Two-Drawer Shaker Blanket Chest

PROJECT PLANNER

Time: 6 days
Special hardware and tools:
(1) 30-in. long, 1½-in. brass-plated piano hinge
(4) 1¼-in. diameter maple Shaker knobs
Dovetailing jig for half-blind dovetails
Wood:
(1) 12-ft 1 × 6 select pine
(1) 6-ft 1 × 8 select pine
Cut 1 × 6 into 4 pieces 36 in. long, and cut 1 × 8 into 2 pieces 36 in. long. Glue up 2 side panels using 2 pieces of 1 × 6 and one piece of 1 × 8 per panel.
(2) 8-ft 1 × 8 select pine
Cut 4 pieces 48 in. long. Glue up 2 panels using 2 pieces per panel for upper front and upper back panels.
(1) 14-ft 1 × 6 select pine
(1) 12-ft 1 × 8 select pine
Cut 1 × 6 into 4 pieces 42 in. long. From 1 × 8 cut 2 pieces 42 in. long. Glue up 2 panels using 2 pieces of 1 × 6 and one piece of 1 × 8 per panel to make storage compartment bottom and lower drawer support panel. Rip remaining piece of 1 × 8 into one piece 1½ in. wide to make middle rail and one piece 1¾ in. wide to make lower rail. Use leftover 1 × 8 to make lower drawer guides and stiles.
(1) 12-ft 1 × 8 select pine
Cut 3 pieces 41 in. long and glue up to make top. Make breadboard edges from remaining piece.
(1) 3/4-in. AC plywood
Trim to 16¾ in. × 39¼ in. for upper drawer support
(1) sheet 4 × 8, 1/4-in.-thick plywood
Cut one piece 18 in. × 39³⁄₁₆ in. for lower back panel. Cut two pieces 16⁵⁄₁₆ in. × 37⁵⁄₁₆ in. for drawer bottoms.
(1) 10-ft 1 × 6 select pine
Cut one piece 42 in. long for upper drawer front. Plane remaining

THIS painted pine blanket chest is based on an antique chest that I found at the Shaker community in Pleasant Hill, Kentucky. It has a deep, lidded storage compartment on top with two good-sized drawers below. The Shakers used pieces like these to store their blankets, coverlets, and quilts, and the chest works just fine for that purpose today.

Allowing for Wood Movement

Wood movement is a factor to consider whenever you work with wide, solid-wood panels, and this blanket chest is a good example of how I cope with some typical wood-movement problems. The joinery allows for wood's natural tendency to change dimension due to seasonal changes in humidity. When humidity goes up in the summer, wood expands. In the winter, in a dry heated house, wood shrinks. Most of this movement occurs *across* the grain; wood moves so little in length that you can safely ignore that factor. You get into trouble when you glue 2 boards together with the grain of one piece at right angles to the grain of the other. This is known as a cross-grain gluing situation and it's a situation you want to avoid. Each board restricts the movement of the other and, after a couple of seasons, either the glue joint or the wood will eventually break.

The decorative "breadboard edges" on the top of the blanket chest are a perfect example of proper joinery (*drawings 2-A and 2-E*). If these edges were simply glued to the top they'd restrict the movement of the top and the top would be likely to split. Instead, the breadboard edges are joined to the top with unglued tongue-and-groove joints pinned with dowels in slotted holes (*drawing 2-E*). This arrangement allows the top to expand and contract freely inside the breadboard edges.

The corner joints are also designed with movement in mind. The grain on the side panels of the chest runs vertically, while the grain on the front and back panels runs horizontally. The panels will move at right angles to each other. If I glue the corner joints together, the front and back panels will probably split. I joined the corners with a

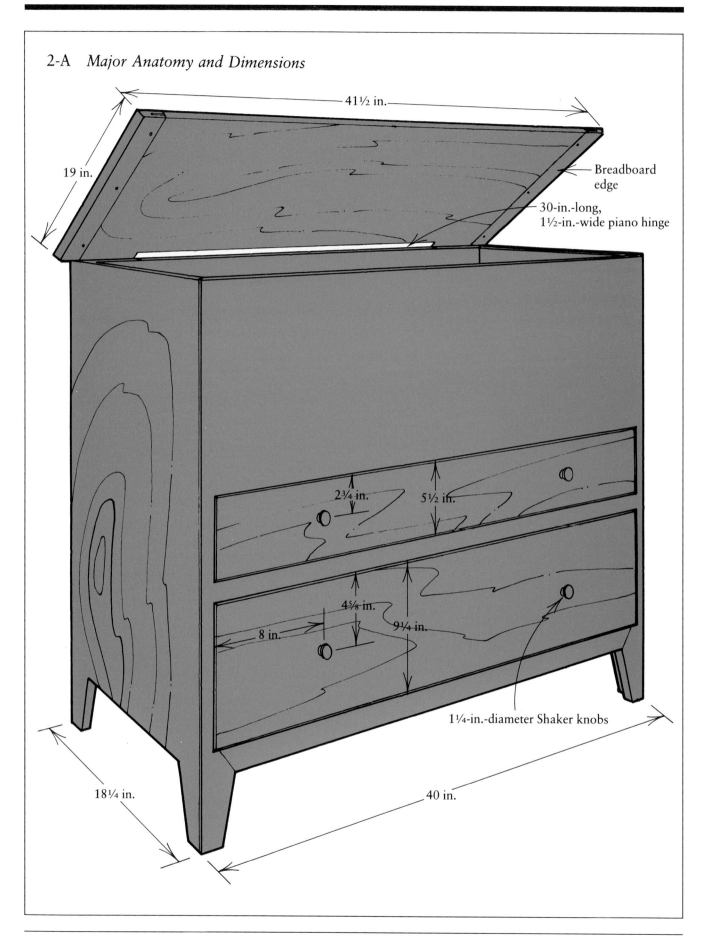

41½ in.

19 in.

Breadboard
edge

30-in.-long,
1½-in.-wide piano hinge

2¾ in.

5½ in.

4⅝ in.

8 in.

9¼ in.

1¼-in.-diameter Shaker knobs

18¼ in.

40 in.

nailed rabbet joint that I find pretty often on original Shaker furniture (*drawings 2-C and 2-D*). Because this joint is nailed, and not glued, the front, back, and sides of the chest are able to move just enough that there isn't much chance of them splitting.

Making the Panels

As with most of the furniture I make, I start the project off by making some panels. I glue up 6 pine panels from 1 × 6 and 1 × 8 select pine (see Project Planner). These panels will make the 2 sides of the chest, the upper front and upper back panels, the bottom of the storage compartment, and the lower drawer support panel. As usual, I always make the panels a little wider and longer than what I need and cut them to size later.

The top of the chest requires a seventh panel. I got really lucky when I picked up the board to make the top. I found a 12-ft 1 × 8 with very straight grain and nice color match across the entire board. What's nice about straight-grained boards like this is that they tend not to warp and twist, so they'll make a good top. From the 1 × 8 I cut three 41-in. lengths, jointed the edges, then edge glued them to make the panel for the top. As I usually do when I glue up wide panels, I alternate the direction of the growth rings on the ends of the boards. The piece left over from the 1 × 8 is large enough to make the 2 breadboard edges for the top.

In addition to the 7 solid-wood panels, I have to cut 2 plywood panels: a 3/4-in.-thick plywood panel for the middle drawer support and a 1/4-in.-thick plywood back.

Sizing the Panels

After scraping off the glue and sanding the panels flat with my belt sander, I'm ready to size them. The first thing is to get a nice straight, square edge, and that's best done on the jointer. I joint one long edge of each panel straight and square.

Next, on my table saw, I rip panels to width. My standard practice is to rip panels 1/32 in. "strong," that is, 1/32 in. wider than I really need. After I rip the panel, I clean up the edge on the jointer, which I keep set to make a 1/32-in. cut. The jointer smooths up any saw marks to give me a perfect edge. This extra 1/32 in. doesn't show up in the written dimensions — I just allow for it when I position my rip fence.

For the side panels, I set the rip fence 17⅞ in. (plus 1/32 in.) from the blade and, with the jointed edge against the rip fence, I rip the 2 side panels to width (*photo 2-1*). I repeat the process to rip the other panels to width, repositioning the fence to give me the finished width for each panel: 13¾ in. for the upper front panel, 13⅜ in. for the upper back panel, 17½ in. for the storage compartment bottom, and 16¾ in. for the lower-drawer support. The top of the chest measures 19 in. wide.

stock to 1/2-in. thickness for upper drawer sides and back.

(1) 10-ft 1 × 10 select pine

Cut one piece 42 in. long for lower drawer front. Plane remaining stock to 1/2-in. thickness for lower drawer sides and back.

2-1 To rip the side panels to width, I set the table saw rip fence 17⅞ in. (plus 1/32 in.) from the blade.

2-2 On my sliding crosscut table I square one end of the panel.

2-3 Then I set the table's adjustable stop for the finished length and butt the squared end of the panel against the stop to crosscut the panel to length.

Once the panels are ripped, then jointed to width, I square up one end of each panel on the table saw with my sliding crosscut table (*photo 2-2*). Then I slide the square end of the panel against the table's adjustable stop, which I've set for the correct panel length, and crosscut each panel to length (*photo 2-3*). The top of the chest is 39¾ in. long. The 2 sides are 35½ in. long. The upper front panel measures 40 in., and the 3 other panels are all 39¼ in. long.

When I'm finished sizing the pine panels, I trim the 3/4-in. plywood drawer-support panel to finished size. It measures 16¾ in. wide and 39¼ in. long (*drawing 2-D*). I still have to size the 1/4-in. plywood back, but I'll do that later when I can measure the assembled chest to get the exact dimensions for the back.

2-4 With a dado head on the table saw, I cut 3 dadoes, 3/4 in. wide and 3/8 in. deep, in each side of the blanket chest.

Milling the Sides

With the panels all sized, the next milling operation is to cut some dadoes in the side panels (*drawing 2-B*). Each side gets 3 dadoes 3/4 in. wide and 3/8 in. deep to support the lower drawer support, the drawer support on which the top drawer rides, and the panel that forms the bottom of the storage compartment.

I set up a dado head on my table saw and adjust it for a 3/4-in.-wide cut. Then I set the blade height to 3/8 in. and position the table saw rip fence 5½ in. away from the dado head to cut the lower-drawer-support dado in both sides. Next, I reposition the fence to cut the top dado for the bottom of the storage compartment. Finally, I cut one more dado in between the other 2 for the plywood drawer support (*photo 2-4*).

With the dadoes complete, I rabbet the front and back edges of each side, as shown in drawing 2-B. Each back edge gets a 3/8-in. by 3/4-in. rabbet. The rabbet on the front edge measures 3/8 in. by 3/8 in. I leave the dado head set up exactly as it was for the dado cuts, but I screw a wooden strip to my rip fence as shown in photo 2-5. The wooden strip allows me to cover part of the dado head cutter to cut rabbets of various widths. With the wooden strip in place on the fence, I set the fence right to the edge of the dado head to cut a 3/4-in.-wide rabbet. When the fence is set, I run a sample cut to make sure the rabbet I cut is exactly 3/4 in. wide. When the setting's right, I mill a rabbet on the back edge of each side, being careful to rabbet the *inside* edges so the sides are a matching pair.

Then I adjust the fence to cut a 3/8-in.-wide rabbet and run another sample. When the setting's right, I mill a 3/8-in. by 3/8-in. rabbet on the front edge of each side.

2-5 A wooden strip screwed to the rip fence allows me to position the fence right over the dado head to cut rabbets of various widths. Here I'm rabbeting the back edge of a side panel.

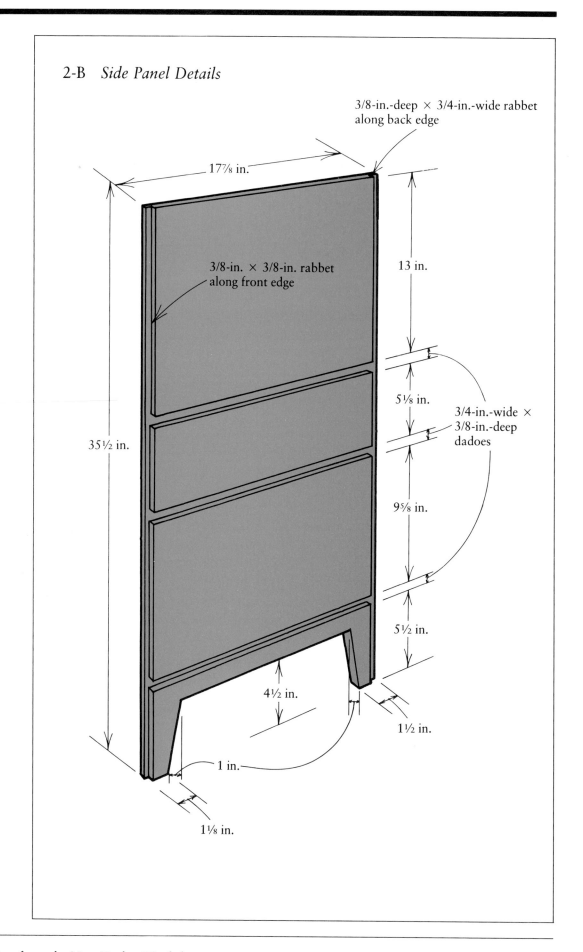

2-B Side Panel Details

3/8-in.-deep × 3/4-in.-wide rabbet along back edge

17⅞ in.

3/8-in. × 3/8-in. rabbet along front edge

13 in.

5⅛ in.

3/4-in.-wide × 3/8-in.-deep dadoes

35½ in.

9⅝ in.

5½ in.

4½ in.

1½ in.

1 in.

1⅛ in.

2-6 I make the horizontal cut for the leg cutout in the sidepieces with my small circular saw. I use a straightedge clamp across the work to guide my small circular saw. I make a plunge cut, pivoting the blade down into the work to start the cut.

With the dadoes and rabbets out of the way, there's one more thing to do to the side panels and that's to make the cutouts that form the legs. I clamp the panel to my workbench and lay out the cutout with a pencil as shown in drawing 2-B, being careful that the sides are a matching pair. I clamp a straightedge clamp across the side and use it as a guide to make the long horizontal cut with my small 5¼-in. circular saw. I offset the clamp from the cutting line by the distance from the blade to the edge of the saw base.

Because this cut starts in from the edge of the board, I have to make a plunge cut, which means I have to lower the spinning blade through the work, then carefully go along the line. I place the front edge of the saw base on the work with the left front corner of the base against the straightedge clamp. With the blade clear of the work, I raise up the guard with my left hand and turn on the saw. Then I slowly lower the blade down into the cut, pivoting the saw on the base's front edge and taking care to keep the left side of the base against the straightedge clamp. When the saw sits flush on the stock, I carefully cut along the line, taking my time because I want a nice, crisp cut (*photo 2-6*). Now I can remove the clamp and make the 2 short angled cuts that form the legs. I make these freehand with the circular saw (*photo 2-7*) and finish off the corners with my trusty old handsaw. A little hand sanding cleans up the saw cuts.

With the sides of the chest complete, I turn my attention to some of the other parts of the chest. The upper front panel, upper back panel, and the panel that forms the bottom of the storage compartment all need to have rabbets milled along one edge (*drawings 2-C and 2-D*). The back panel and storage compartment bottom get 3/8-in. by 3/8-in. rabbets, and my table saw still happens to be set to make just that cut. I mill a rabbet on the inside of the bottom edge of the upper back panel and the bottom rear edge of the storage compartment bottom. For the upper front panel, I mill a 3/4-in.-wide

2-7 I make the 2 short angled cuts that form the legs by cutting freehand with the circular saw.

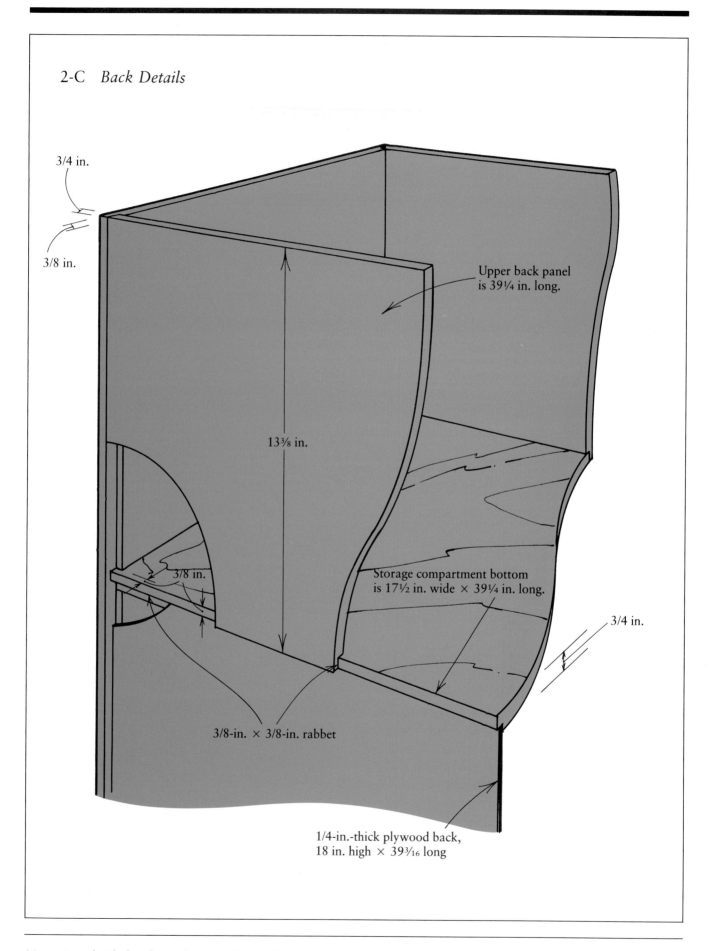

3/4 in.

3/8 in.

Upper back panel
is 39¼ in. long.

13⅜ in.

3/8 in.

Storage compartment bottom
is 17½ in. wide × 39¼ in. long.

3/4 in.

3/8-in. × 3/8-in. rabbet

1/4-in.-thick plywood back,
18 in. high × 39³⁄₁₆ long

2-8 I glue the bottom shelf support and the storage compartment bottom into their respective dadoes and nail them in place with some 4d finish nails.

by 3/8-in.-deep rabbet on the inside of the bottom edge, to overlap the storage compartment bottom. On each end of the front panel, I mill a 3/8-in. by 3/8-in. rabbet (*drawing 2-D*).

Now it's just about time to do a little assembly, but first, I finish sand all the inside surfaces of the storage compartment that will show on the finished chest. Now I'm ready to go. I put some glue in the top dado and on one end of the storage compartment bottom panel. I fit the end of the panel into the dado, making sure to keep the rabbeted edge facing down and to the rear of the chest, and nail it in place with some 4d finish nails. The next piece to go in is the lower drawer support. I brush some glue in the bottom dado and on the end of the shelf and nail it in place. I repeat the procedure to fasten the other side of the chest (*photo 2-8*).

The 3/4-in. plywood drawer support comes next. For this step, I flip the chest over so it's front-side up on my workbench. In this position, it's easier to locate the front edge of the drawer support. Because this panel is plywood, I have to treat it a little differently than the solid-wood panels I just installed. I don't want to put glue along the entire joint because that gets me into a cross-grain gluing situation (plywood doesn't move as much as solid wood). I want the sides to be free to move, so I'll just put a little glue at the front corners of the plywood panel to keep it fixed (*photo 2-9*) and drive a couple of 4d nails in each joint to hold it in place. The thin nails have just enough give to let the sides of the chest expand and contract.

Now I'm ready to put on the 1/4-in. plywood back. I flip the chest around again on the bench so the back side faces up, and I measure the inside of the opening with my tape measure. I always cut the panel 1/16 in. less than the distance between the rabbets to allow me a little freedom in case the panel is out of square.

2-9 To avoid a cross-grain gluing situation between the plywood shelf support and the sides of the chest, I don't put glue along the entire joint. Just a little glue at the front corners and a few nails keep it fixed in the joint.

2-10 With the 1/4-in. plywood back in place, I tack the top edge to the edge of the storage compartment bottom. Then I place a framing square on the back, move the sides in or out a little until things are square, then nail the back all around.

2-11 The bottom edge of the upper back panel gets a 3/8-in. by 3/8-in. rabbet. This allows it to overlap the compartment bottom, so there's no visible gap from inside the chest.

Now I cut the panel on the table saw to its finished dimensions of 18 in. by 39³⁄₁₆ in. (*drawing 2-C*). I spread a little glue on the back edges of the shelves and side panels and put the panel in place. With some 1-in. brads in my pneumatic nailer, I tack the top edge of the panel to the storage compartment bottom. With a framing square to check for square, I move the sides in or out a little to square up the case and tack the plywood back to the sides, plywood drawer support, and lower-drawer support (*photo 2-10*).

There's just one more piece for the back of the blanket chest, and that's the upper back panel. The bottom edge gets a 3/8-in. by 3/8-in. rabbet so it will overlap the bottom of the storage compartment (*drawing 2-C and photo 2-11*). That way, if the bottom panel shrinks, I won't see a gap on the back inside edge of the chest. As I mentioned, no glue at the corners, just a few 4d nails, maybe 3 or 4 along each corner. For good measure, I shoot a few brads along the bottom edge of the panel.

Now I'll just flip the whole case over again so I can nail on the upper front panel. No glue, remember.

Stiles and Rails

Each side of the chest has a stile that extends from the upper front panel to the floor. It's 1 in. wide along the side of the drawer openings. Then, at the top of the lower rail it angles down to the bottom edge of the rail. At this point, it's 2½ in. wide. From there it tapers down to 1½ in. wide at the foot (*drawing 2-D*).

To make the stiles, I cut 2 pieces of 1× stock about 3 in. wide and 24 in. long. I mill a 3/8-in. by 3/8-in. rabbet along one edge to fit over the side panels. Next, I square up one end on my miter box and mark the other end for length. To do this, I place the stile in position on the chest with the square end butted against the bottom

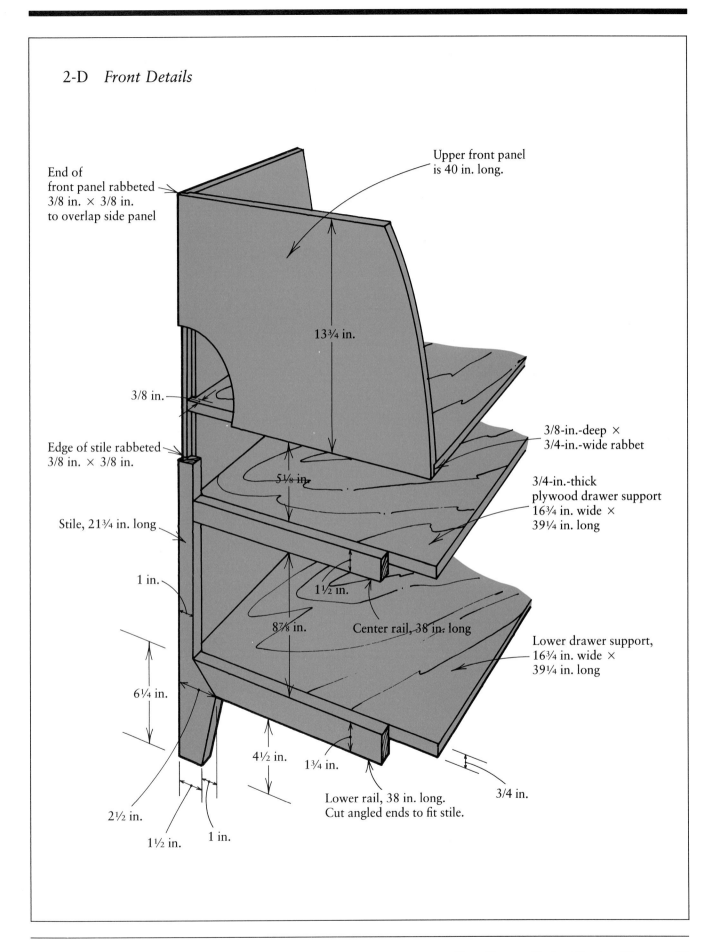

End of
front panel rabbeted
3/8 in. × 3/8 in.
to overlap side panel

Upper front panel
is 40 in. long.

13¾ in.

3/8 in.

Edge of stile rabbeted
3/8 in. × 3/8 in.

3/8-in.-deep ×
3/4-in.-wide rabbet

3/4-in.-thick
plywood drawer support
16¾ in. wide ×
39¼ in. long

5⅛ in.

Stile, 21¾ in. long

1 in.

1½ in.

Center rail, 38 in. long

8⅞ in.

Lower drawer support,
16¾ in. wide ×
39¼ in. long

6¼ in.

4½ in.

1¾ in.

3/4 in.

2½ in.

1½ in.

1 in.

Lower rail, 38 in. long.
Cut angled ends to fit stile.

edge of the upper front panel. Using my square as a guide, I mark the bottom end to length and cut it on the miter box.

I make the 2 angled cuts at the foot first, cutting them freehand with my small circular saw. Then I set the table saw rip fence for a 1-in. cut and rip the 1-in. section that runs along the drawer openings (*photo 2-12*). Finally, I pass the tapered foot section over the jointer to clean up the saw marks from the circular saw (*photo 2-13*). I finish the other stile in the same way and attach both stiles to the chest with glue and 1-in. brads.

The top rail is easy, a 1½-in.-wide piece with straight cuts on either end (*drawing 2-D*). I spread some glue along the front edge of the plywood drawer support and nail the rail in place with some 4d finish nails.

The bottom rail is a bit more involved because I have to make 2 angled cuts where the rail meets the stiles (*drawing 2-D*). I need to know what angle to cut, and I use my sliding bevel gauge to find out. Problem: When I try to slide my bevel gauge into the corner to measure the angle, it hits the stile and I can't get a true reading. As shown in photo 2-14, I use a little piece of scrap wood as a spacer so I can set the gauge to the correct angle.

At my power miter box, I use my bevel gauge to set the angle of the cut (*photo 2-15*). Now I make a cut on one end of the rail and place that end against the stile so I can mark the other end for length. When I make the second angled cut, I like to leave the rail just a little bit long. It's always easy to trim it back later for a perfect

2-12 Each stile has a 1-in.-wide section that runs along the sides of the drawer openings. After completing the foot cuts, I rip the 1-in.-wide section, stopping the cut where it meets the top of the angled cut.

2-13 A quick pass over the jointer cleans up the saw marks on the bottom angled cut of the stile.

2-14 The ends of the bottom rail must be angled to fit against the stiles. I need to measure the angle, but the blade of my sliding bevel gauge won't fit all the way into the corner. I use a little scrap of wood as a spacer so I can set the gauge to the correct angle.

fit. When the rail fits, I brush on some glue and nail it in place with some 4d finish nails.

One more thing. I nail a couple of 3/4-in. by 3/4-in. cleats to the underside of the plywood shelf to serve as drawer guides for the bottom drawer (*drawing 2-G*). These cleats will keep the bottom drawer from rocking as I pull it out.

Now I just sand everything smooth and flush with my random orbit sander. This tool is great for sanding the stiles, rails, and front panel flush because it doesn't leave any scratch marks when I sand across opposing grain. That's about it for the body of the blanket chest. All that's left now is the top.

Completing the Top

The first milling operation for the top is to make the 5/16-in. tongue on the ends of the panel for the breadboard edges (*drawing 2-E*). I do that on the table saw with the dado head and the wooden strip screwed to the rip fence. I raise the dado head a little less than 1/4 in. above the table and set the fence to cut a 5/8-in.-wide tongue. I make a sample cut on a piece of 1× stock, then flip it over and cut the other side. The resulting tongue should be exactly 5/16 in. thick. If necessary, I adjust the blade height up or down until I get a 5/16-in. tongue. When the setting's right, I mill one side of the tongue, then flip it over and cut the other side.

The next step is to make a corresponding groove in the breadboard edges. The trick here is to have a groove that's a snug fit on the tongue and perfectly centered. If it isn't centered, it will take lots

2-15　I use the sliding bevel gauge to set my miter box to the angle I measured from the stile.

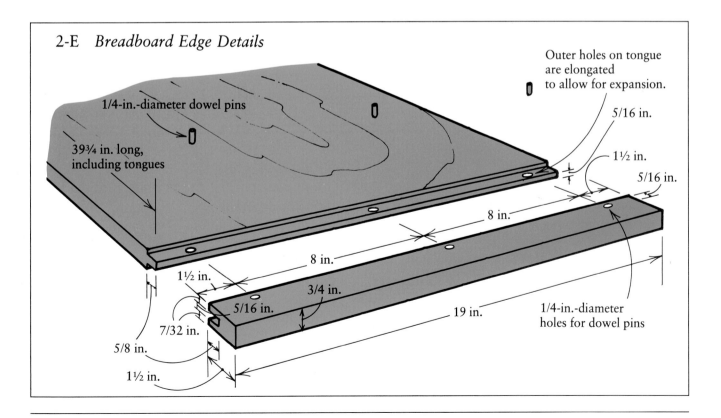

2-E　*Breadboard Edge Details*

Outer holes on tongue are elongated to allow for expansion.

1/4-in.-diameter dowel pins

39¾ in. long, including tongues

5/16 in.

1½ in.

5/16 in.

8 in.

8 in.

3/4 in.

1½ in.

5/16 in.

7/32 in.

5/8 in.

1½ in.

19 in.

1/4-in.-diameter holes for dowel pins

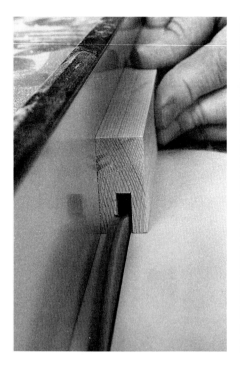  

2-16 The breadboard edges need a perfectly centered groove to fit the tongue on the top. I set the dado head for a groove of 1/4 in. and set the rip fence so the distance between the blade and the fence is a little less than 1/4 in. Then I cut a groove, flip the piece around, and make a second pass with the opposite side of the stock against the fence. Result? A perfectly centered groove.

2-17 Three 1/4-in. dowels fasten each breadboard edge to the top. I clamp the breadboard edges to the top with a piece of scrap underneath to minimize tearout. Then I drill the dowel holes with a 1/4-in. brad-point bit.

2-18 The 2 outside holes in each tongue must be slots so the top can expand and contract. After drilling the holes, I elongate the 2 outer holes by rocking the drill back and forth.

of sanding to make the breadboard edges nice and even with the surface of the top.

I have a little trick to help center the groove. I set my dado head up so it cuts a groove a little bit narrower than I need. But I very carefully align the rip fence so that the distance between the fence and the dado head is just right — in this case, about 7/32 in. Now I mill a groove in the breadboard edge, flip the piece around, and make a second pass, this time with the opposite side of the stock against the fence (*photo 2-16*). I end up with a groove that's perfectly centered, every time. (As with most machine setups, I always run a sample cut to test the setup.)

As I mentioned before, the breadboard edges are secured to the top with 1/4-in. dowels — 3 on each side. The dowel holes go clear through the top. I set up my top on the bench, clamp the 2 breadboard edges in place with pipe clamps, and slip a piece of scrap underneath to minimize tearout when the drill breaks through (*photo 2-17*). With a 1/4-in. brad-point bit in my drill, I bore 3 holes in each side at the locations shown in drawing 2-E.

Next, I want to elongate the 2 outside holes on each end of the top, so the top can expand and contract on either side of the center dowel. I remove the breadboard edges and use my drill, rocking the drill from side to side to elongate the holes (*photo 2-18*). Now I clamp the breadboard edges in place again to install the dowels. I put just a little bit of glue at the top of each dowel — enough to hold it in place but not so much that it will be glued all the way through and restrict the movement of the top. Then I tap the dowels home with a hammer. When the glue is dry, I'll sand the dowels flush with the top.

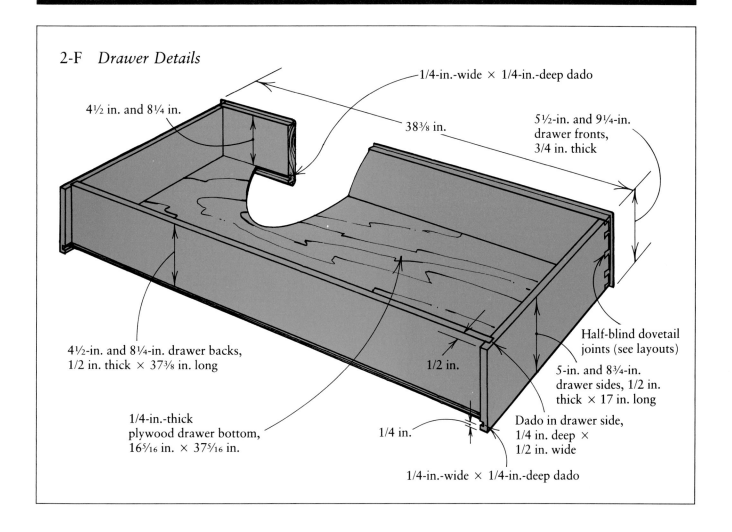

2-F   Drawer Details

1/4-in.-wide × 1/4-in.-deep dado

4½ in. and 8¼ in.

38⅜ in.

5½-in. and 9¼-in. drawer fronts, 3/4 in. thick

4½-in. and 8¼-in. drawer backs, 1/2 in. thick × 37⅜ in. long

1/2 in.

Half-blind dovetail joints (see layouts)

5-in. and 8¾-in. drawer sides, 1/2 in. thick × 17 in. long

1/4-in.-thick plywood drawer bottom, 16⁵⁄₁₆ in. × 37⁵⁄₁₆ in.

1/4 in.

Dado in drawer side, 1/4 in. deep × 1/2 in. wide

1/4-in.-wide × 1/4-in.-deep dado

Making the Drawers

The 2 drawers are different in depth, but all the construction details are the same for both drawers. Each drawer front is a piece of 3/4-in.-thick pine. For the drawer sides and backs I plane some 3/4-in. stock down to a 1/2-in. thickness using my portable thickness planer. I joint and rip all the drawer stock to width and trim the ends to the lengths shown in drawing 2-F. I also cut the 1/4-in. plywood bottom panels to size, using the same technique I always use for sizing panels on the table saw. I think the drawers look better if the face grain on the plywood runs across the width of the drawer rather than front to back.

On the table saw, using my dado head and the wooden auxiliary fence, I mill a 1/4-in.-wide by 1/2-in.-deep rabbet around all 4 edges of the drawer front so that it overlaps the face frame of the chest (*drawing 2-G*).

Next, I mill 1/4-in. by 1/4-in. grooves on the sidepieces and the bottom edge of the drawer front to accept the plywood drawer bottom (*drawing 2-F and photo 2-19*). I mill the side grooves first, then move the rip fence 1/4 in. farther from the dado head to cut the

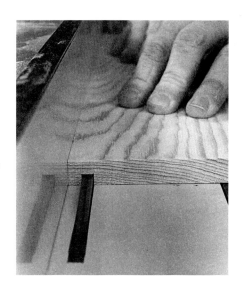

2-19 The 1/4-in. plywood drawer bottoms fit into 1/4-in. by 1/4-in. grooves milled in the drawer sides (shown here) and along the bottom front edge of the drawer fronts.

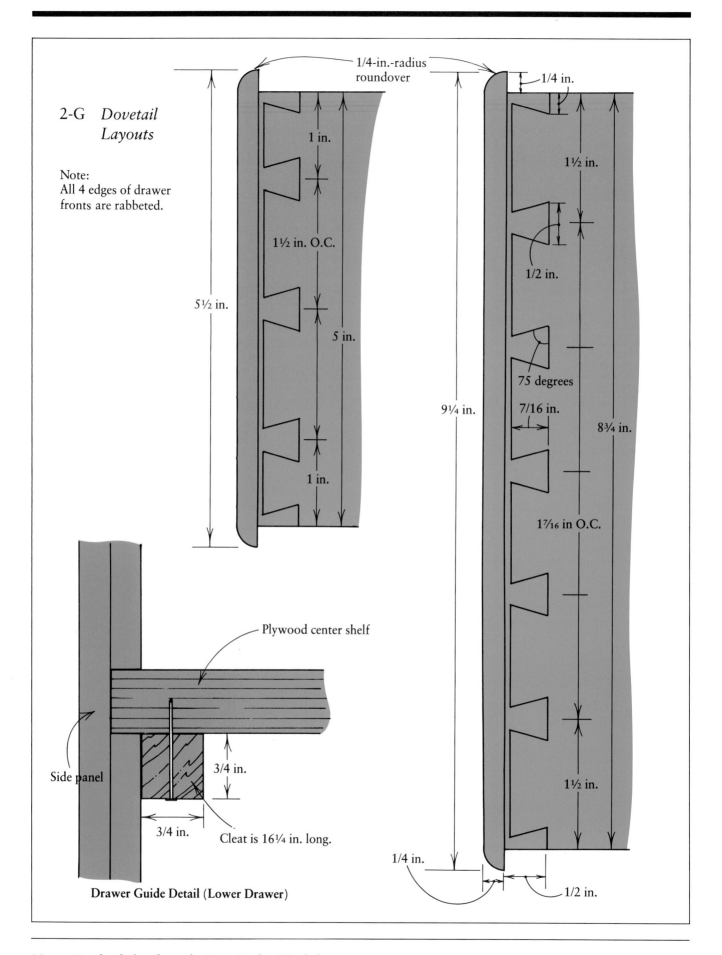

2-G *Dovetail Layouts*

Note:
All 4 edges of drawer fronts are rabbeted.

1/4-in.-radius roundover

1 in.

1½ in. O.C.

5½ in.

5 in.

1 in.

1/4 in.

1½ in.

1/2 in.

75 degrees

7/16 in.

9¼ in.

8¾ in.

1⁷⁄₁₆ in O.C.

1½ in.

1/4 in.

1/2 in.

Plywood center shelf

Side panel

3/4 in.

3/4 in.

Cleat is 16¼ in. long.

Drawer Guide Detail (Lower Drawer)

2-20 I mill a 1/2-in.-wide dado, 1/4 in. deep, at the back end of the drawer sides, to house the backs of the drawers.

groove in the drawer front. The next step is to mill a 1/4-in.-deep by 3/4-in.-wide dado at the back end of each sidepiece to help secure the back of the drawer (*photo 2-20*).

The sides of the drawer are joined to the front with half-blind dovetails (*drawing 2-G*). The Shakers would have cut these joints by hand, but I'm a firm believer in cutting dovetails with a dovetailing jig and a router. Every manufacturer's dovetailing jig is a little different, so I won't go into detail about how I set up my jig to cut the joints. Suffice it to say that on my jig, I have to cut the tails in the sidepieces first (*photo 2-21*). Next, I cut the pins in the drawer fronts (*photo 2-22*). You can use any spacing you like for the pins and tails. The spacing I used is shown in drawing 2-G.

The last thing I have to do before I can assemble the drawers is round over the front edges of the drawer fronts. To do that, I use my router table with a 1/4-in. roundover bit. As usual, I cut the end grain first, feeding the stock from right to left against the rotation of the bit. Assembly is the next step, but first I give the drawer parts a good finish sanding on all surfaces, inside and out.

2-21 With my dovetailing jig and a router, I cut the dovetail tails in one side of the drawer.

2-22 The router does a quick job of cutting the corresponding pins in the drawer front.

Assembling the Drawers

The first step in the assembly process for the drawers is to put a little bit of glue on all the mating surfaces of the dovetails and tap the joints together. Next, I'm ready for the back. I put a little glue in the side dadoes and secure the back with some 1-in. brads in each end. Now, with the drawer facedown on the bench, I just slip the bottom piece of plywood in. I turn the drawer upside down on the bench, check for square with my framing square, and tack the bottom to the drawer back with some brads. A little sanding to clean up the dovetails, and the drawers are complete, ready for the knobs. I locate and drill the holes for the knobs (*drawing 2-A*), but I don't install them until after I've painted the chest.

To attach the top to the chest, I use a 30-in. length of 1½-in.-wide surface-mounted, brass-plated piano hinge, which I screw in place with my drill/driver (*drawing 2-A and photo 2-23*).

And Finally, the Finish

For the inside of the chest, where blankets might be stored, I brush on 3 coats of a water-soluble satin polyurethane. This will do a good job of protecting the wood. I like to use a disposable foam brush for applying this finish, and I sand lightly with either 320- or 600-grit wet-or-dry paper between coats.

The exterior of the chest gets a color coat of acrylic latex enamel, but before I put that on, I brush on a coat of primer. I have the paint store tint the primer a light gray color by adding a little universal black color. I find that this helps the final coat cover better. When the primer's dry, I sand lightly with 220-grit paper and brush on 2 coats of the latex enamel — a nice old-timey brick color. Somehow, I think that the Shakers would approve.

2-23   The lid of the blanket chest swings on a 30-in.-long, 1½-in. brass-plated piano hinge. I install it with screws, using my drill/driver.

THREE

Shaker Washstand

BACK in the old days, every home had a washstand or two, with a big porcelain bowl and a pitcher full of water to splash on your sleepy face when you tumbled out of bed in the morning. Today washstands are decorative — a nice piece of furniture for showing off some flowers, antiques, or a prize bowl-and-pitcher set.

I patterned my washstand after a nineteenth-century beauty I found at the Hancock Shaker Village. Like the original, it's made of pine with a nice raised-panel door at the bottom and a drawer for some smaller items. The sides and the front of the counter, or top part of the washstand, flare out at a 5-degree angle — a nice decorative touch that makes an otherwise plain piece look very elegant. These angled sides are joined with through dovetails at the corners. Aligning these angled dovetails was the only thing I found mildly difficult about making this piece. The rest of the project is pretty straightforward.

Making Panels

The first thing to do is to glue up some panels — 7 in all. One for the backsplash, one for the countertop, 2 for the sides, and one each for the drawer support, the middle shelf, and the bottom shelf of the washstand (See Project Planner and *drawings 3-A, 3-B, 3-C, and 3-E*). All the panels are made of 3/4-in. pine (1 × 6s and 1 × 8s) edge glued together and reinforced with compressed hardwood biscuits.

When the clamps come off the panels, I scrape off the excess glue with my scraper and belt-sand the panels flat. Then I joint and rip the panels to the finished widths shown in the drawings. As usual, I joint one long edge of each panel straight and square, then rip the other edge 1/32 in. "strong" on the table saw. Then I go back to the jointer and take off that extra 1/32 in. While the table saw makes a pretty smooth cut, the jointer cleans up any saw marks and gives me a nice, clean edge and a panel that's exactly the width that I need.

Next I crosscut all the panels except the backsplash and counter-

Time: 6 days
Special hardware and tools:
(2) 2-in. brass butt hinges
(3) 3/4-in.-diameter Shaker knobs
Dovetailing jig for through and half-blind dovetails
Wood:
(1) 5-ft 1 × 8 select pine
(1) 10-ft 1 × 6 select pine
Cut 1 × 8 into 2 pieces 30 in. long and cut 1 × 6 into 4 pieces 30 in. long. Glue up 2 panels for washstand sides, edge gluing 2 pieces of 1 × 6 and one piece of 1 × 8 for each panel.
(1) 6-ft 1 × 8 pine
(1) 12-ft 1 × 6 pine
Cut 1 × 8 into 3 pieces 24 in. long. Cut 1 × 6 into 6 pieces 24 in. long. Glue up 3 panels for drawer support, middle shelf, and bottom shelf using 2 pieces of 1 × 6 and one piece of 1 × 8 for each panel.
(1) 12-ft 1 × 8 select pine
(1) 8-ft 1 × 6 select pine
Cut 2 pieces of 1 × 8 26 in. long and one piece of 1 × 6 26 in. long and edge glue these pieces together for countertop.
Cut one piece of 1 × 8 28 in. long and one piece of 1 × 6 28 in. long and edge glue together for backsplash.
Cut one piece of 1 × 6 30 in. long and rip into one piece 3¾ in. wide for counter front and one piece 1½ in. wide for back cleat.
Cut 2 pieces of 1 × 8 27 in. long for stiles. Make face-frame bottom rail from remaining piece of 1 × 6.
(1) 12-ft 1 × 10 select pine
Cut 2 pieces 21 in. long for counter sides.
Cut one piece 15 in. long for door panel.
Rip remainder into one piece 4¾ in. × 86 in. Cut one piece 4¾ in. × 21 in. for drawer front. Plane remainder to 1/2-in. thickness for drawer sides and back. Make door

stiles and rails from remaining 3/4-in.-thick stock.

(1) 1/4-in. plywood

Cut one piece 21³⁄₁₆ in. × 24½ in. for back panel.

Cut one piece 15⁵⁄₁₆ in. × 19⁵⁄₁₆ in. for drawer bottom.

top to length. For this project I used my new factory-made sliding crosscut table. It works much the same as the homemade panel cutters I use so often for squaring up panels, but the factory table has a handy built-in tape measure and a stop system that's really convenient for cutting panels to length.

With the sliding table in place on my table saw and the blade set to the correct height, I square up one end of each panel. Next I cut the panels to length. I set the stop on the sliding crosscut table to give me the length that I want, butt the squared end of the panel against the sliding table's stop, and cut the other end to length.

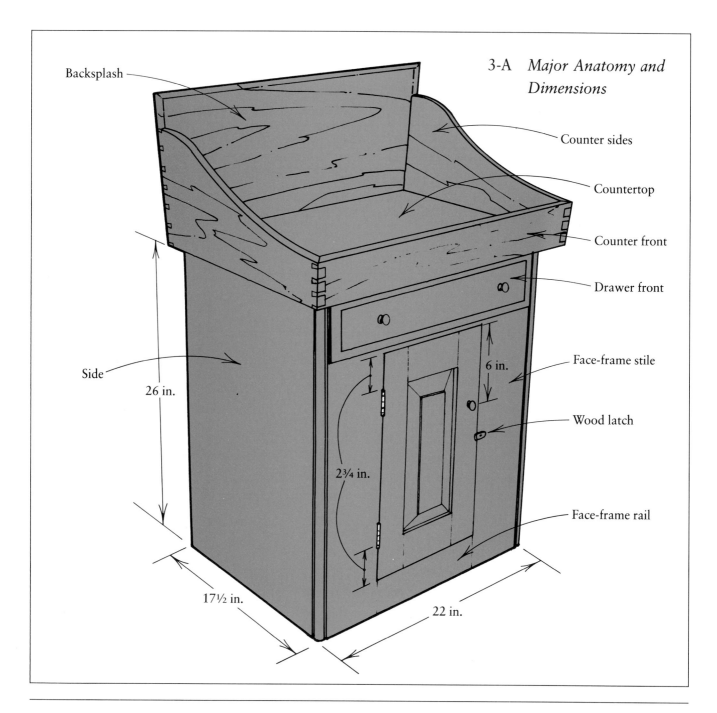

3-A *Major Anatomy and Dimensions*

Backsplash

Counter sides

Countertop

Counter front

Drawer front

Side

26 in.

Face-frame stile

6 in.

Wood latch

2¾ in.

Face-frame rail

17½ in.

22 in.

Side Dadoes and Rabbets

The two shelves and the drawer support fit into dadoes milled in the sides of the washstand (*drawings 3-B, 3-C, and 3-D*). I cut these dadoes on the table saw with my adjustable dado head. I adjust the dado head for a 3/4-in.-wide dado and raise the cutter to make a cut 3/8 in. deep. As usual, I run a sample dado in a piece of scrap to test the fit on one of the shelves — it should be not too tight, not too loose. Then I set the rip fence 4½ in. away from the cutter and mill the upper dado in each side panel for the drawer support, guiding the top of each side panel against the rip fence.

For the next set of dadoes, I set the rip fence 2 in. away from the cutter and mill the dadoes for the bottom shelf — one on each side panel (*drawing 3-D*). Finally, I set the rip fence 11¼ in. from the dado head and mill the dadoes for the middle shelf, keeping the bottom edge of each panel against the rip fence (*photo 3-1*).

The back of the washstand is a piece of 1/4-in. plywood that fits into a 3/8-in. by 3/8-in. rabbet milled on the inside edge of each side panel (*drawing 3-B*). I cut this rabbet on the table saw with my dado head, but first I screw a wooden auxiliary fence to my rip fence. This strip of wood protects the rip fence from the cutter and allows me to cover part of the dado head with the fence to cut a narrow rabbet. This wooden fence is reusable. When I have to make a new one, I screw the strip to the rip fence. Then I raise the spinning dado head slowly to make a circular cut on the underside of the auxiliary fence, being extremely careful not to hit the metal rip fence with the blade.

With the dado head set for a 3/8-in.-deep cut, I position the wooden fence to cover all but 3/8 in. of the dado head. I run a sample rabbet on some scrap stock to check the setup, then mill a 3/8-in. by 3/8-in. rabbet on the back inside edge of each side panel (*photo 3-2*).

3-1 I mill the 3/4-in.-wide dadoes in the sidepieces with a dado head on the table saw. Here I'm cutting the dado for the middle shelf.

3-2 I mill a 3/8-in. by 3/8-in. rabbet on the back inside edge of each side panel for the plywood back panel.

Assembling the Carcass

After finish sanding the shelves and the insides of the side panels, I'm ready for a little assembly. I spread some glue in the dadoes and install the 2 shelves and the drawer support. The front edges of the middle and bottom shelves line up flush with the front edges of the side panels (*drawing 3-C*). The front edge of the drawer support projects 3/4 in. beyond the front edges of the side panels as shown in drawing 3-B. A few 4d finish nails from my pneumatic nailer hold the whole thing together — I find that clamps are not necessary here (*photo 3-3*).

Now I'm ready to put on the 1/4-in. plywood back, but first I have to measure the carcass and cut the plywood panel to size. With the carcass facedown on the bench, I measure across the back and subtract 1/16 in. from the distance between rabbets — 21³⁄₁₆ in., in

3-3 Some glue and some 4d nails from my pneumatic nail gun hold the carcass together.

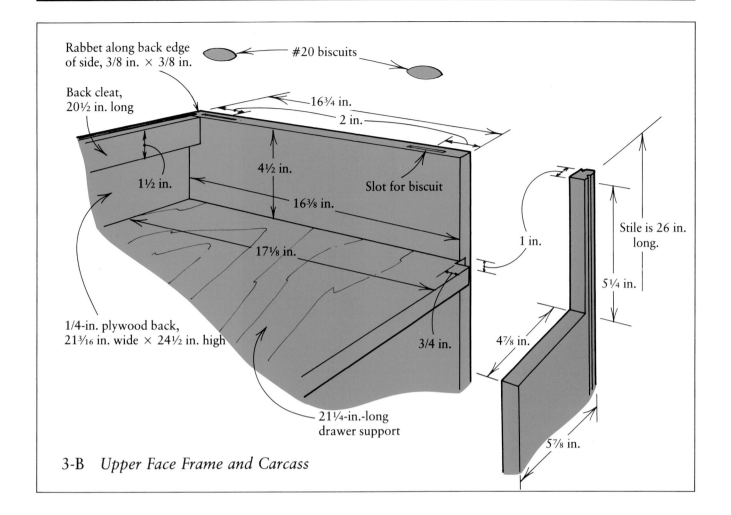

Rabbet along back edge of side, 3/8 in. × 3/8 in.

#20 biscuits

Back cleat, 20½ in. long

16¾ in.

2 in.

1½ in.

4½ in.

16⅜ in.

Slot for biscuit

17⅛ in.

1 in.

Stile is 26 in. long.

5¼ in.

1/4-in. plywood back, 21³⁄₁₆ in. wide × 24½ in. high

3/4 in.

4⅞ in.

21¼-in.-long drawer support

5⅞ in.

3-B   *Upper Face Frame and Carcass*

this case. I rip the plywood to width and cut it to length with my sliding crosscut table. Next, I brush a little glue in the rabbets as well as the back edges of the shelves and the drawer support and put the plywood panel in place. I hold the top edge of the panel even with the tops of the side panels. Then I place a framing square on the back to check the carcass for square and tack the panel in place with some 1-in. brads.

While the carcass is still facedown on the bench, I install a 1×2 cleat on the inside top edge of the plywood (*drawing 3-B*). This cleat reinforces the plywood back of the washstand and provides a place for the countertop to rest (*drawing 3-B*). The ends of the cleat just butt against the sides of the washstand. I spread glue on the cleat and the plywood and drive a few brads through the plywood and into the cleat. Then I drive a couple of 4d finish nails through the sides of the washstand into each end of the cleat.

Making the Stiles

Now I can turn my attention to the front of the carcass. There are 2 stiles on the front, one on each side, that run from the floor to the top of the carcass. At the top, these stiles are cut out to fit around

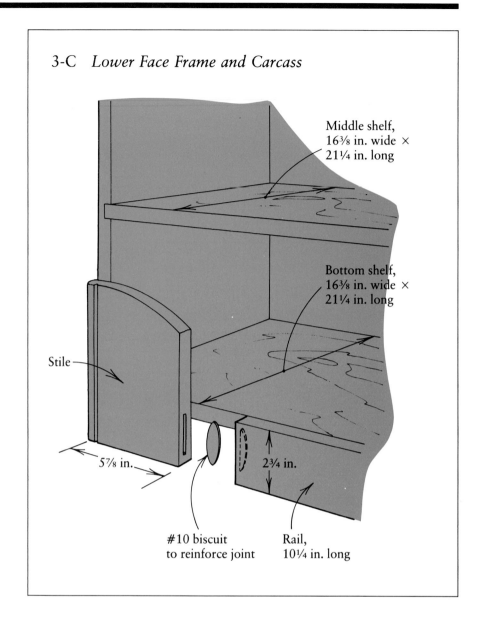

3-C *Lower Face Frame and Carcass*

Middle shelf,
16⅜ in. wide ×
21¼ in. long

Bottom shelf,
16⅜ in. wide ×
21¼ in. long

Stile

5⅞ in.

2¾ in.

#10 biscuit
to reinforce joint

Rail,
10¼ in. long

the drawer support panel and form the opening for the drawer (*drawing 3-B*). The corners of the drawer support panel must be notched to receive the stiles. With the carcass faceup on the bench, I use my dovetailing saw to cut a 3/4-in. by 1-in. notch at each front corner of the drawer support panel as shown (*drawing 3-B and photo 3-4*).

I rip the stiles from 3/4-in. pine. I joint one long edge on the jointer. Then I set my table saw rip fence 5⅞ in. from the blade and rip the stiles to width. Then, with the table saw miter gauge, I square up one end of each stile and cut the stiles to their finished length of 26 in.

Now I have to make the cutouts in the stiles that form the drawer opening (*drawing 3-B*). With my tape measure and a square, I mark off the cutouts — 4⅞ in. wide and 5¼ in. long — drawing lines with my square and a pencil. To make the rip cut on the right-hand

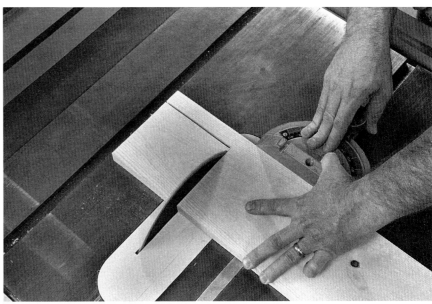

3-4 The upper drawer support projects 3/4 in. from the front edges of the side panels. The 2 front corners of this drawer support get 3/4-in. by 1-in. notches to receive the stiles.

3-5 The tops of the stiles are cut out to form the drawer opening. I make these cuts on the table saw. A rip cut first, stopping at the pencil line, then the crosscut, shown here. I stop the cut when it meets the kerf from the rip cut.

stile I set the table saw rip fence 1 in. to the right of the blade. I raise the blade to a height of 2 in. and make a rip cut 5¼ in. long, stopping the cut when the blade reaches the pencil line. For the left-hand stile, I set the rip fence to the right of the blade, measuring 4⅞ in. to the far side of the blade to make the stop rip cut on the left-hand stile. These rip cuts form the 1-in.-wide section along the outer edge of each stile.

To complete the cutouts, I make the crosscuts on the table saw, using the miter gauge to feed the stock into the blade (*photo 3-5*). On the backs of the stiles, the kerfs will be overcut, due to the radius of the saw blade, but this will face the inside of the cabinet, where it won't be seen.

Finishing the Face Frame

A rail 2¾ in. wide and 10¼ in. long joins the 2 stiles at the bottom of the washstand. I joint and rip this rail from 3/4-in. pine and crosscut it to length on my power miter box.

To strengthen the butt joints where the rail ends meet the stiles, I put a #10 biscuit in each joint (*drawing 3-C*). To mark for the biscuit slots, I place the stiles and the rail in position on the front of the carcass and draw a pencil line across each butt joint. Now I take the pieces apart and, with my biscuit joiner, cut the slots in the stiles and rail ends. I also finish sand the inside edges of the stiles and the top edge of the rail.

With the biscuit slots cut and the edges all sanded, I'm ready to fasten the stiles and rails to the carcass. The left-hand stile goes on first. I brush glue along the front edge of the left side and on the edges of the shelves where they'll be covered by the stile. Then I place the left-hand stile in place on the carcass. Before I nail the stile

3-6 The front of the washstand is a face frame with 2 stiles and a rail at the bottom. I reinforce the butt joint where the rail meets the stile with a #10 hardwood biscuit. I made pencil marks across the joint to mark the slot locations.

in place, I check to see that the edge of the stile is flush with the side of the carcass. I just reach around the edge and feel with my fingers. When it's flush, I nail the stile to the shelves and side with 4d finish nails. I'm careful to hold the nails in about 3/8 in. from the corner of the stile when nailing along the edge so that I don't hit the nails with my router bit later when I rout a decorative V groove on the corners.

The next step is to nail the rail in place. I brush some glue on the front edge of the bottom shelf and a little bit more in the biscuit slot in the left-hand stile. A #10 biscuit goes in the slot. Working quickly, I put some glue on the left end of the rail and some more in the slot. Now I assemble the joint and nail the rail to the bottom shelf with three 4d finish nails.

Next, I brush glue in the other 2 biscuit slots, put the biscuit in place, and assemble the joint (*photo 3-6*). Making sure that the right-hand stile is flush with the side of the carcass, I nail it in place and, as I did with the left stile, hold the nails in about 3/8 in. from the corner. Before I can rout the corners, I use my random orbit sander to sand the edges of the stiles flush with the sides of the washstand.

Routing the Corners

The 2 front corners of the washstand get a decorative treatment that involves 3 separate router cuts for each corner (*drawing 3-D*). First, with the washstand faceup on the bench, I round over the outside corner of each stile using a 1/4-in.-radius roundover bit with a pilot bearing. The bearing rides against the side of the washstand. As always, I move the router from left to right, against the rotation of the bit.

I make the second and third cuts with a 90-degree V-grooving bit and a fence to guide the router (*photo 3-7*). I set the fence 5/8 in. from the point of the bit, to cut a V groove with the center of the V

3-D Dado Layout for Sides

Note: All dadoes are 3/8 in. deep.

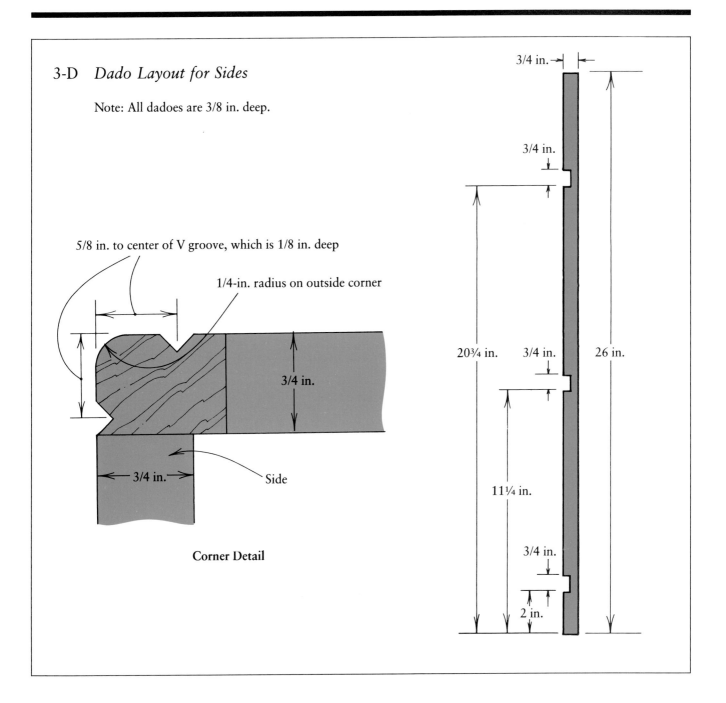

5/8 in. to center of V groove, which is 1/8 in. deep

1/4-in. radius on outside corner

3/4 in.

3/4 in.

Side

Corner Detail

3/4 in.

3/4 in.

3/4 in.

20¾ in.

26 in.

11¼ in.

3/4 in.

2 in.

3-7 The 2 front corners of the washstand get a decorative routed profile that requires 3 separate cuts. The first cut rounds the corner with a 1/4-in. roundover bit. The second cut cuts a V groove on the side of the carcass with a 90-degree V-grooving bit. The third cut (shown here) cuts a V groove on the front of the stile. The fence rides along the side of the washstand to guide the cut.

located 5/8 in. in from the corner (*drawing 3-D*). I make a test cut on some scrap to get the setting right. Then I turn the washstand on its side and cut a V groove along the side, guiding the router fence against the front of the stile.

Now I turn the washstand faceup on the bench to make the third cut that completes the corner. I mill another V groove on the front of the stile, guiding the router fence against the side of the washstand (*photo 3-7*). I repeat the 2 V-groove cuts to complete the opposite corner of the washstand.

That about does it for the base of the washstand. The counter, or top of the washstand, comes next.

Making the Counter

As I mentioned before, the sides and front of the counter flare outward at a 5-degree angle. This angle makes things just a little bit tricky.

The first piece to start with is the backsplash. When I glued up the panels for the washstand, I made a panel approximately 12¾ in. wide and 28 in. long for the backsplash (see Project Planner). I joint and rip this panel to 11½ in., the finished width of the backsplash (*drawing 3-E*).

Next I cut the ends of the backsplash to a 5-degree angle as shown in drawing 3-E. The finished backsplash measures 25 in. along the bottom edge, and I start by measuring off this length along the bottom edge of the backsplash panel. Then, with my adjustable sliding bevel set to a 5-degree angle, I draw pencil lines to mark the angled cuts, one at each end of the 25-in. line. To make these cuts, I set my table saw miter gauge to 5 degrees and cut one end of the backsplash (*photo 3-8*). Then I flip the board around, tilt the miter gauge 5 degrees to the other side of zero, and cut the other end of the backsplash.

3-8   The ends of the backsplash must be cut at a 5-degree angle. I make the cuts on the table saw by setting the miter gauge to 5 degrees.

3-E *Countertop Details*

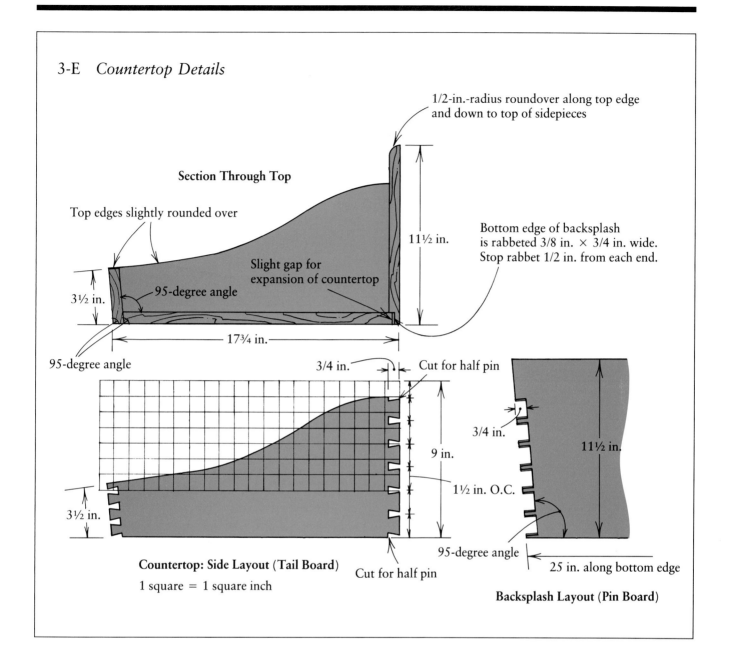

Section Through Top

1/2-in.-radius roundover along top edge and down to top of sidepieces

Top edges slightly rounded over

Bottom edge of backsplash is rabbeted 3/8 in. × 3/4 in. wide. Stop rabbet 1/2 in. from each end.

11½ in.

3½ in.

Slight gap for expansion of countertop

95-degree angle

95-degree angle

17¾ in.

Countertop: Side Layout (Tail Board)
1 square = 1 square inch

3/4 in.

Cut for half pin

9 in.

1½ in. O.C.

3½ in.

Cut for half pin

3/4 in.

11½ in.

95-degree angle

25 in. along bottom edge

Backsplash Layout (Pin Board)

The front of the counter is the same length as the backsplash and gets the same treatment — 5-degree cuts on either end. From the 3¾-in.-wide piece of 1 × 6 left over from ripping the cleat (see Project Planner) I joint and rip a 3⅝-in.-wide piece that's 30 in. long. But before I cut the ends to length, I bevel the bottom edge of this front piece on the jointer (*drawing 3-E*).

To bevel the edge, I tilt the jointer fence 5 degrees, set the depth of cut to 1/16 in., and make 2 passes over the jointer to complete the bevel. When I'm finished jointing the bevel, the front piece is exactly 3½ in. wide across the front face. The fence on my jointer tilts *toward* the table, so I keep the *inside* face of the stock against the fence. Some jointer fences only tilt *away* from the table. In this case, I'd keep the *outer* face of the stock against the fence.

3-9 I use my dovetailing jig to rout the through dovetails on the counter sides. I position the jig's adjustable fingers to give me the spacing I want. Then I rout the tails on the back ends of the sidepieces using a dovetailing bit and a guide collar on my router.

3-10 With the tails complete, I switch to a straight bit and flip my jig's fingers around. Then I clamp the backsplash in the jig with the angled end firmly against the underside of the finger bar to rout the dovetail pins on the ends of the backsplash.

Now I can make the angled end cuts on the table saw, using the miter gauge just as I did with the backsplash.

The sidepieces, too, get a 5-degree bevel on the bottom edge. I joint this edge before I cut the ends of the sidepieces to length. Then, on the table saw, I cut the back ends of the sidepieces off square and make a 5-degree angled cut on the front of each sidepiece (*drawing 3-E*).

The next step in making the sidepieces is to lay out the curves and cut them to shape with my jigsaw (*drawing 3-E*). I clean up the edges with a drum sander and label the sides "left" and "right" with a pencil. Now I'm ready to rout a few dovetails.

Routing the Dovetails

The dovetails come next. I mill these with my through dovetailing jig and a router. Routing the dovetails is the easy part — that goes really fast. Setting up the jig, however, takes a little longer. No matter how many times I've used my dovetailing jig, I always go back to the manual to check — and double-check — the procedure and my setup.

Let's start with the tails on the sidepieces. First, I set up my router with a guide collar and a 1/2-in.-diameter, 8-degree dovetailing bit. Setting the router aside for now, I position the adjustable fingers on my dovetailing jig to give me the pin and tail spacing shown in drawing 3-E. There's a half pin at the top and a half pin at the bottom, with 5 pins spaced 1½ in. O.C. (on center), and 6 tails. When the setup is right, I clamp the sidepiece in the jig and rout the tails on the back end (*photo 3-9*). I repeat the process to rout the tails on the other sidepiece.

The matching pins for the backsplash are the next thing to tackle. I flip the fingers on my dovetailing jig around and switch to a 5/16-in.-diameter straight bit to rout the pins. There's nothing tricky about the angle. I just clamp the end of the backsplash up against the underside of the jig's fingers, and the joints will line up. I mill the pins on both ends of the backsplash (*photo 3-10*).

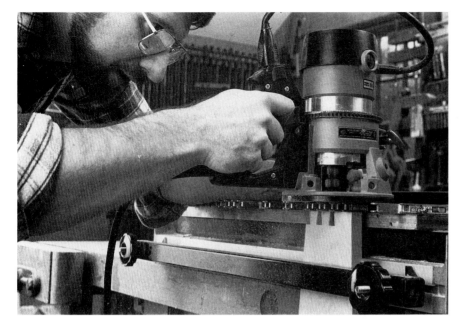

3-11 I switch back to a dovetailing bit to rout the tails on the front ends of the sidepieces. I clamp the counter side in the jig with the end positioned firmly against the underside of the finger bar.

3-12 The matching pins in the front piece are cut with a straight bit. Note the extra-wide "pin" to the right. This will be cut away later by hand to form a 1/2-in.-wide pin and a miter at the top of the joint.

The dovetails at the front of the counter are a little unusual because they have a miter joint at the top. I liked this detail on the original Shaker washstand, and I decided to carry it through on my version. Stop for a minute and study the drawing . . . it's easier than it looks (*drawings 3-F and 3-F detail*).

As shown in drawing 3-F, the joint has 3 full tails, 2 full pins spaced 1 in. O.C. off the bottom, and a 1/4-in.-wide half pin at the bottom. It's the *top* of the joint that warrants a closer look. The miter at the top is sawn out by hand after routing the pins and the tails to create a modified "top pin." I'll explain how in a minute.

Back to the dovetailing jig. I start with the tails on the sidepieces. I reinstall a 1/2-in.-diameter dovetailing bit in my router and adjust the fingers of the jig to give me the pin and tail spacing shown in drawing 3-F. When I've got things set up properly, I rout the tails in both sidepieces, making sure I end up with a "half tail" at the top of each piece (*photo 3-11*).

A quick switch to a 5/16-in.-diameter straight bit and a flip of the fingers on my dovetailing jig and I'm ready to rout the pins in the front piece (*photo 3-12*). Here, too, I make sure that I have the extra-wide pin at the *top* of the front. When I'm finished routing, I have a 1/4-in.-wide half pin at the bottom, two 1/2-in.-wide pins in the middle, and an extra-wide pin at the top.

Mitering the Corners

The joint won't go together at this stage because the extra-wide "pin" on the top of the front piece keeps the joint from closing up. That's easy to fix.

With my combination square, I draw a 45-degree line on the top of the "half tail" on each of the sidepieces (*drawing 3-F*). With my

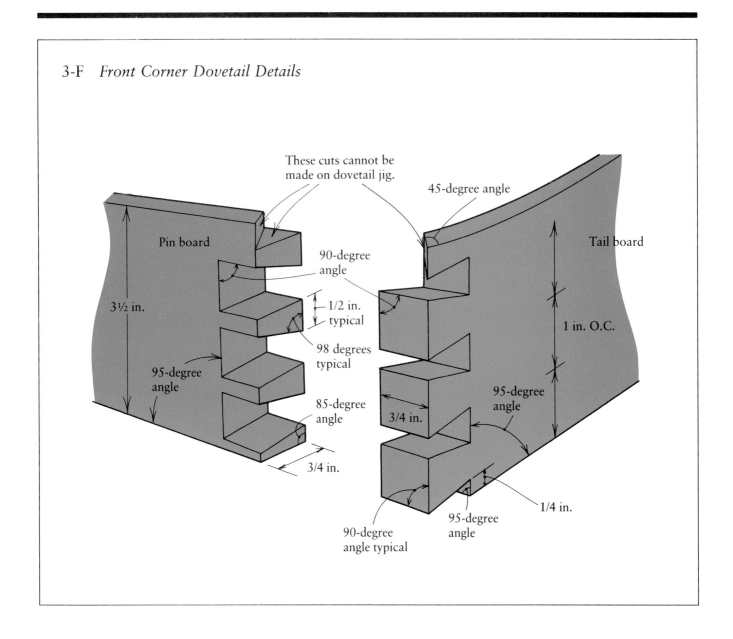

These cuts cannot be
made on dovetail jig.

45-degree angle

Pin board

Tail board

90-degree
angle

3½ in.

1 in. O.C.

1/2 in.
typical

98 degrees
typical

95-degree
angle

85-degree
angle

3/4 in.

95-degree
angle

3/4 in.

1/4 in.

90-degree
angle typical

95-degree
angle

3-13 The front corner dovetails are mitered at the top. After routing the dovetails I saw the miter by hand. I miter the counter sidepieces first. I lay out a 45-degree miter on the top tail and saw straight down to form a miter.

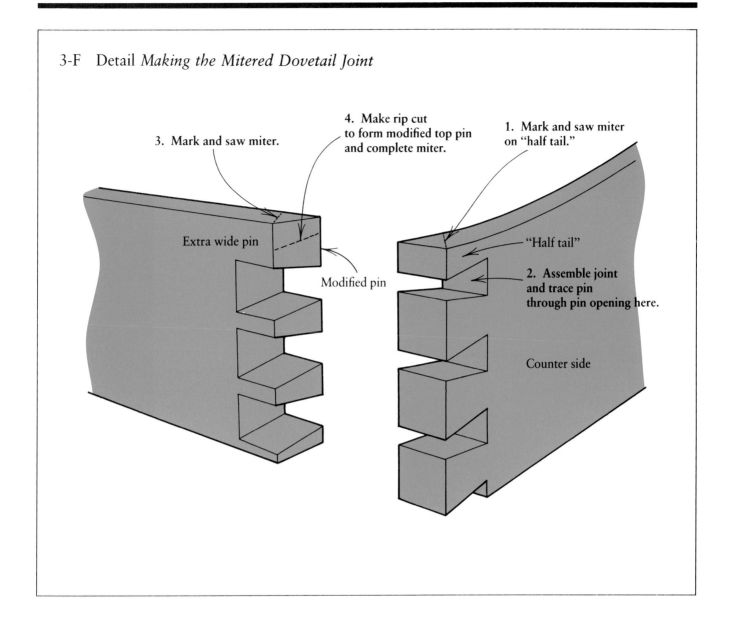

3. Mark and saw miter.

4. Make rip cut to form modified top pin and complete miter.

1. Mark and saw miter on "half tail."

Extra wide pin

Modified pin

"Half tail"

2. Assemble joint and trace pin through pin opening here.

Counter side

dovetailing saw, I saw down along this line, nipping off the inside corner of this narrow tail to create a 45-degree miter (*photo 3-13*).

The mating miter on the front piece of the counter is a little more complicated because it requires 2 cuts to complete. The first cut is a 45-degree crosscut, sawing down from the top edge of the stock. The second cut is a short rip cut sawing in from the end of the extra-wide top pin to free up the chip. This second cut also creates the top side of the 1/2-in.-wide "modified top pin." It's a difficult thing to describe, but if you study drawing 3-F for a minute, you'll see what I mean.

First, I assemble the joint as far as I can. With a pencil that's sharpened to a long, skinny point I mark the top edge of the modi-fied top pin on the end grain of the counter front piece by tracing through the pin opening in the sidepiece. Then I disassemble the pieces and mark the 45-degree miter on the top edge of the stock.

3-14 It takes 2 saw cuts to miter the front piece. On the top edge I lay out a 45-degree miter and saw down from the top edge of the board. The second cut (shown here) is a short rip cut that frees up the chip, completes the miter, and also forms a 1/2-in.-wide pin (note the pencil line to the right of the saw).

3-15 I round over the top and side edges of the backsplash with a 1/2-in.-radius roundover bit, stopping at the line where the side and back meet.

To make the second cut that completes the miter, I clamp the front piece of the counter end-up in my vise. I hold my dovetailing saw at a 45-degree angle and saw down the line I traced on the end grain (*photo 3-14*). A few short strokes and the scrap piece is free. I repeat the process to miter the other end of the front piece.

With the miters complete, the dovetails should go together. If not, the miters may need a little trimming to allow the joint to close. With the joints assembled, I make a light cut with my dovetailing saw straight down the miter joint. This trims a little bit of wood from both sides of the joint and will allow the joint to close perfectly.

Now that all 4 dovetail joints fit nicely together, I can even up the top edges where the sidepieces meet the front. I do this with a plane or a rasp, taking care not to tear out the grain. If the bottom edges don't line up, I true them up with a plane.

Next, I disassemble the counter and round over the top edges with a router. For rounding the top and side edges of the backsplash, I use a 1/2-in.-radius roundover bit (*drawing 3-E and photo 3-15*), being careful not to rout below the point where the sides meet the backsplash. For rounding the top edges of the sides and front, I use a 3/8-in.-radius roundover bit, but I only let part of the cutter project below the router base — I just want to knock the corners off.

There's just one more thing to do before I glue up the counter. I mill a 3/8-in.-deep by 3/4-in.-wide rabbet along the inside bottom edge of the backsplash. This rabbet allows the countertop to expand and contract without opening up a gap where the back edge of the countertop meets the backsplash. This rabbet is a stopped rabbet — the ends of the rabbet stop 1/2 in. shy of the backsplash ends (*photo 3-16 and drawing 3-E*). I use a 1/2-in.-diameter bit and make 2 passes to complete the rabbet. For the first pass, I set the router fence to cut the top edge of the rabbet. For the second pass, I reposition the fence so the bit removes the rest of the wood.

Assembling the Counter

Time for a little assembly, but first, I finish sand the inside surfaces of all the counter pieces. Now I'm ready to spread some glue on the pins and tails and tap the counter together with my deadblow mallet. A couple of clamps across the front and back will pull in the sides to close up the joints and hold things together while the glue sets (*photo 3-17*).

The countertop has to fit inside the counter "frame" that I just glued together. The front and side edges of this countertop need to be beveled 5 degrees to match the outward flair of the counter sides and front. I joint the back edge of the countertop panel straight and square on the jointer, then tilt my table saw blade 5 degrees to bevel the front edge and sides. With the counter "frame" right-side up on the bench, I fit the back edge of the countertop into the rabbet in the backsplash. Then I lower the front edge into place, tapping the

countertop down until it's seated at the bottom. I want a 1/8-in. gap between the back of the countertop and the rabbet in the backsplash. Fitting the countertop is a cut-and-fit process, and it takes me a few tries to get it just right. When it fits, I shoot a few 4d finish nails through the front, sides, and backsplash to hold the countertop in the frame, making sure the 1/8-in. gap is at the back edge of the countertop. No glue here. I want the countertop to be free to expand and contract.

My random orbit sander with a 150-grit disk makes short work of sanding the dovetails flush and smooth. I smooth out the transition where the sides meet the backsplash and sand all the edges by hand. That about does it; the countertop is complete.

Frame-and-Panel Door

The washstand has a little frame-and-panel door with 2 stiles, 2 rails, and a small raised panel that fits into grooves milled in the stiles and rails. The frame is joined with pinned mortise-and-tenon joints — the traditional joint for this application.

First, I joint and rip the stiles and rails to width. The stiles are 2½ in. wide and the rails are 2¾ in. wide. I cut the rails and stiles to length on my power miter box. The stiles are 17¾ in. long. The length of the rails, including the tenons, is 8⅝ in.

The next thing to do is to mill the panel groove in the stiles and rails. On the table saw, I set up my dado head for a 1/4-in.-wide cut. Then I raise the cutter 3/8 in. above the table. I position the rip fence so it's 1/8 in. from the dado head and run a groove in a sample to test the setup. The groove should be 1/4 in. wide and 3/8 in. deep, located 1/8 in. from the edge of the stock (*drawing 3-H*). If necessary, I make any adjustments to the dado head or fence.

Before I start cutting, I mark the front face of each stile and rail so I can keep track of things. Then I mill the panel groove in the stiles and rails, keeping the *back* side of the stock against the rip fence and taking care to keep the stock flat against the fence. I run the groove right to the ends of each frame member.

3-16 The inside bottom edge of the backsplash gets a 3/8-in. by 3/4-in. rabbet to house the back edge of the counter. The rabbet stops 1/2 in. short of the backsplash ends.

3-17 To assemble the counter frame, I brush some glue on the dovetails and tap them together with a mallet. A couple of clamps tighten up the joints and hold things together while the glue dries.

3-18 I cut the mortises in the door stiles with a 1/4-in. hollow-chisel mortising attachment on my drill press. Note that the mortise is located in the panel groove.

Mortising the Stiles

The mortises come next. A 1/4-in. hollow-chisel mortising attachment on my drill press makes short work of the job (*photo 3-18*). I cut two 1/4-in.-wide mortises in each stile, 1¾ in. deep and 1⅞ in. long. The mortises are located within the panel groove itself and start 1/2 in. in from the ends of the stile.

Beveling the Stiles and Rails

On the original Shaker washstand, the inside edges of the stiles and rails are beveled — a decorative detail that sets off the panel nicely. I decided to reproduce this detail on my own washstand door.

To mill the bevel on the stiles and rails, I tilt the fence on my jointer 15 degrees and adjust the infeed table for a 1/16-in. depth of cut. Then I bevel the front, inside edge of each stile and rail, making 2 passes on each piece. As I mentioned before, the fence on my jointer tilts toward the table, so I keep the back side of each frame member against the fence for this cut (*photo 3-19*). On a jointer whose fence tilts away from the table, I'd keep the front side of the stiles and rails against the fence instead.

Door-Rail Tenons

Next come the tenons on the rails, and I make these on the table saw. First I set up to cut the tenon shoulders. I mount a smooth-cutting blade on the saw and put the miter gauge in its slot, ready for business.

The tenons are all 1¾ in. long, and I use a wooden gauge block to ensure that all 4 tenons are exactly the same length. The gauge block is just a piece of wood clamped to the table saw rip fence slightly forward of the blade (that is, toward the operator). I place a rail against the miter-gauge head and slide the rail to my right until the end stops against the gauge block. Then I move the miter gauge forward toward the blade to make the shoulder cut (*photo 3-20*). Moving the rip fence toward or away from the blade will change the length of the tenon. When the rail contacts the blade, the end should no longer be touching the gauge block. It might seem simpler just to butt the rail against the rip fence itself, but it isn't safe to crosscut narrow stock with the end touching the rip fence. The risk of a kick-back is high.

Back to the tenons. I make the shoulder cuts on the backs of the rails first. I raise the blade for a 1/8-in.-deep cut, position the fence (and the gauge block) to make a 1¾-in.-long tenon, and run a sample cut to check the setup. Then I cut the shoulders on the back sides of all 4 tenons. I make a couple of shoulder cuts in some scrap stock, too, as samples to test the next few setups.

The shoulder cuts on the fronts of the stiles and rails are a little more complicated because they have to be angled to match the bevel I milled on the inside edges of the stiles and rails (*drawing 3-G*).

I move the rip fence farther to the right so I can now cut on the left end of the rail, still butting the right-hand end of the rail against the gauge block. Because the rails are so short, I need to screw a long wooden auxiliary fence to my miter gauge fence. Then I tilt the saw blade 15 degrees to the right. I raise the blade to make a 3/8-in.-deep cut and make a trial cut on one of my sample pieces. The angled cut should line up with the first shoulder cut on the opposite side of the stock (*drawing 3-H*). I move the rip fence in or out until a sample cut comes out right. Then I make the angled shoulder cuts on all 4 rail ends (*photo 3-21*).

Now I'm ready to cut away the tenon to form the 3/8-in. haunches on the tenons (*drawing 3-G*). These haunches fill the

3-19 I mill a decorative bevel on the front inside edges of the stiles and rails. I tilt the jointer fence 15 degrees to make this cut, keeping the back side of the frame piece against the fence.

3-20 A gauge block clamped to the table saw rip fence determines the length of the tenon shoulder cuts. I butt the end of the rail against the guide block (at left), then feed the stock forward into the blade to cut the tenon shoulders on the back side of the rail.

3-21 The front shoulder cuts must be angled to match the 15-degree chamfer on the stiles. I tilt the saw blade 15 degrees, move the fence to the right, and make angled shoulder cuts on the front side of the rail.

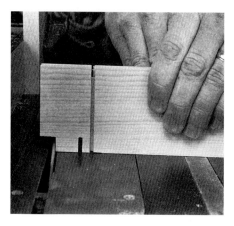

3-22 To form the 3/8-in.-long haunches on the rail tenons, I raise the table saw blade 1/2 in. and make multiple crosscuts to nibble out the waste.

grooves in the stiles, so you don't see gaps at the top and bottom of the door. The haunch cuts are easy. I raise the table saw blade 1/2 in. above the table, stand the rails on edge against the miter-gauge fence, and make multiple crosscuts to nibble out the waste (*photo 3-22*). I use the gauge block to make the first cut that forms the haunch.

The next thing I want to do is cut the cheeks of the tenons. Because the tenons aren't centered on the rail, there'll be 2 setups. First I'll set up for the cheek that's on the front side of the door.

I raise the table saw blade a little less than 1¾ in. above the table and clamp one of my sample pieces in my table saw tenoning jig. I move the jig toward or away from the blade until the saw blade cuts a cheek 3/8 in. from the front of the stock. Then I cut the front cheek on all 4 tenons (*photo 3-23*).

For the second setup, I move the tenoning jig so the blade cuts the second cheek 1/8 in. from the back of the rail. I run a sample cut to check the setup. The tenon should be exactly 1/4 in. wide and a nice slip fit in the stile mortises. When I'm satisfied with the fit of my sample tenon, I make the second cheek cut on all 4 tenons.

The tenons should all fit into their mortises easily — not too tight, not too loose. If they're too tight, I either file the cheeks with a rasp to make the tenons a little thinner or I adjust the tenoning jig so I can shave off just a hair on the table saw. If they're much too loose, I glue veneer to one of the cheeks to make the tenon a little fatter.

Raising the Panel

You can raise a door panel a lot of different ways. You can use a table saw, a router — even a plane, but nothing beats the shaper. It does the best job. I used my shaper and a 4.9-in.-diameter raised panel cutter to cut the field on the door panel (*photo 3-24*).

Before raising the panel, of course, I have to joint, rip, and crosscut the panel to its finished dimensions: 5⅝ in. wide and 12¾ in.

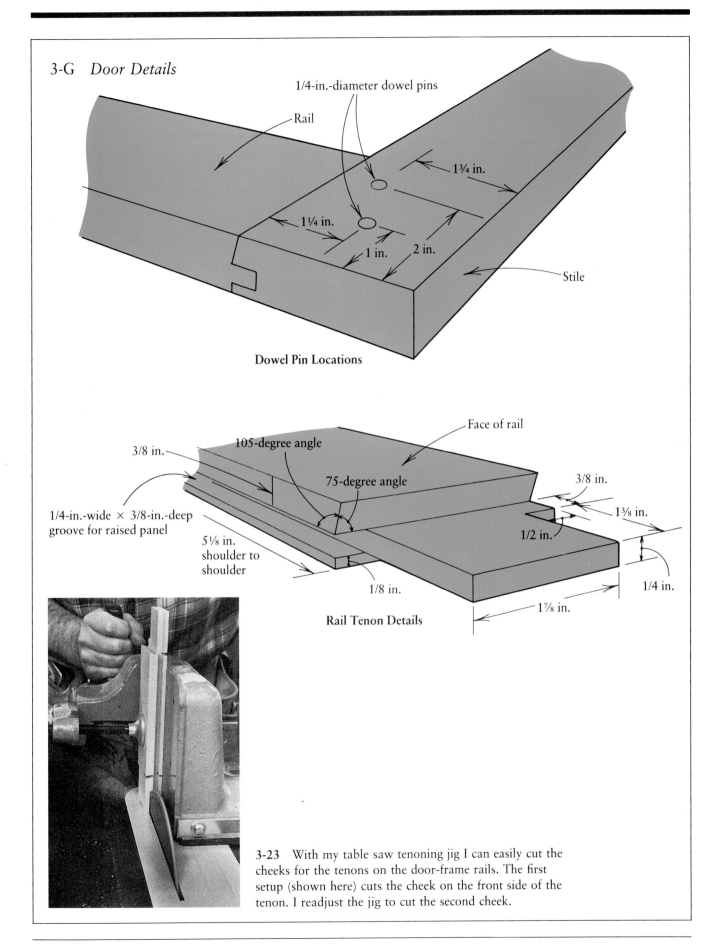

3-G Door Details

1/4-in.-diameter dowel pins

Rail

1¾ in.

1¼ in.

1 in.

2 in.

Stile

Dowel Pin Locations

Face of rail

3/8 in.

105-degree angle

75-degree angle

3/8 in.

1⅜ in.

1/2 in.

1/4-in.-wide × 3/8-in.-deep groove for raised panel

5⅛ in. shoulder to shoulder

1/8 in.

1/4 in.

1⅞ in.

Rail Tenon Details

3-23 With my table saw tenoning jig I can easily cut the cheeks for the tenons on the door-frame rails. The first setup (shown here) cuts the cheek on the front side of the tenon. I readjust the jig to cut the second cheek.

3-24 The shaper with a raised-panel cutter does the best job of raising the field around the door panel. A plastic safety guard covers the cutter and an adjustable hold-down keeps the panel flat against the table. The finished panel has a 1/4-in. tongue around the edge.

3-25 The drawer front gets a decorative chamfer on the top, bottom, and sides. I made a plywood jig that rides on my table saw rip fence to allow me to chamfer the ends of the drawer front safely. I position the fence to the left of the blade and tilt the saw blade 15 degrees to make the cut.

long. Then I set up the shaper to make a 1/4-in.-thick tongue around the edge of the panel.

Assembling the Door

Now I'm ready to dry-assemble the door and see how things fit. If the panel is too large, it will prevent the frame from coming together. The panel shouldn't bottom out in its groove — there should be a gap of about 1/8 in. all around (*drawing 3-H*). If necessary, I trim off some of the panel tongue on the table saw.

Before gluing things together for keeps, I finish sand the panel and all the stiles and rails. Then I brush some glue in the mortises and on the tenons and put the door together. The panel just floats in the groove without glue. I want it to be free to expand and contract.

When the frame is assembled, I drill two 1/4-in.-diameter holes through each tenon and glue in some 1/4-in. dowels to reinforce the joints (*drawing 3-G*). When the glue's dry, I saw the ends of the dowels off flush with my dovetailing saw. Then I sand the dowels flush with my belt sander. Now I sand all the door rails and stiles one more time with my random orbit sander.

The finishing touch is to bevel the latch-side edge of the door 5 degrees so it doesn't hit the stile when I open or close it. I tilt the jointer fence 5 degrees and bevel one edge (*drawing 3-H*).

Making the Drawer

The washstand drawer is a simple one. The drawer front is a piece of 3/4-in.-thick pine, rabbeted on the bottom and sides so it overlaps the face frame of the washstand. It's joined to the sides with half-blind dovetails, which I cut with a router. The back of the drawer fits into dadoes cut in the drawer sides, and the bottom is a piece of 1/4-in. plywood.

For the drawer sides and backs I plane some 3/4-in. stock down to a 1/2-in. thickness using my portable thickness planer. I joint and rip all the drawer stock to width and trim the ends to the lengths shown in drawing 3-I. I also cut the 1/4-in. plywood bottom panel to size, using the same technique I always use for sizing panels on the table saw.

First, on the table saw, I set up my dado head to mill a 1/4-in. by 1/4-in. groove along the inside bottom edges of the drawer sides and drawer front (*drawing 3-I*). Note that the groove in the drawer front is 1/2 in. from the bottom edge. Next, I set up the dado head for a 1/2-in.-wide cut and mill a 1/2-in.-wide dado at the back end of each drawer side to house the back of the drawer.

Next, with the dado head still set for a 1/2-in.-wide cut, I attach my wooden auxiliary fence to the table saw rip fence and position the fence to mill a 1/4-in. by 7/16-in. rabbet along the bottom and sides of the drawer front (*drawing 3-I*).

I cut the half-blind dovetails with my dovetailing jig and a router, cutting the tails in the drawer sides first and the pins in the drawer

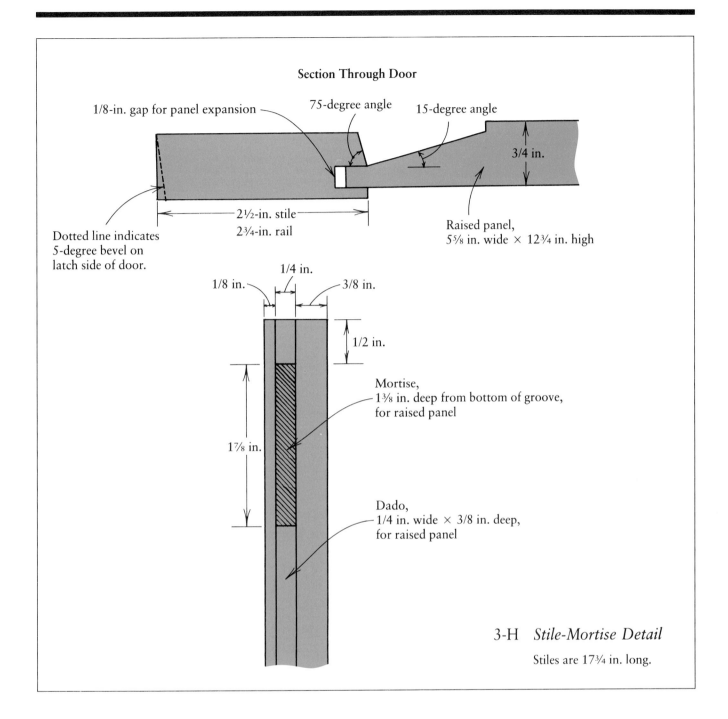

Section Through Door

1/8-in. gap for panel expansion

75-degree angle

15-degree angle

3/4 in.

Dotted line indicates 5-degree bevel on latch side of door.

2½-in. stile
2¾-in. rail

Raised panel,
5⅝ in. wide × 12¾ in. high

1/4 in.

1/8 in.

3/8 in.

1/2 in.

Mortise,
1⅜ in. deep from bottom of groove,
for raised panel

1⅞ in.

Dado,
1/4 in. wide × 3/8 in. deep,
for raised panel

3-H *Stile-Mortise Detail*
Stiles are 17¾ in. long.

front next. I adjust the fingers of my dovetailing jig to give me 2 full pins, spaced 1½ in., as shown in drawing 3-I, with a half pin at the top and bottom.

After the dovetails are cut I "raise" the edges of the drawer front on the table saw. I made a plywood jig that rides on my rip fence and works just like a tenoning jig to hold the drawer vertically on end so I can bevel the ends of the drawer front safely (*photo 3-25*). I position the rip fence to the left of the blade and tilt the saw blade 15 degrees. I raise the blade a sufficient height and bevel the edges and ends of the drawer front. I clean up the saw marks with my random orbit sander and finish sand all the drawer parts inside and out.

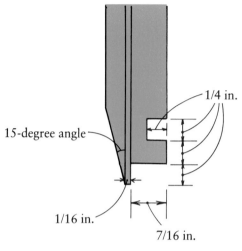

1/4 in.

15-degree angle

Drawer Front Details
Note: Top edge of drawer front is not rabbeted.

1/16 in.

7/16 in.

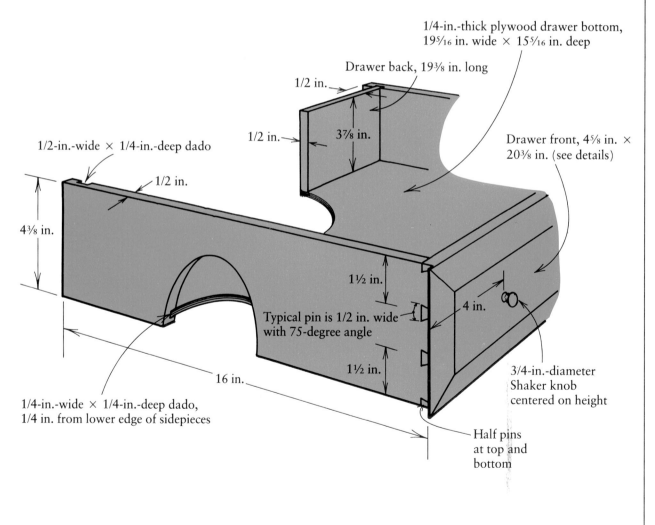

1/4-in.-thick plywood drawer bottom, 19⁵⁄₁₆ in. wide × 15⁵⁄₁₆ in. deep

Drawer back, 19³⁄₈ in. long

1/2 in.

1/2 in.

3⁷⁄₈ in.

Drawer front, 4⁵⁄₈ in. × 20³⁄₈ in. (see details)

1/2-in.-wide × 1/4-in.-deep dado

1/2 in.

4³⁄₈ in.

1½ in.

4 in.

Typical pin is 1/2 in. wide with 75-degree angle

1½ in.

3/4-in.-diameter Shaker knob centered on height

16 in.

1/4-in.-wide × 1/4-in.-deep dado, 1/4 in. from lower edge of sidepieces

Half pins at top and bottom

3-26 I brush some glue in the slots, put in some biscuits, and lower the counter into position on the sides.

Now I'm ready to glue the drawer together. I brush some glue on all the mating surfaces of the dovetails and tap the joints together. Now I'm ready for the back. I put glue in the side dadoes and secure the back with some 1-in. brads in each end. Now I slip the plywood bottom into the groove. I check for square with my framing square and tack the bottom to the drawer back with some brads. Some sanding to clean up the dovetails and I'm ready to install the knobs. I locate and drill the holes for the knobs. I put a little glue on the knob tenons and tap them into their holes with a mallet.

Mounting the Counter

With my biscuit joiner, I cut two #20-size biscuit slots in the top of each side and 4 matching slots in the bottom of the countertop (*drawing 3-B*). I glue in the biscuits and glue the countertop to the sides of the washstand (*photo 3-26*), clamping if necessary.

Hanging the Door

There's just one thing left to do, and that's to hang the door. I screw the butt hinges in position where I want them (not on the beveled edge of the door) and outline the hinge with a utility knife. Then I remove the hinges and cut the mortises with a chisel and mallet. I score the outline of the mortise with the chisel first. Then I make a few vertical cuts with the chisel to score the depth of the mortise. Finally, I chisel out the waste between these cuts to complete the mortise.

I cut mortises on both the door stile and the washstand stile and screw hinges in their mortises. The door is now free to swing. I drill a hole for a knob and glue it in place. Last of all, I make a little

3-27 The finishing touch, after hanging the door, is a little wooden turn latch, which I install with a brass round-head screw.

wooden turn latch from a piece of scrap and screw it in place on the stile with a brass roundhead screw (*photo 3-27*). Not too tight — the latch must be able to turn.

The Finishing Touch

The finishing scheme for my washstand calls for painting the bottom a nice, "old timey" putty color. On the countertop, I planned to apply a clear, satin finish. Paint might chip, and I didn't want to cover up the dovetails after all that work.

I finished the counter with three coats of satin, water-based polyurethane — a clear, durable finish that won't yellow with age. I apply the finish with a disposable foam brush, sanding between coats with 320- to 600-grit paper. After the first coat is dry, I fill the nail holes in the counter with a colored putty stick that matches the pine. I give the underside of the countertop one coat of finish to reduce the chance of cupping.

The base of the cabinet gets a coat of latex primer. When the primer is dry, I sand the piece lightly with 220-grit paper and fill the nail holes with glazing compound. Now for the top coat. Two coats of acrylic latex paint — a color just like the Shakers might have used. In fact, the name of the color I bought is "Hancock Gray." Maybe they named it after Hancock Shaker Village.

FOUR

Shaker Wall Clock

PROJECT PLANNER

Time: 2 days
Special hardware and tools:
(2) 3/4-in.-diameter Shaker knobs
(4) 1⅛-in. × 2-in. brass butt hinges and screws
(1) Battery-powered quartz clock movement with hands and hardware
(1) 9-in.-square paper dial with 7-in.-diameter time ring
(2) 5/16-in.-diameter magnetic catches
(1) 7⁹⁄₁₆-in. × 8¹⁄₁₆-in. single-strength glass
Thickness planer
Wood:
(1) 7 ft 1 × 12 walnut
Plane to 9/16-in. thickness. Cut one piece 3 ft long for back. Cut one piece 2 ft long and rip into one piece 2⅝ in. wide for top and bottom of case, and one piece 4⅜-in. wide for top and bottom trim pieces. From remaining 2-ft length: Rip 2 pieces 2¹⁄₁₆ in. wide for lower-door stiles. Rip one piece 1¹¹⁄₁₆ in. wide for lower-door rails. Rip one piece 1⁷⁄₁₆ in. wide for upper-door rails. Rip one piece 1³⁄₁₆ in. wide for upper-door stiles.

(1) 5 ft 1 × 8 walnut
Rip a strip 3/4 in. wide and mill into 2 pieces of 1/4-in. quarter round 60 in. long for moldings. From remainder: Cut one piece 31 in. long, rip in half, and plane to 1/2-in. thickness for sides of case. Cut one piece 17 in. long and plane to 5/16-in. thickness for lower-door panel. Cut one piece 1¹³⁄₁₆ in. wide and plane to 1/2-in. thickness for divider rail. Make trim strip and cleats from scrap.

(1) 3/8-in. plywood
Cut 10-in. × 10-in. piece to make backer for paper dial and quartz clock movement.

THE Shakers didn't carry pocket watches. They didn't need them. They told time by the ringing of a bell. It would wake them in the morning and call them at mealtimes or to worship. What clocks they did have were very special and reserved for special places. This elegant walnut wall clock is based on an original clock made in 1840 by Isaac N. Youngs, a furniture-maker at the Shaker community in Mount Lebanon, New York. Youngs made 6 clocks that year, according to the notes that he kept in his "Clock Maker's Journal." Three of these clocks, including the one that inspired my version, are now in the collection at Shaker Hancock Village in Pittsfield, Massachusetts.

I really liked the proportions of the original clock, so I decided to stick to the design as much as possible. I did make a few changes, however. The original clock has a spring-driven pendulum movement with wooden gears. I could have installed a windup movement in my clock, but I decided to go with a battery-powered quartz movement instead. It's less expensive than a mechanical movement, more accurate, and (best of all) it never needs winding. Quartz movements are available at hobby stores, clock stores, mail-order companies, and some woodworking stores. Since my clock has no interesting works to look at, I also eliminated the two small, glass windows in the sides of the original clock case.

Planing the Wood

When I bought the wood for the clock, the thinnest walnut I could find was 3/4 in. thick. Since I want to stick to the original design and use 9/16-in., 1/2-in., and 5/16-in. stock, I need to thin it down. I could stand the boards on edge and rip them on my table saw or band saw (this technique is known as "resawing"), but I'd end up with a pretty rough surface that would be difficult to sand smooth. It's easier and faster just to run the boards through my thickness planer (*photo 4-1*).

First, I'll plane the 1 × 12 to a thickness of 9/16 in. (see Project Planner). I set my planer to take a light cut (about 1/32 in. or so)

4-1 The parts of the clock case vary in thickness from 5/16 in. to 9/16 in. I could find only 3/4-in.-thick walnut so I thinned down the stock on my thickness planer. Here I'm surfacing a piece of 1 × 12 that will be cut into various parts of the clock. A dust-collection attachment helps to keep the shop clean.

4-A *Major Anatomy and Dimensions*

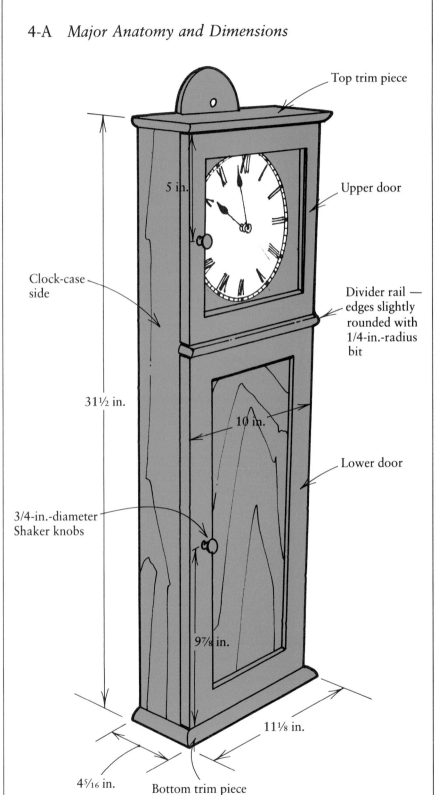

Top trim piece

Upper door

Divider rail — edges slightly rounded with 1/4-in.-radius bit

Lower door

Clock-case side

5 in.

31½ in.

10 in.

3/4-in.-diameter Shaker knobs

9⅞ in.

11⅛ in.

4⁵⁄₁₆ in.

Bottom trim piece

Note: Upper and lower doors hang on a pair of 2-in. × 1⅛-in. butts mortised into front edge of clock-case side and back of door stile. Align one edge of butt hinge with inner edge of door rail.

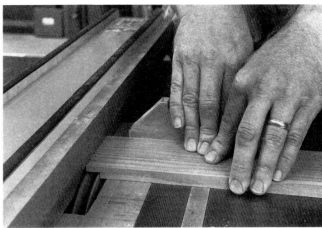

and run the board through the planer. After the first pass, I raise the table another 1/32 in. and flip the board over to plane the opposite side. I continue to plane alternate sides of the board until I reach the thickness I want. By taking an equal amount off each side, I end up with a board that has uniform moisture content. This means that I won't end up with cupping later.

The walnut 1 × 8 gets sawn up into parts of varying thickness, so I can't plane the entire board at once. I'll cut out the pieces first, then plane them to the thicknesses specified in the Project Planner. Note that the rough dimensions given there are 1/16 in. wider than the width of the finished part. To size the piece, I simply need to joint the edges — one pass on each long edge. Since I keep my jointer set for a 1/32-in. cut, 2 passes takes off the extra 1/16 in. of material. This technique saves time since I only have to rip the stock once — when I rough it out.

Making the Clock-Case Sides

The next thing I want to do is make the sides of the clock case. I joint both long edges of the two 1/2-in.-thick by 31-in.-long pieces I milled from the 1 × 8 (see Project Planner) to end up with 2 pieces exactly 3⅛ in. wide.

Next I'll cut each sidepiece to length. I square up one end on my power miter box. Then I measure off the length and cut both sides to their finished length of 30⅜ in.

The back of the clock case fits into rabbets cut along the back inside edges of the sidepieces (*drawing 4-B*). There are also rabbets at the top and bottom of each sidepiece for the top and bottom of the clock case. I mill those rabbets with a dado head on my table saw.

I mill the 1/4-in. by 9/16-in. rabbets along the back edges first. First I protect my table saw rip fence with an auxiliary wooden fence. Then I set up my stack dado head for a 3/4-in.-wide dado. I position the wooden fence so it covers part of the dado head, exposing 9/16 in. of the cutter (*photo 4-2*). I make a cut in scrap stock to

4-2 The back of the clock case fits into 1/4-in. by 9/16-in. rabbets in the sides of the case. To mill these rabbets, I attach a wooden fence to my rip fence and position it to cover all but 9/16 in. of the dado head.

4-3 Without changing the setting I used to cut the rabbets, I mill a rabbet on each end of the sidepieces. I feed the stock into the blade with my miter gauge.

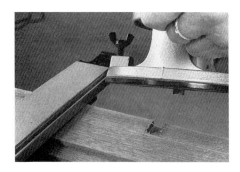

4-4 The divider rail fits into 1/2-in. by 7/8-in. dadoes in the sides of the case. I rout these short dadoes by guiding the router base against a straightedge clamp.

4-5 I assemble the sides, top, and bottom of the case by gluing the dado joints and fastening them together with some 3/4-in. brads from my pneumatic brad nailer.

check the blade height and width, then I mill a rabbet along one edge of each sidepiece.

Without changing the fence or dado-head setup, I cut the rabbets on both ends of each sidepiece (*photo 4-3*). I use my miter gauge to feed the stock into the dado head, making sure that I cut the dado on the same face as the rabbet.

There's one more milling step for the sides of the case. I need to cut a short dado in each sidepiece for the ends of the divider rail — the horizontal piece that separates the upper and lower doors (*drawings 4-A and 4-B*). These dadoes don't run across the full width of the sidepiece, so I'll mill them with a router instead of on the table saw.

I lay out the 1/2-in.-wide by 7/8-in.-long dadoes with a pencil and square. I set up my router with a 1/2-in.-diameter straight bit and adjust it for a 1/4-in.-deep cut. Then I clamp the sidepiece firmly in place on my bench and position a straightedge clamp squarely across the work to guide the base of my router for making the cut (*photo 4-4*). The distance from the layout line to the straightedge equals the distance from the router bit to the edge of the router base. I guide the base of the router against the straightedge clamp to cut the dado. I square up the rounded corners of each dado with a chisel.

Putting the Case Together

Next, I joint the top and bottom of the clock case to width and cut these 2 pieces to length (*drawing 4-B*). I also joint the divider rail to its finished, 1¾-in. width. Then I finish sand the inside surfaces of the clock-case sides, as well as the inside surface of the top and bottom of the case.

Now I'm ready for a little assembly. I brush some glue on the top and bottom rabbets in the two sidepieces and put the top and bottom pieces of the case in place. On the front of the case, I want to make sure that the edges of the top and bottom are flush with the edges of the sides. When the edges are flush, I shoot in a few 3/4-in. brads with my pneumatic brad nailer (*photo 4-5*). If any glue squeezes out of the joints, I wipe it off with a damp sponge.

The ends of the divider rail project 1/16 in. beyond the sides of the clock case. I measure and mark the length and trim the rail ends on my miter box. I have to cut a 5/16-in. by 7/8-in. notch at each end of the rail to overlap the sides of the case (*drawings 4-A and 4-B*). On the table saw, since my dado head is still installed, I raise my dado head 7/8 in. above the table, place the rail against the miter gauge, and cut a notch in each end (*photo 4-6*).

The front edge and ends of this divider rail need to be slightly eased, or rounded over. I do this with my router, which I've set up with a 1/4-in. roundover bit. I only reveal a little of the bit because I don't want to cut a full quarter round. I rout around the ends and front of the divider on both the top and bottom edges.

After finish sanding the divider, I'm ready to glue it in place. I

4-B   *Clock-Case Details*

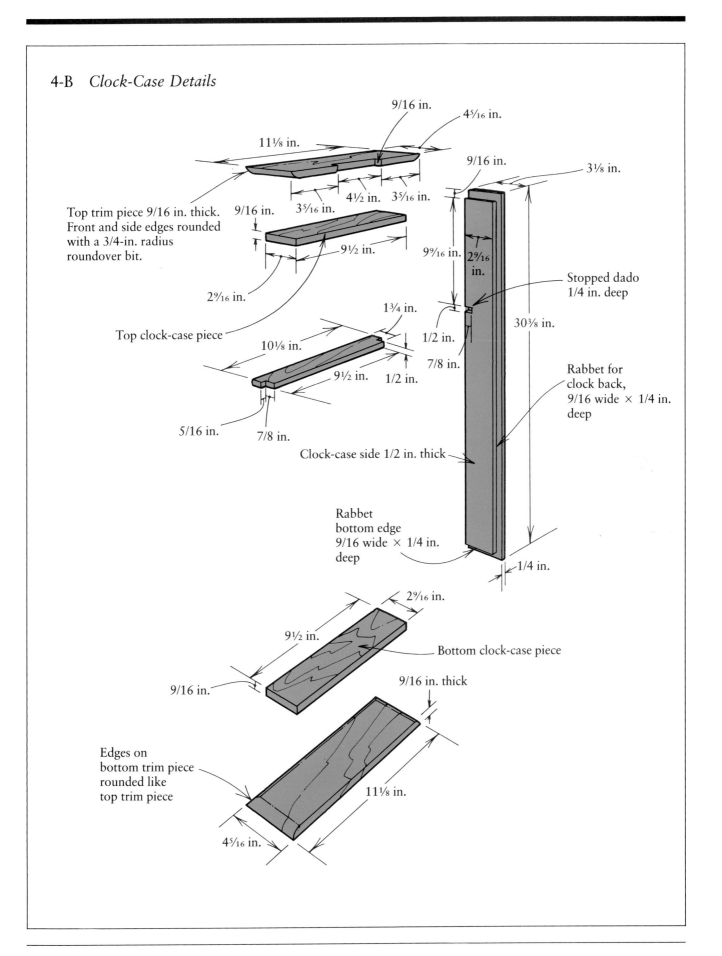

9/16 in.

4⁵/₁₆ in.

11⅛ in.

9/16 in.

3⅛ in.

Top trim piece 9/16 in. thick. Front and side edges rounded with a 3/4-in. radius roundover bit.

9/16 in.

3⁵/₁₆ in.

4½ in.

3⁵/₁₆ in.

9½ in.

9⁹/₁₆ in.

2⁹/₁₆ in.

Stopped dado 1/4 in. deep

30⅜ in.

2⁹/₁₆ in.

Top clock-case piece

1¾ in.

10⅛ in.

9½ in.

1/2 in.

1/2 in.

7/8 in.

Rabbet for clock back, 9/16 wide × 1/4 in. deep

5/16 in.

7/8 in.

Clock-case side 1/2 in. thick

Rabbet bottom edge 9/16 wide × 1/4 in. deep

1/4 in.

2⁹/₁₆ in.

9½ in.

Bottom clock-case piece

9/16 in. thick

9/16 in.

Edges on bottom trim piece rounded like top trim piece

11⅛ in.

4⁵/₁₆ in.

4-6 The ends of the divider rail are notched to overlap the case sides. I raise the dado head 7/8 in. above the saw table and cut these notches using my miter gauge to support the stock.

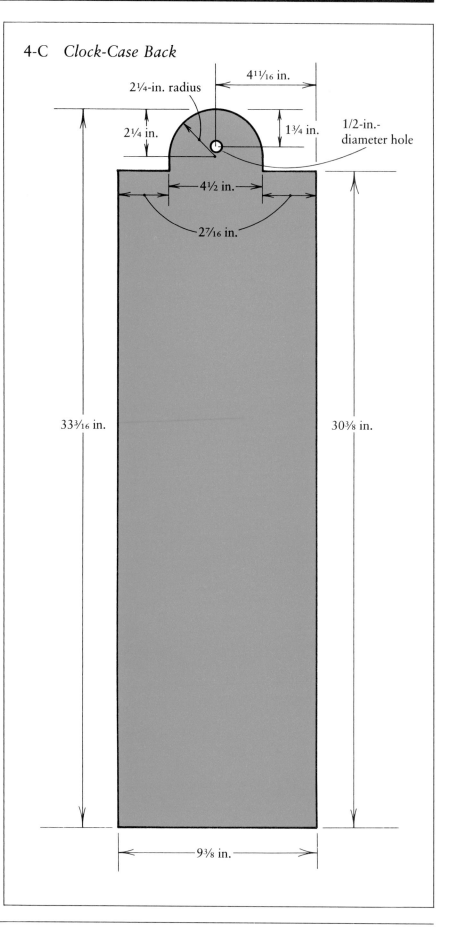

4-C   Clock-Case Back

2¼-in. radius

4¹¹⁄₁₆ in.

2¼ in.

1¾ in.

1/2-in.- diameter hole

4½ in.

2⁷⁄₁₆ in.

33³⁄₁₆ in.

30⅜ in.

9⅜ in.

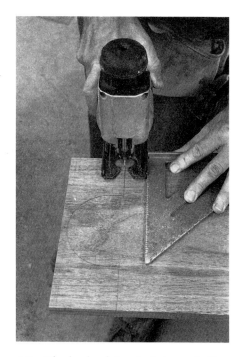

4-7 The back of the clock has a half-round part at the top where the clock will hang on the wall. I lay out the arc with a compass and cut out the shape with my jigsaw. I make the 2 straight cuts first, guiding the saw against the edge of my square.

brush a little glue in the dadoes, install the divider, and tack it in place by shooting 2 brads through the side of the case into each end of the rail.

Cutting Out the Back

The next thing to do is to cut the back to size and saw out the half-round portion at the top, where the clock will hang on the wall (*drawings 4-A and 4-C*). I've already roughed out a 3-ft-long piece of 1 × 12 to make the back (see Project Planner). With the clock case facedown on my bench, I measure across the dadoes in the sides to determine the final width for the back. I joint one long edge and rip the back 1/8 in. narrower than the distance between the rabbets — in this case, 9⅜ in. Next, I square up the bottom end on the table saw with my homemade panel cutter.

With a square and a compass, I lay out the half-round portion at the top (*drawing 4-C*). I clamp the back with the end hanging off my bench and cut out the shape with my jigsaw. I make the straight cuts first, guiding the saw's base against the edge of my square so the cuts are nice and straight (*photo 4-7*). Then I cut out the round part (*photo 4-8*). I sand the edges smooth with my small, electric pad sander.

Now I'll drill a hole for hanging the clock. I back up the stock with a piece of scrap wood and drill a 1/2-in.-diameter hole (*drawing 4-C*).

I fasten the back of the clock to the case with nails only. I don't want to use any glue because the back is likely to shrink in width. If I glued it in place, it would probably split.

With the back in position, I nail it to the bottom piece with a single nail in the middle of the back. Then I nail the other end to the top piece with a single nail. So the back will be free to shrink without splitting, I nail through the sides of the case instead of the back. I tip the clock case on one side and nail through the side, driving the nails into the edge of the back. I do the same thing on the opposite side of the case. It's important to hold the back tight in the rabbets when nailing — clamping it in place isn't a bad idea.

The top and bottom trim pieces are the next 2 parts to install on the clock case (*drawings 4-A and 4-B*). I joint and rip these pieces to a width of 4⁵⁄₁₆ in., then cut both pieces 11⅛ in. long.

The top and bottom trim pieces are shaped on their front edge and ends (*drawings 4-A and 4-B*). To mill this shape, I use my router table and a 3/4-in.-radius roundover bit. I don't expose the entire bit — part of the cutting edge remains below the router-table surface, as shown in photo 4-9. I mill the ends first, then the long, front edge. I sand the cuts smooth with my pad sander.

The top trim piece has to have a notch cut in the middle to fit around the half-round hanger part of the back (*drawing 4-B*). To mark the cut, I place the top trim piece on top of the clock case, center it, and use a square to mark the cutout. Then I cut the notch

4-8 With the straight cuts complete, I saw out the round part with the jigsaw. I clean up the cuts with a pad sander.

4-9 To mill the rounded shape on the top and bottom trim pieces, I set up my router with a 3/4-in.-radius roundover bit. I rout the ends first, then the front edge. Note that only a portion of the bit is exposed above the table.

4-10 The back edge of the top trim piece needs a notch to fit around the half-round part of the back. I raise the dado head 9/16 in. above the table and nibble out the 4½-in.-wide notch, supporting the stock against my miter gauge.

4-11 I mill a 3/16-in. by 7/16-in. rabbet along the inside edge of the stiles and rails for both the upper and lower doors. I cut the rabbet in 2 passes.

with a dado head on the table saw. I raise the blade 9/16 in. above the table and make repeated crosscuts with the miter gauge to nibble out the 4½-in.-long notch (*photo 4-10*). Now I can glue and nail the top and bottom trim pieces to the case (*drawings 4-A and 4-B*).

Making the Doors

Now I'm ready to start working on the doors. The door frames are joined with mortise-and-tenon joints. The top door has a glass panel in it while the bottom door has a wooden panel. Both of these panels fit into rabbets cut in the stiles and rails and are held in place with a small, quarter-round molding.

First, I joint all the stock for the stiles and rails to finished width (*drawings 4-D and 4-E*). The lower-door rails are 1⅝ in. wide. The lower-door stiles are 2 in. wide. The rails for the upper door are 1⅜ in. wide, and the upper-door stiles are 1⅛ in. wide. Then I square up one end of each frame member on my miter box and cut each one to the length shown in the drawings, remembering to allow for the tenons on the rails (*drawings 4-D and 4-E*).

With the stiles and rails cut to size, I'm ready to mill the rabbets for the panels. The rabbets on both doors are the same size — 3/16 in. by 7/16 in. (*drawing 4-D, rabbet detail*). I could cut these rabbets on the table saw with my dado head, but I decided to mill them on my router table instead. I set up my router table with a 3/8-in. rabbeting bit and run sample cuts in a piece of scrap wood until I get the setting right. Then I mill a rabbet along one edge of all 8 door-frame pieces (*photo 4-11*). I mill the rabbet in 2 passes. For the first pass, the bit is raised only 3/16 in. above the table. I raise the height to 7/16 in. for the second pass.

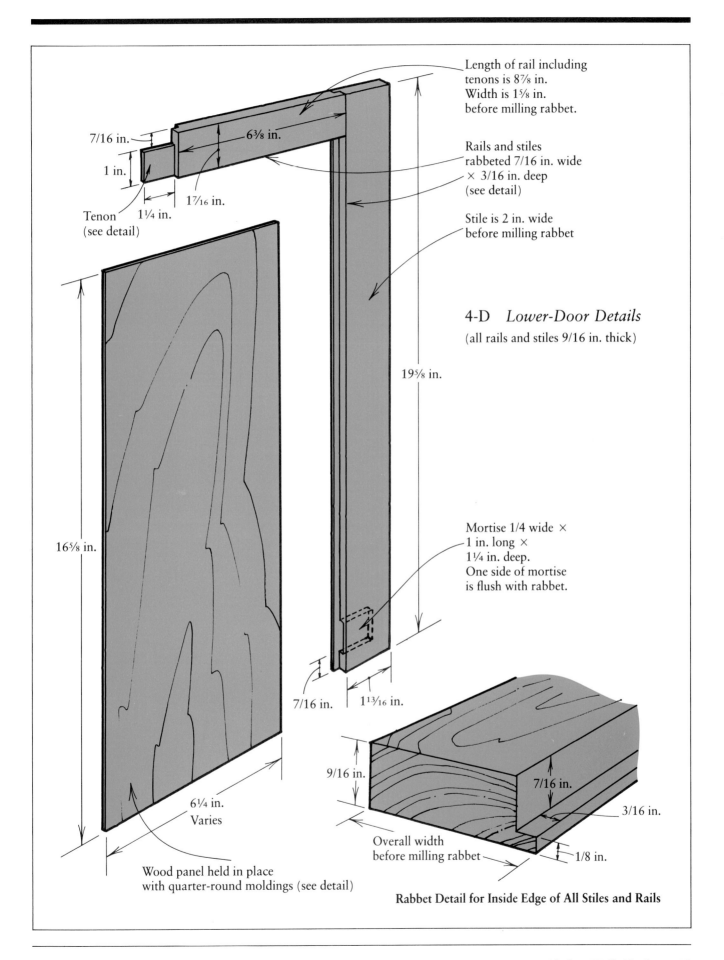

Length of rail including
tenons is 8⅞ in.
Width is 1⅝ in.
before milling rabbet.

7/16 in.

6⅜ in.

Rails and stiles
rabbeted 7/16 in. wide
× 3/16 in. deep
(see detail)

1 in.

Tenon
(see detail)

1¼ in.

1⁷⁄₁₆ in.

Stile is 2 in. wide
before milling rabbet

4-D   *Lower-Door Details*

(all rails and stiles 9/16 in. thick)

19⅝ in.

Mortise 1/4 wide ×
1 in. long ×
1¼ in. deep.
One side of mortise
is flush with rabbet.

16⅝ in.

7/16 in.

1¹³⁄₁₆ in.

9/16 in.

7/16 in.

3/16 in.

6¼ in.
Varies

Overall width
before milling rabbet

1/8 in.

Wood panel held in place
with quarter-round moldings (see detail)

Rabbet Detail for Inside Edge of All Stiles and Rails

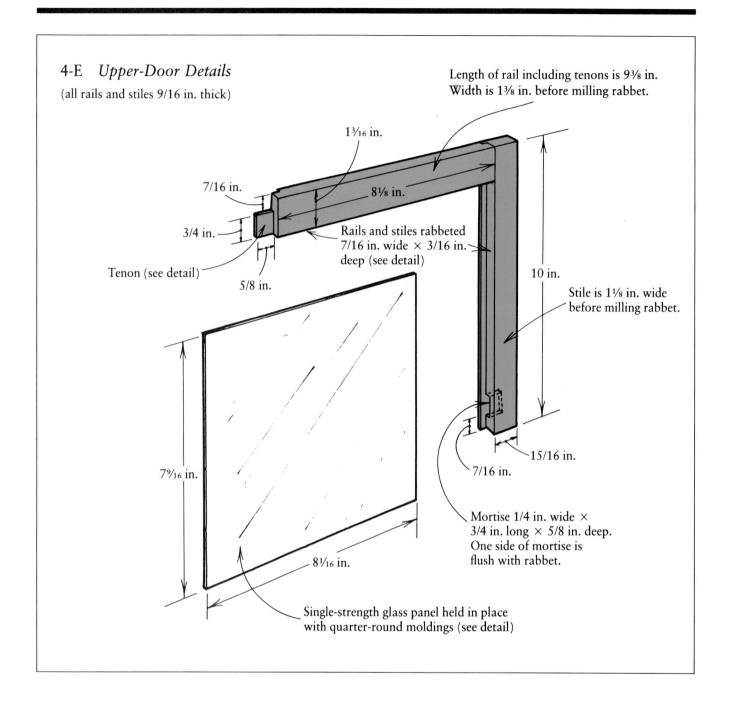

4-E Upper-Door Details

(all rails and stiles 9/16 in. thick)

Length of rail including tenons is 9⅜ in.
Width is 1⅜ in. before milling rabbet.

1³⁄₁₆ in.

7/16 in.

8⅛ in.

3/4 in.

Tenon (see detail)

5/8 in.

Rails and stiles rabbeted
7/16 in. wide × 3/16 in.
deep (see detail)

10 in.

Stile is 1⅛ in. wide
before milling rabbet.

15/16 in.

7/16 in.

7⁹⁄₁₆ in.

8¹⁄₁₆ in.

Mortise 1/4 in. wide ×
3/4 in. long × 5/8 in. deep.
One side of mortise is
flush with rabbet.

Single-strength glass panel held in place
with quarter-round moldings (see detail)

Mortises and Tenons

With the rabbets milled in the stiles and rails, the next step is to lay out and cut the mortises in the stiles. With a pencil, square, and rule, I lay out the 1/4-in.-wide mortises on each stile (*drawings 4-D and 4-E*). Then I cut the mortises using the hollow-chisel mortising attachment for my drill press (*photo 4-12*). I set the depth stop on the drill press to limit the depth of the mortises. The mortises for the lower door are 1¼ in. deep. The upper-door mortises measure 5/8 in. deep.

The tenons come next. The tenon shoulders are a little tricky because the shoulders on the back side of the doors must be offset 3/16

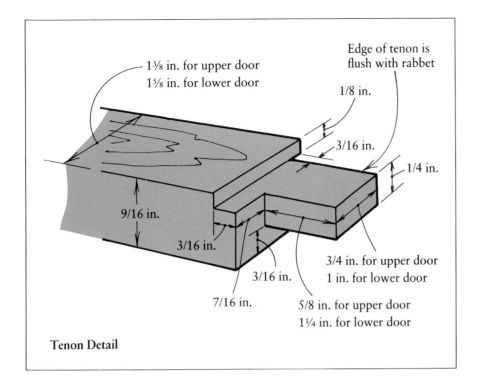

1⅜ in. for upper door
1⅝ in. for lower door

Edge of tenon is flush with rabbet

1/8 in.

3/16 in.

1/4 in.

9/16 in.

3/16 in.

3/16 in.

7/16 in.

5/8 in. for upper door
1¼ in. for lower door

3/4 in. for upper door
1 in. for lower door

Tenon Detail

in. to account for the width of the rabbet in the stiles. This is easy enough to do on the table saw.

To ensure that the tenons will all be the same length, I use a wooden gauge block for making the shoulder cuts. The gauge block is just a piece of wood clamped to the table saw rip fence slightly forward of the blade (that is, toward the operator). I place a rail against the miter-gauge head and slide the rail to my right until the end butts against the gauge block. Then I move the miter gauge and rail forward toward the blade to make the shoulder cut (*photo 4-13*). When the rail contacts the blade, the end should no longer be touching the gauge block. Moving the rip fence will adjust the length of the tenon.

First, I'll cut the tenon shoulders on the lower-door rails. With the gauge block in place, I raise the blade 3/16 in. above the table to cut the shoulders on the front sides of the tenons. I position the fence so the gauge block is 1¼ in. from the *left* side of the blade and make a sample cut to check the setup. The shoulder cut should be 3/16 in. deep and 1¼ in. from the end of the stock. I make any necessary adjustments and cut the front shoulder on both ends of each rail (*photo 4-13*).

To cut the shoulder on the back of the rails, I just move the rip fence 3/16 in. further away from the blade. Then I lower the blade to a height of 1/8 in. and cut the back shoulders on both ends of each rail (*photo 4-14*).

The procedure is the same for cutting the shoulders on the upper-door rails. The only difference is that the tenons are shorter. For the front shoulder cuts, I set the fence so the gauge block is 5/8 in. from

4-12 The door frames are joined with mortise-and-tenon joints. I cut the mortises in the stiles with the hollow chisel mortising attachment on my drill press.

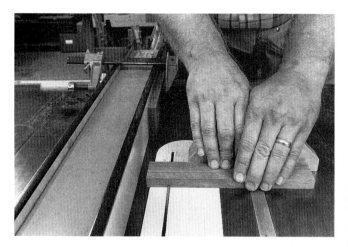

4-13 To make the shoulder cuts for the door-rail tenons, I clamp a guide block to my rip fence. With the rail against my miter gauge, I butt the end of the rail against the block, then move the rail forward into the blade to make the cut. Here I'm cutting a shoulder on the front side of the rail.

4-14 The shoulder on the back side of the rail is offset 3/16 in. from the front shoulder cut to account for the rabbet in the stile. I move the rip fence 3/16 in. farther away from the blade to make the back shoulder cuts.

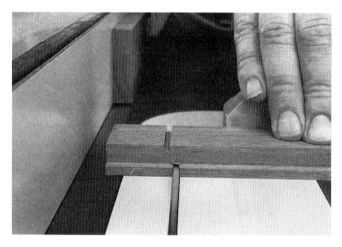

4-15 To nibble away the tenon haunches, I make multiple crosscuts with my miter gauge.

4-16 The tenons are offset slightly toward the back of the rail. I make the back cheek cut first (completed in photo). Then I lower the blade height 3/16 in. and move the tenoning jig 1/16 in. closer to the blade to cut the front cheeks. Here I'm making the cheek cut on the front of the rail.

the left side of the blade. I move it 3/16 in. farther away to cut the shoulders on the backs of the rails.

Note that the mortises are set in from the ends of the stiles. I have to cut a notch, or "haunch," on each tenon. I do this on the table saw by making multiple crosscuts to nibble away the haunch (*photo 4-15*). I set the blade to a height of 7/16 in. and support the rail against the miter gauge to make the cuts, making sure to keep the rabbeted edges up.

The cheek cuts come next. As usual, I do this on the table saw with my tenoning attachment. Note that the tenons aren't centered in the middle of the rails — they're offset 1/16 in. toward the back side of the door.

First I make the cheek cut on the back sides of the upper-door rails. I set the blade height to 13/16 in. and cut all 4 cheeks. Then I raise the blade height to 1⁷⁄₁₆ in. and cut the cheeks on the back sides of the lower-door rails.

Now I'm ready to cut the front cheeks. I move the tenoning jig 1/16 in. closer to the blade and set the blade height to 1¼ in. to cut the front cheeks on the lower-door rails (*photo 4-16*). Then I lower the blade height to 5/8 in. to make the cheek cuts on the front sides of the upper-door rails.

After I do a little finish sanding on the inside edges of the doors, I'm ready to glue the door frames together.

Assembling the Doors

The Shakers would have pegged their mortise-and-tenon joints together, but I think that modern yellow glue alone will be strong enough for such lightweight doors. Working on one door at a time, I brush glue on the tenons and in the mortises and assemble the joints, clamping the frame to pull the joints together tight while the glue sets up (*photo 4-17*). With a framing square, I check the doors for square before setting them aside to dry.

Routing the Hinge Mortises

When the glue is dry, I scrape off any excess. Now I'm ready to cut the hinge mortises in the back of the door stiles and the front edge of the clock-case side. Since there are 8 mortises to cut in all, I decided to make a jig so I could cut the mortises with a router.

To make the jig, I screw 2 pieces of plywood together — one piece of 3/4-in. and one piece of 1/2-in. ply — to make a piece that's 1¼ in. thick. I square up the edges and cut the jig to a 10-in. length. Then I cut a notch in one edge that's 1/16 in. larger all around than the mortise I need to cut. Unlike the other router mortising jigs featured in this book, which have the notch located in the middle of the plywood's edge, this jig has the notch located about 1⅜ in. from one end. This is necessary in order to cut the mortises in the side of the clock case that are close to the divider rail and the top and bottom trim pieces.

4-17   Then I clamp the frames to pull the joints together tight.

4-18 I made a mortising jig to rout the hinge mortises for the doors. The guide collar on the router rides around a notch that's 1/16 in. larger all around than the mortise I need. A small piece of wood screwed to each end of the jig serves as an edge guide to position the jig. The stops pivot on the screws so both sides of the jig may be used.

4-19 After routing the hinge mortises in the doors, I mark the mortises on the case using the layout marks for the door mortises as a guide. I place the doors in position on the case and use a square and a pencil to extend the mortise centerlines from the door to the sides of the case.

I need to be able to use both sides of the mortising jig, so I also had to modify the edge guide I normally use on this type of jig. Instead of a strip of wood nailed along the edge of the plywood, I screwed 2 small pieces of wood to the edge of the jig (*photo 4-18*). These pieces pivot on their screws and function as edge guides no matter which side of the jig faces up. Because the edge guides always hang down, they stay out of the way of the router.

I'll rout the mortises in the doors first. I fit out my router with a 5/8-in. O.D. guide collar and a 1/2-in.-diameter straight bit and set the depth of cut to match the thickness of the hinge. Then I mark the center of each mortise on the back side and edge of the stile.

With the door clamped flat on my bench, I place the jig over the door and slide the edge stops up against the edge of the stile. I move the jig to align the center mark of the notch with my layout mark on the door. Then I clamp the jig in place and rout the mortise on the back of the stile, guiding the collar around the inside of the notch (*photo 4-18*). I repeat this process to rout the other hinge mortises in both doors. I square up the corners with a chisel before I move on to the case mortises.

So there'll be no surprises later, I'll mark the mortises on the case using the layout marks for the door mortises as a guide. I place the doors in position on the clock case and use a square and a pencil to extend the door-mortise centerlines downward onto the sides of the case (*photo 4-19*), and then onto the edge. When I've marked off these centerlines, I clamp the jig in position to rout each mortise. I finish them up by squaring off the corners with a chisel.

Before I install the door frames to the case, I finish sand both sides of the door frames and the outside of the clock case with my random orbit sander. The brass hinge screws are soft, so I take the precaution of drilling pilot holes in the wood before installing the hinges. A piece of tape around the bit acts as a depth stop to keep me from drilling clear through the door. Then I install the hinges and the door frames, being careful not to overtighten the delicate brass screws that hold the hinges in place.

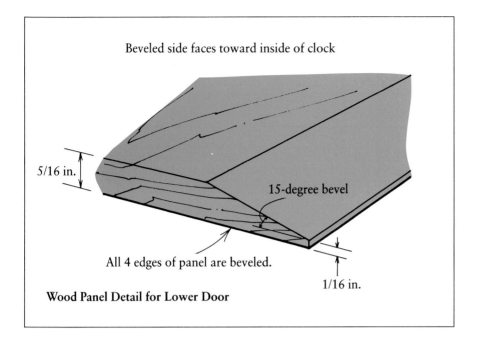

Beveled side faces toward inside of clock

5/16 in.

15-degree bevel

All 4 edges of panel are beveled.

1/16 in.

Wood Panel Detail for Lower Door

Now for the magnetic catches that secure the doors. Both doors get a magnetic catch, centered along the height of the door. With a 5/16-in.-diameter brad-point bit, I drill two 9/16-in.-deep holes in the middle of the case-side edge — one for each door. I screw the threaded magnetic inserts into the holes with a screwdriver. On the back side of each door, I screw on the small plate that comes with the insert.

Making the Lower-Door Panel

The panel in the bottom door is 5/16-in.-thick walnut, with the edges beveled to a thickness of 1/16 in. I install the panel with the beveled side facing in. When you look at the front of the door, the panel appears to be flat.

To size the panel, I measure the distance across the rabbets in the stiles. I subtract 1/8 in. from this measurement and joint and rip the panel to this dimension — in this case, 6¼ in. wide. Then I square up one end of the panel on the table saw using my homemade panel cutter. Going back to the door frame, I measure the distance across the 2 rail rabbets and cut the door panel just 1/16 in. shorter.

With the panel cut to size, I'm ready to bevel the edges on the table saw. I made a plywood panel-raising jig that rides on my rip fence and works much like a tenoning jig to hold the panel vertically on edge so I can bevel the ends and edges of the panel safely (*photo 4-20*). I position the rip fence to the left of the blade, put the jig over the fence, and clamp the panel against the jig's stop. Then I tilt the saw blade 15 degrees, raise the blade a sufficient height, and bevel the ends and the edges of the door panel (*photo 4-20*). I clean up the saw marks with my sander and finish sand the front and back of the panel.

4-20 For beveling the ends and edges of the door panel, I made a plywood panel-raising jig that rides on my rip fence and works much like a tenoning jig to hold the panel so I can bevel the ends and edges safely. I position the fence to the left of the blade and tilt the saw blade 15 degrees.

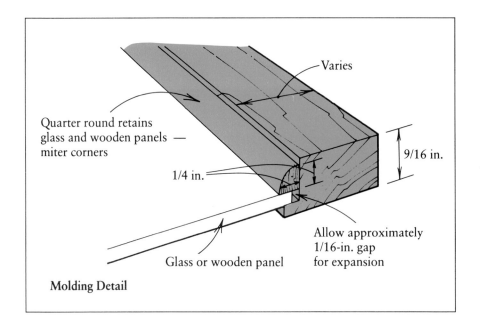

Quarter round retains
glass and wooden panels —
miter corners

Varies

9/16 in.

1/4 in.

Allow approximately
1/16-in. gap
for expansion

Glass or wooden panel

Molding Detail

Making the Moldings

I need to make some tiny moldings to hold the door panel and the glass in the door-frame rabbets. I want a 1/4-in. quarter round. Obviously, I can't mill a piece of stock this small. So I mill the quarter-round profile on a long 3/4-in.-square piece of stock, then rip the narrow moldings from this larger piece.

I set up my router table with a 1/4-in. roundover bit and a couple of homemade feather boards to hold the stock tight against the fence and the table (*photo 4-21*). I take the 3/4-in.-square strip of walnut that I ripped from the edge of the 1×8 and round off 2 adjacent corners.

4-21 The first step to making the small quarter-round moldings that hold the door panels in place is to round off 2 adjacent corners of a 3/4-in.-square piece. I set up my router table with a 1/4-in.-radius roundover bit and two homemade featherboards to hold the stock firmly against the table and fence.

Next, on the table saw, I rip the moldings to width. I set my rip fence 1/4 in. from the blade and use a feather board to hold the stock tight against the fence. I raise the blade about 3/8 in. above the table. With the rounded corners of the stock down on the table, I make a rip cut along the length of the piece. Then I flip the stock end-for-end and make a second rip cut on the opposite side of the stock. The piece is now hollowed out in the middle with sides that are 1/4 in. thick.

To complete the moldings, I position the rip fence 1/2 in. from the left side of the blade and raise the blade to a height of 1 in. Then, with the open part of the U facing left, I rip the 3/4-in.-square strip, slicing off 2 long 1/4-in. moldings on the left side of the blade (*photo 4-22*). I lightly sand the moldings by hand before I cut them to length.

From these 2 strips I use my utility knife to cut 8 pieces of molding for the upper and lower doors. I cut them about 1/8 to 1/4 in. longer than I need. I suppose I could miter all these corners with the utility knife, but my "wood trimmer" does a great job (*photo 4-23*). It works like a horizontal guillotine and cuts a perfect miter. I spend a little time dry-fitting the moldings around both doors.

Now I can put the glass and wood door panels in their rabbets, tacking the molding strips to the rabbets with some glue from my hot-glue gun (*photo 4-24*). I apply the glue, squeeze each molding in place with my fingers, and hold it until the glue cools and sets. I glue the moldings only to the door frame, not the wood panel. Any excess squeezeout can be trimmed off with a utility knife after the glue has set.

There are a few other pieces to install in the clock case. First, there are the 3 cleats to which the plywood backer board will be attached (*drawing 4-F*). I rip these cleats from 3/4-in. scrap. I joint the

4-22 I finish the moldings on the table saw. First, I raise the blade to a 1/2-in. height, set the rip fence 1/4 in. from the blade, and make a rip cut on both sides of the strip with the rounded corners down on the table. Then I raise the blade, set the rip fence 1/2 in. from the far side of the blade, turn the strip on its side, and make the cut shown here. It rips off two 1/4-in., quarter-round moldings.

4-23 I miter the ends of the moldings on my wood trimmer.

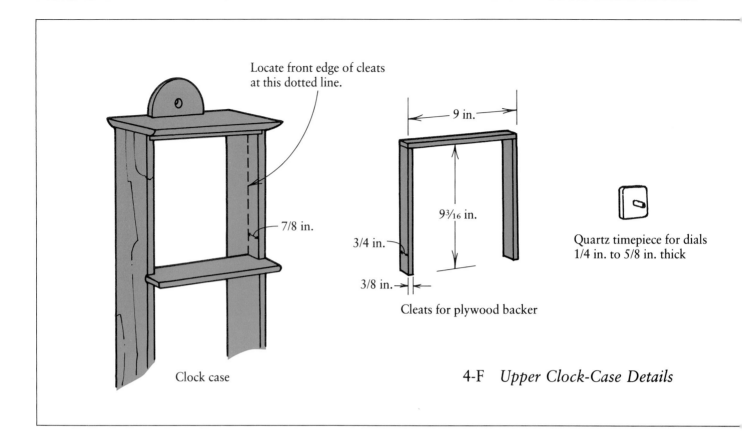

Locate front edge of cleats at this dotted line.

7/8 in.

Clock case

9 in.

9³⁄₁₆ in.

3/4 in.

3/8 in.

Cleats for plywood backer

Quartz timepiece for dials 1/4 in. to 5/8 in. thick

4-F   *Upper Clock-Case Details*

4-24 Hot glue works well to fasten the moldings to the rabbets in the door frame. The moldings hold the glass panel in the upper door and the wood panel in the lower door.

edges and plane them to a 3/8-in. thickness. Then I cut off 3 pieces to make the cleats: one piece 9 in. long and 2 pieces 9³⁄₁₆ in. long. I also cut a fourth strip of walnut, 3/8 in. by 9/16 in. by 9 in. long. This little trim strip goes in later, after I install the clock face.

I nail the 3 cleats to the inside of the clock case, setting them back 7/8 in. from the front edges of the sides (*drawing 4-F and photo 4-25*). Then I mark and drill 1/4-in.-diameter holes for the knobs that go on each door.

There's just one last piece of wood to cut for the clock. That's the 10-in.-square piece of 3/8-in. plywood — the backer board for the paper dial. I square up and size the plywood on the table saw. Then I drill a 3/8-in.-diameter hole for the shaft that holds the hands of the clock (*drawing 4-F*).

Oiling the Clock Case

I finished my clock with a Danish oil finish that I darkened a little by adding some walnut oil stain. I brush on the stain, let it soak in for a while, then wipe off the excess with a rag. After the first coat is dry, I fill all the nail holes with a colored putty stick that matches the stain. For the second and subsequent coats, I apply the oil with a rag, then rub the surface with 600-grit wet-and-dry sandpaper. When the oil starts to feel tacky, I wipe off the excess with a clean rag. Over the next few days I apply 5 more coats of oil in the same way.

The only turned knobs I could find were maple. To get them dark

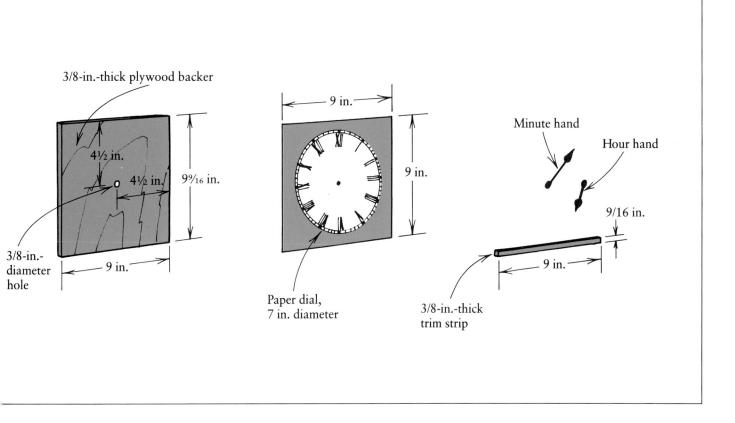

3/8-in.-thick plywood backer

4½ in.

4½ in.

9 9/16 in.

3/8-in.-diameter hole

9 in.

9 in.

9 in.

9 in.

Paper dial,
7 in. diameter

Minute hand

Hour hand

9/16 in.

9 in.

3/8-in.-thick
trim strip

enough to match the walnut, I drop them into a cup full of stain and let them soak for a couple of hours. That should do the job.

Installing the Movement

When the last coat of finish is thoroughly dry, I'm ready to install the plywood backer, the paper dial, and the quartz movement.

First, I put the shaft of the quartz movement through the hole in the plywood and put on the nut that holds the movement in place. Then I tack the plywood backer to the cleats in the case with some 3/4-in. brads. Next, I remove the nut that holds the movement in place, apply a drop of hot glue at the 4 corners of the backer board to keep the paper dial from curling, and put it in place. Now the dial goes on over the shaft. I carefully press the paper down against the plywood so there are no wrinkles.

The hands go on next: the hour hand first, then the minute hand. Last of all, the little nut that holds the hands in place. I thread this onto the shaft and tighten it with my fingers. The very last thing is the little piece of trim that fills the gap between the paper dial and the divider rail. I just tack that in place with some brads.

That about does it. When I have to change the battery in a year or so, I can just reach up from the lower door to replace it. You know, I have a hunch that this clock is a piece that's going to get handed down for quite a few generations in my family.

4-25 With my brad nailer, I fasten the 3 cleats to the inside of the clock case. These cleats support the plywood backer to which the paper dial face will be glued.

FIVE

Harvest Table

T HE inspiration for this harvest table came from an antique drop-leaf table I saw on a visit to the Shaker Museum in Old Chatham, New York. The original Shaker table is unusually long. When the leaves are up it could probably seat 12 people, maybe more. When you stop and think that a typical Shaker "family" might have 80 to 100 members to feed at mealtimes, you can understand why they needed such long tables.

My family isn't *quite* that large, so I designed my harvest table to seat 6 to 8 people comfortably. When the leaves are up, the table is about 39 in. wide and 71¾ in. long. I wanted to be able to store chairs underneath the table when the leaves are down — an idea I borrowed from the original Shaker table — so I designed the table with relatively narrow leaves.

I made my table from cherry, one of the prettiest North American hardwoods. The fixed, center section of the top is glued up from three 6-ft lengths of 1×8 cherry (see Project Planner). 1 in. × 8 in. are nominal dimensions only. I bought my cherry surfaced 4 sides (S4S). The actual dimensions of the 1×8 boards are 3/4 in. thick and 7½ in. wide.

Gluing the Top

I want the best possible match for figure and color on the top of the table, so I spread the 3 boards for the top on my bench and spend some time looking them over. First, I look at the ends of the boards and orient the growth rings so they alternate down, up, down (this minimizes the effect of cupping across the entire top). Then I move the boards around until I get the best match I can, still making sure that the growth rings alternate on adjacent boards. When I have the boards arranged the way I want them, I mark the boards with a pencil so I can reassemble them in the same order.

As I checked the edges of my boards for straightness (I used a 6-ft-long level), I found that one of the boards had a very slight bow (*photo 5-1*). It would be difficult to remove this bow on the jointer, because the board is so much longer than my jointer table. I

PROJECT PLANNER

Time: 3–4 days
Special hardware and tools:
(6) 1½-in.-wide drop-leaf hinges
Wood lathe and turning tools
Duplicating attachment for lathe (optional)
 Corner chisel (optional)
Wood:
(1) 30-in. length, 8/4 × 10 cherry
Rip and joint 4 pieces 1¾ in. square for legs.
 (1) 14 ft 1×6 cherry
Cut 2 pieces 64½ in. long; rip and joint to 5-in. width for long rails. Cut 2 pieces 18½ in. long; rip and joint to 5-in. width for short rails.
 (1) 4 ft 1×6 pine
Cut one piece 20 in. long for center support. Make corner blocks from scrap.
 (2) 6 ft 1×10 cherry
Square one end of each piece and cut to 71¾ in. length for drop leaves.
 (3) 6 ft 1×8 cherry
Joint and edge glue 3 pieces together to make a panel approximately 21½ in. × 71¾ in. for top.

5-1 When I checked the tabletop boards for straightness I found that one of my cherry boards had a slight bow.

5-2 I straighten out the concave edge by jointing halfway in from each end to take off the high spot at each end. Then I joint the entire edge to straighten it out.

5-3 With the jointed edge against my table saw fence, I rip off the convex edge then joint it smooth on the jointer.

5-4 With biscuits and glue in the joints, I clamp the 3 boards for the top together. Alternating the clamps, down, up, down, up ensures that the top won't bow from the clamp pressure.

straightened out the concave edge by jointing in halfway from each end (*photo 5-2*). I followed up with a pass along the entire edge. Then I ripped off the convex edge on the table saw (*photo 5-3*). Finally, I ran this sawed edge over the jointer to smooth it. The other boards were all pretty straight, so I simply jointed all the long edges on the jointer.

The next step is to mark and cut biscuit slots in the mating edges. I place the boards together edge to edge and make pencil marks every 9 to 10 in. along the joints to mark the location of the biscuit slots. Then I line up the index mark of my biscuit joiner with these pencil marks and cut the slots.

With the slots all cut, I'm ready for glue. I stand the 3 boards on edge on my bench. Then I brush glue on 2 mating edges and put some in the biscuit slots. Working fast, before the glue sets, I put glue on the biscuits, put a biscuit in each slot, and assemble the joint. Next, I brush glue on the other 2 mating edges, put in the biscuits, and put the third board in place. I clamp the 3 boards together with

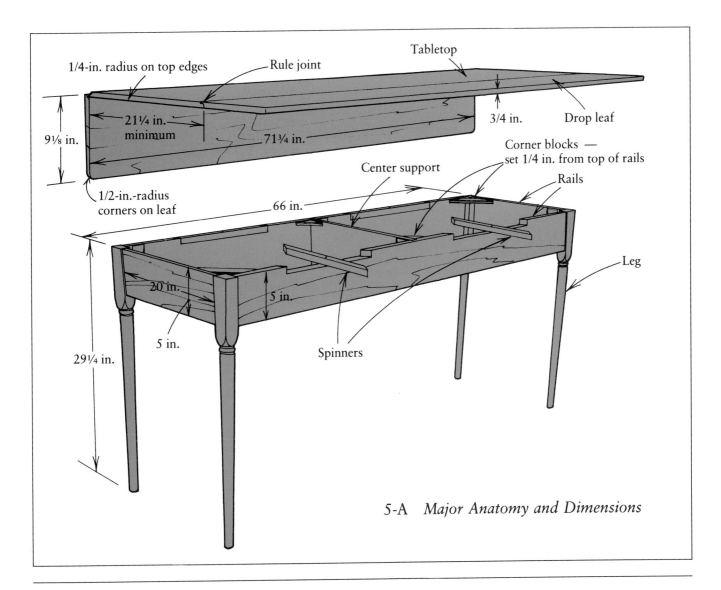

5-A   *Major Anatomy and Dimensions*

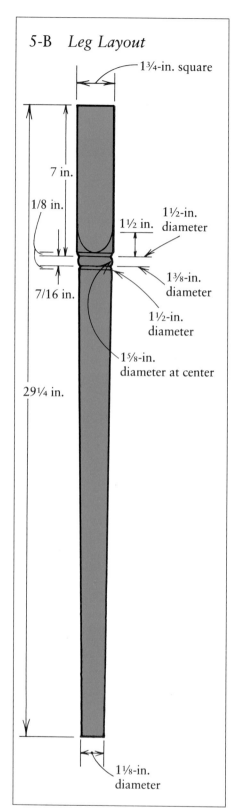

5-B Leg Layout

1¾-in. square

7 in.

1/8 in.

1½ in.

1½-in. diameter

7/16 in.

1½-in. diameter

1⅜-in. diameter

1½-in. diameter

1⅝-in. diameter at center

29¼ in.

1⅛-in. diameter

pipe clamps, alternating adjacent clamps: under, over, under, over (*photo 5-4*). This minimizes the tendency of the top to bow from the clamp pressure. I tighten the clamps just enough to squeeze out some glue. Now I'll put the top aside for awhile to work on the leaves.

I make each leaf from 1 × 10 cherry (see Project Planner). I joint one long edge and rip each leaf to its finished width of 9⅛ in. "strong," then joint the sawn edges to remove any saw marks. I square up the ends of the leaves on my radial-arm saw, trimming the length to 71¾ in.

Preparing the Leg Blanks

When it came to designing the legs, I had a lot of different choices. The legs on original Shaker harvest tables vary in style from simple, tapered legs to elegant turned legs. I compromised by making a turned, tapered leg with a decorative bead near the top (*drawing 5-B*).

I cut the leg blanks from a 30-in.-long piece of 8/4 × 10 cherry (8/4, pronounced "eight quarter," is lumberyard terminology for 2-in.-thick hardwood.). First, I joint one edge of the stock. Then, I set my table saw rip fence 2 in. from the blade and rip the cherry into four 2-in.-square blanks. On the jointer, I square up 2 adjacent faces on each blank. Then I run the blanks through my portable thickness planer to end up with leg blanks that are 1¾ in. square.

The next step is to square up the ends of the leg blanks on my power miter box. Because of the way I set up the template for my lathe duplicator, it was necessary for me to cut the leg blanks a little long for turning and trim them to finished length afterward. So, when I trim the ends now, I end up with a blank that's about 29¾ in. long. If I intended to turn the legs by hand, without the duplicator, I'd just trim the blanks now to their finished 29¼-in. length (*drawing 5-B*).

With the ends of the leg blanks squared off, I mark the ends for the lathe centers. I draw diagonal lines across the corners on the ends of each blank. X marks the spot for the centerpoint. I remove the drive center from the lathe headstock, place the centerpoint on the center of the X, and whack it with a mallet to engage the drive center's spurs in the wood. I repeat the process on the other end with the tailstock center.

The legs have a 7-in.-long square section at the top, with a bead detail underneath (*drawing 5-B*). I measure off 7 in. from the top end of each blank and mark the point where the square section meets the bead. With a square, I draw pencil lines around all 4 sides of each blank at this point. I draw another pencil line around the blank 5½ in. from the end to mark the starting point for rounding the corners of the square section (*drawing 5-B*).

Before I turn the legs, I like to knock off the corners on the band saw so I don't have to remove all that wood on the lathe. I tilt my band saw table 45 degrees and set a fence to position the blank so the blade just knocks off the corner (*photo 5-5*). Then I saw off all 4 corners to make a rough octagon shape. I stop the cut when the saw blade reaches the pencil lines that mark the start of the square part of the leg. Then, with a backsaw, I cut straight down on these pencil lines to remove the scrap.

Turning the Legs

I turn the legs in 2 steps: First, I rough out the taper with a gouge. Then I complete the turning with my lathe duplicator. When I have to make multiple turnings I find that the duplicator is faster than turning freehand and it guarantees that all 4 legs will be exactly the same.

The duplicator requires me to make a hardboard template that matches the profile of the leg. I draw out the profile on a piece of 1/4-in. hardboard and saw out the shape on the band saw. This template clamps in a holder mounted above the turning. A follower on the duplicator rides the edge of this template to guide the cutter as shown in the photos.

With the leg blanks ready to go, I mount one between centers on the lathe with the bottom end facing the tailstock. With a 3/4-in. gouge I rough out the taper (*photo 5-6*). At the top of the leg, I just round off the stock where the turned detail will be. At the bottom end, I turn down to a diameter of about 1¼ in. I rough out all 4 legs in the same way.

Now I switch to my lathe duplicator for the finish turning. With a square, carbide cutter in the tool holder, I turn the taper (*photo 5-7*). Then I exchange the square cutter for a triangular-shaped carbide cutter to turn the detail at the top of the leg (*photo 5-8*). When I've completed the leg, I mount another in the lathe and start with the triangular cutter, which is still in the tool holder. Then I switch to the straight cutter again to turn the taper. This method minimizes the number of times I have to switch the cutters. Because of my template setup, I can't cut all the way up against the tailstock center, so I end up with an unturned section at that end that I'll trim off later (*photo 5-9*).

Sanding the legs is the next step. The duplicator's cutter leaves tool marks that have to be sanded off. It's fastest to sand the legs right on the lathe. I increase the speed of my lathe for sanding — about 1,750 to 2,000 RPM. I start with 80-grit sandpaper and switch to progressively finer grits, finishing up with 180-grit paper. I hold the sandpaper on the underside of the leg to keep from jamming my fingers if the sandpaper catches (*photo 5-9*). When the tool marks are gone and the leg feels smooth, I switch off the lathe and sand the taper by hand with 180-grit paper, sanding with the grain of the leg, to remove cross-grain scratches.

I turn and sand each leg, one at a time. Then I clamp each leg in my vise and, with a handsaw, trim each leg to the correct length, taking off the little unturned section at the bottom of each leg. After

5-5 Before I turn the legs on the lathe, I like to knock off the corners on the band saw. I tilt the band saw table 45 degrees and set the fence so the blade just cuts off the corner.

5-6 Turning the legs is a 2-step process: roughing with a gouge, and finishing with my duplicator attachment. Here I rough out the taper with a 3/4-in. gouge.

5-7 After roughing out the legs with a gouge, I switch to my lathe duplicator for the finish turning. I use a square carbide cutter in my lathe duplicator to turn the tapered part of the leg. A follower on the duplicator rides the edge of a hardboard template to guide the cutter beneath.

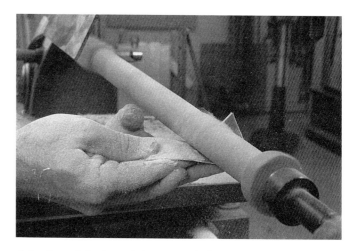

5-9 I sand the legs right on the lathe, holding the sandpaper under the leg to avoid the risk of jamming my fingers. I start with 80-grit and work up to 180-grit paper. I saw off the unturned section at the bottom of the leg (right) to trim the leg to length.

5-8 After turning the taper, I switch to a triangular carbide cutter for turning the detail at the top of the leg.

5-10 The rails of the table are joined to the legs with mortise-and-tenon joints. I use a hollow-chisel mortising attachment and a 3/8-in. bit to cut the mortises on my drill press.

trimming, the legs should all be exactly the same length — 29¼ long.

Cutting the Leg Mortises

The rails of the table are joined to the legs with mortise-and-tenon joints. I cut the mortises in the legs first, then cut the rail tenons to fit the mortises. Each leg has 2 mortises, located on adjacent sides of the leg.

With a rule, a square, and a pencil, I lay out the 3/8-in.-wide mortises on the tops of each leg. As shown in drawing 5-C, the 4¼-in.-long mortises are set in 5/16 in. from the corner of the leg and 3/8 in. from the top. After laying out the mortises, I double-check to make sure I've located the mortise on adjacent sides of each leg. While I'm drawing layout lines on the legs, I also lay out the hole centers for the 1/4-in.-diameter dowels that will pin the mortise-and-tenon joints together. Each joint gets 2 dowel holes, and these holes go on the outside faces of the leg (*drawing 5-C*).

I cut the mortises on my drill press with a hollow-chisel mortising attachment and a 3/8-in. bit (*photo 5-10*). I set the depth stop on the drill press to cut the mortises 1 in. deep.

Rails and Tenons

The rails of the harvest table are 3/4 in. thick and 5 in. wide. I start with 1 × 6 cherry stock and cut the rails to length on the miter box, a little longer than the length I need. Then I joint one long edge and rip the rails to a 5-in. width plus 1/32 in., or "1/32 in. strong," as we say. A pass on the jointer removes this extra 1/32 in. and gives me a clean edge. Then, on my miter box, I cut the rails to their finished

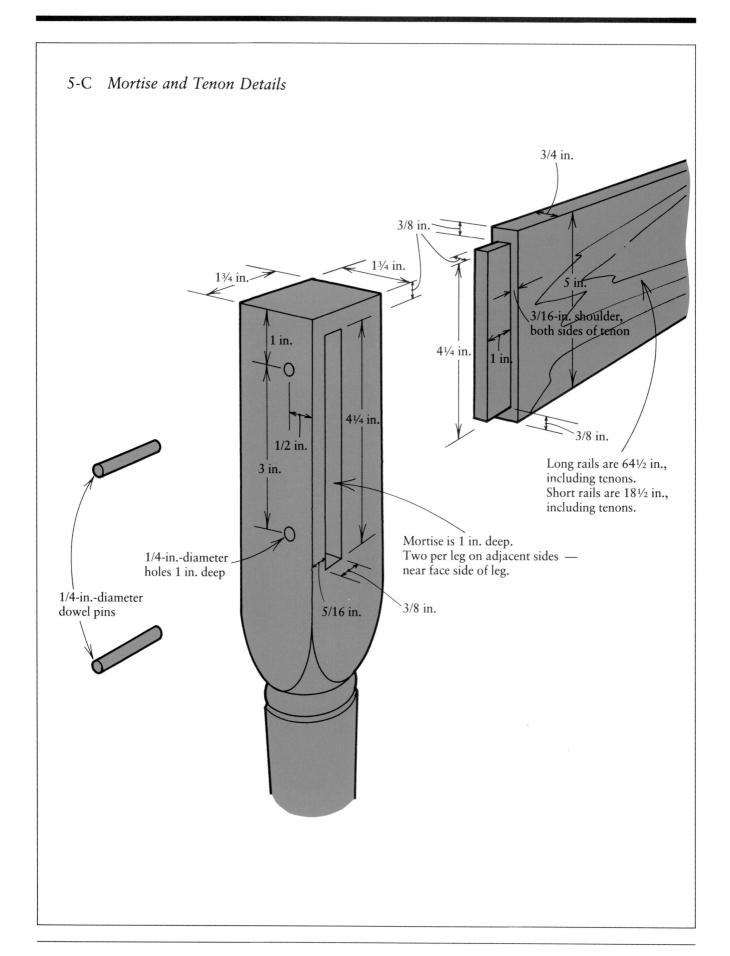

3/4 in.

3/8 in.

1¾ in.

1¾ in.

5 in.

4¼ in.

1 in.

3/16-in. shoulder, both sides of tenon

1 in.

3/8 in.

1 in.

1/2 in.

4¼ in.

3 in.

Long rails are 64½ in., including tenons.
Short rails are 18½ in., including tenons.

1/4-in.-diameter holes 1 in. deep

Mortise is 1 in. deep.
Two per leg on adjacent sides — near face side of leg.

1/4-in.-diameter dowel pins

5/16 in.

3/8 in.

length, remembering to include the 1-in.-long tenon at either end — 64½ in. for the 2 long rails and 18½ in. for the 2 short rails.

Cutting the tenons on the table saw comes next. The first thing I do is screw an extension to the head of my miter gauge to make it easier to support the long rails when I cut them (*photo 5-11*). The extension is just a piece of 3/4-in.-plywood about 36 in. long and 4 in. wide. I screw the extension to the miter-gauge head, with about 7 in. projecting to the right of the blade. Then I make a cut through the fence and screw a stop block exactly 1 in. from the kerf — the length of my tenon.

The first tenon cut is the 3/16-in.-deep shoulder cut on each face of the rail (*drawing 5-C*). I raise the blade 3/16 in. above the table and make a test cut in a piece of scrap exactly the same thickness as my rail stock to check the setting. Then, with the end of the rail butted against the stop block, I make a shoulder cut on each face, keeping the rail flat on the table (*photo 5-11*). I repeat this shoulder cut on all 4 rails.

Without changing anything except the height of the blade, I next make the cuts that form the top and bottom shoulders of the tenon. I raise the blade to a height of 3/8 in. and make the cuts with the rail standing on edge.

With the shoulder cuts complete, I'm ready to make the cuts that form the cheeks of the tenons. For this procedure, I use my table saw tenoning attachment. This accessory has a runner that fits in the miter-gauge slot and has a built-in clamp that holds stock securely in a vertical position as I feed the stock forward into the blade.

For cutting the cheeks, I raise the blade to a height of 1 inch. Then I cut a test tenon in 3/4-in. scrap stock and adjust the tenoning jig in or out as necessary to vary the thickness of the tenon. I try the

5-11 I cut the shoulders for the rail tenons on the table saw. I screw a long plywood extension to my miter-gauge head to support the long rails for the cut. A stop block determines the length of the tenon. I set the blade height to 3/16 in. and make a shoulder cut on each side, butting the end against the stop block. Then I raise the blade height to 3/8 in. and make a shoulder cut on each edge of the rail.

5-12 Cutting the tenon cheeks on the table saw requires me to stand the long rails on end in the tenoning jig. My cast-iron tenoning jig is strong and heavy enough to clamp these rails securely, but this may not be safe with a homemade tenoning jig. An alternate approach is to cut the cheeks on the radial-arm saw with the rail lying flat on the table.

5-13 To complete the tenons, I make 2 rip cuts with my dovetailing saw to form the top and bottom of each tenon.

test tenon in the leg mortises and keep making adjustments until I get the fit I want — a smooth slip fit, not too loose and not too tight. When the fit is right, I mount a rail in the tenoning jig and cut the cheeks, first one side, then the other. The tenons are identical on all 4 rails.

As you can see from photo 5-12, this procedure requires me to stand the long rails on end to cut the cheeks. I'm able to clamp these long rails securely in my heavy, cast-iron tenoning attachment. However, this may not be safe with a homemade tenoning jig. And if the shop ceiling is low, there may not be room to stand the long rails on end. An alternative method is to cut the tenon cheeks with a dado head on the table saw. Lay the rail flat on the table and use the miter gauge to make multiple crosscuts to cut the cheeks. Another alternative is to cut the cheeks on the radial-arm saw with the rail lying flat on the table. Raise the radial-arm saw blade 9/16 in. above the table and make multiple crosscuts to complete each cheek.

There's just one more step before the tenons are complete. I lay out the top and bottom of each tenon and, with a dovetailing saw, I make 2 rip cuts on each rail end to form the top and bottom of the tenon (*photo 5-13*).

Installing the Center Support

In the middle of the table, there's a 19-in.-long center support (*drawings 5-A and 5-E*). The ends of the support fit into 3/8-in. by 3/4-in. dadoes in each long rail. I made the center support from a piece of 1 × 6 pine that I jointed and ripped to a 5-in. width.

Each long rail gets a dado in the middle. I lay out the dadoes on the worst face of each rail (since the dadoes will face inside). Then I cut the dadoes on the table saw with my dado head set for a 3/4-in.-wide cut that's 3/8-in. deep. I support the rail against the miter gauge to make the cut (*photo 5-14*).

Making the Spinners

The leaves of the table are supported by 16-in.-long wooden spinners — 2 on each side of the table — that turn out to hold up the leaves (*drawings 5-A, 5-D, and 5-E*). The ends of the spinners are cut at a 45-degree angle so they line up flush with the rails when you turn them back into place to let down the leaves.

I cut the spinners right out of the 2 long rails. I clamp the 2 rails together, side by side, and stand them on edge on my bench. With a tape, a square, and a pencil, I mark out the spinners on the top edge of each rail with 45-degree angles at each end, as shown in drawings 5-D and 5-E. I mark the pivot point for each spinner by measuring in 16 in. from each tenon shoulder as shown in drawing 5-E. On the side of each rail, I draw a line 1¼ in. from the top of the rail, running parallel to the top. This line marks the bottom edge of the spinner slot.

Before I cut out the spinners, I drill 3/32-in.-diameter pilot holes

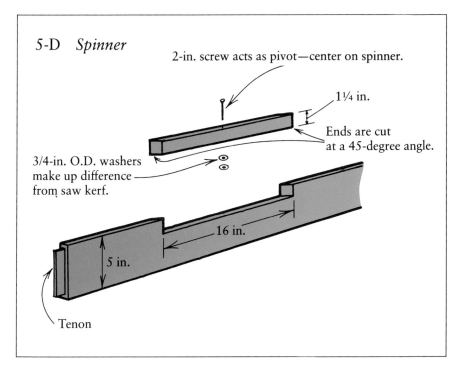

5-D *Spinner*

2-in. screw acts as pivot—center on spinner.

1¼ in.

Ends are cut
at a 45-degree angle.

3/4-in. O.D. washers
make up difference
from saw kerf.

16 in.

5 in.

Tenon

5-14 Each long rail gets a 3/4-in.-wide dado in the middle to house the ends of the center support. I cut these 3/8-in.-deep dadoes with a dado head on the table saw, using the miter gauge to feed the rail into the blade.

about 2 in. deep for the pivot screws on which the spinners will turn (*photo 5-15*). Then, I countersink the top of the hole to recess the screw head.

Now I'm ready to cut along the bottoms of the spinners. I position the table saw rip fence to the right of the blade so it's exactly 1¼ in. away from the *left* side of the blade. I've found that the best way to make the cut is to lower the table saw blade all the way and position the rail firmly against the rip fence with the spinner located over the blade. I hold the rail firmly in place, keeping my hands well

5-15 The drop leaves are supported by 2 wooden spinners in each long rail. I mark out the spinners and then drill a 2-in.-deep hole on the pivot point of each spinner before cutting them out on the table saw.

5-16 I cut along the bottom of the spinners on the table saw. I set the fence 1¼ in. from the left side of the blade and lower the blade all the way. I hold the rail against the fence (hands well away from the layout lines), switch on the saw, and raise the blade through the wood.

5-17 I continue raising the blade until the front of the blade touches the front layout line. Then I move the rail forward to complete the cut, stopping when the back of the blade touches the back layout line. I switch off the saw and wait until the blade stops before I remove the rail.

5-18 To separate the spinners from the rail, I make a 45-degree angled cut at each end with a dovetailing saw.

5-19 The spinners pivot on a bugle-head screw threaded into the rail. Two washers underneath reduce friction and make up the thickness of the saw kerf from the table saw blade.

away from the layout lines. Then I switch on the saw and slowly raise the blade up through the wood until the front of the blade touches the layout line that marks the front end of the spinner (*photos 5-16 and 5-17*). Then I move the rail forward until the blade cuts to the rear layout line. I switch off the saw at this point and cut the other spinners in the same way. I finish cutting out the spinners by making the angled cuts at the ends with my dovetailing saw (*photo 5-18*). I clean up the sawed edges with sandpaper.

The pivot mechanism for the spinners couldn't be simpler (*photo 5-19*). I put a couple of washers under the spinner to minimize friction and make up the thickness of the saw kerf. I enlarge the hole in the spinner to a 3/16-in. diameter and then fasten the spinner to the rail with a 2-in.-long bugle-head screw as a pivot. That's all there is to it.

5-20 When the 2 long-rail assemblies are pinned, I join them by gluing the short rails into their mortises. I apply enough clamp pressure to close up the joint, then drill for the dowel pins and glue them in place.

Now I'm ready to finish sand the rails and spinners. I don't spend much time on the inside faces of the rails, but I'm careful to relieve the sharp corners on the spinners and their notches, where fingers are likely to touch.

Assembling the Base

Now for a little assembly. First, I glue the 2 long sides of the table together, one at a time. I place one long rail on my bench with the center-support dado facing down. Then I place a leg at either end, making sure that the mortises are oriented properly — one mortise facing the rail tenon, the second mortise facing down. Now I brush glue on the tenons and a little in the mortises and assemble the joints. With an extra-long pipe clamp, and some pieces of scrap wood to protect the legs, I apply just enough pressure to pull the joint tightly together (shorter pipe clamps can be joined together with threaded pipe couplers to make a longer clamp). Next, in each joint, I drill two 1/4-in.-diameter dowel holes 1 in. deep on the centers I marked earlier. I put a little glue in these holes and tap in a 1/4-in. dowel to pin the joint securely. I assemble the other long side of the table in the same way. When the glue is dry, I use my belt sander to sand the ends of the dowels flush.

I complete the base assembly by gluing, clamping, and pinning the 2 short rails in their mortises. At this stage, I find it helpful to work with the table upside down on my bench (*photo 5-20*). After clamping up the mortises, I glue the center crosspiece in its dadoes. I shoot in a few 4d finish nails to reinforce the crosspiece dado joints.

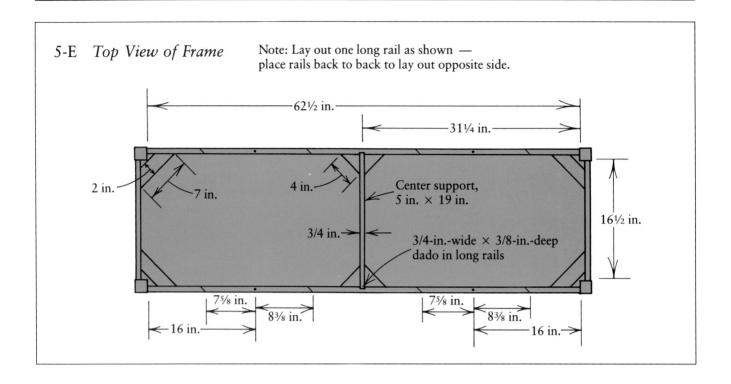

5-E *Top View of Frame*

Note: Lay out one long rail as shown —
place rails back to back to lay out opposite side.

62½ in.

31¼ in.

2 in.

7 in.

4 in.

Center support,
5 in. × 19 in.

3/4 in.

3/4-in.-wide × 3/8-in.-deep
dado in long rails

16½ in.

7⅝ in.

8⅜ in.

7⅝ in.

8⅜ in.

16 in.

16 in.

5-21 The top of the table is secured to the base by screws through pine corner blocks. I glue and screw the 4 long outer corner blocks to the inside corners of the rails. The tops of the blocks are 1/4 in. below the rail edge.

Installing the Corner Blocks

The top of the table is held in place with screws installed through 8 pine corner blocks fastened to the rails and the crosspiece (*drawing 5-E*). These corner blocks also add some strength to the frame. The 4 outer corner blocks are 2 in. wide and 7 in. long with 45-degree cuts on the ends. The 4 inner corner blocks are right triangles measuring 4 in. along the base (*drawing 5-E*).

I cut these corner blocks from the remainder of the 1×6 board I bought to make the center support (see Project Planner). To make the blocks, I rip the remaining length of 1×6 pine into 2 long pieces 2 in. wide. Then I set my power miter box for a 45-degree angle and cut off the corner blocks one by one.

I glue and screw the 4 long outer blocks to the inside corners of the rails — 2 screws in each block (*photo 5-21*). The 4 inner blocks get glued and nailed in the corners between the center support and the rails. I recess all the blocks about 1/4 in. below the tops of the rails so that the screws that secure the top can pull the top down tight against the rails.

Completing the Top and Leaves

Now I'm ready to finish off the tabletop. First I scrape off the excess glue with my paint scraper and sand the top flat and smooth on both sides with my belt sander. With my random orbit sander, I finish sand the face that will show. I also sand the underside of the top where it overhangs the base.

After sanding, I rip the top to width on my table saw, taking off as little wood as possible to get a straight edge. Then, with my

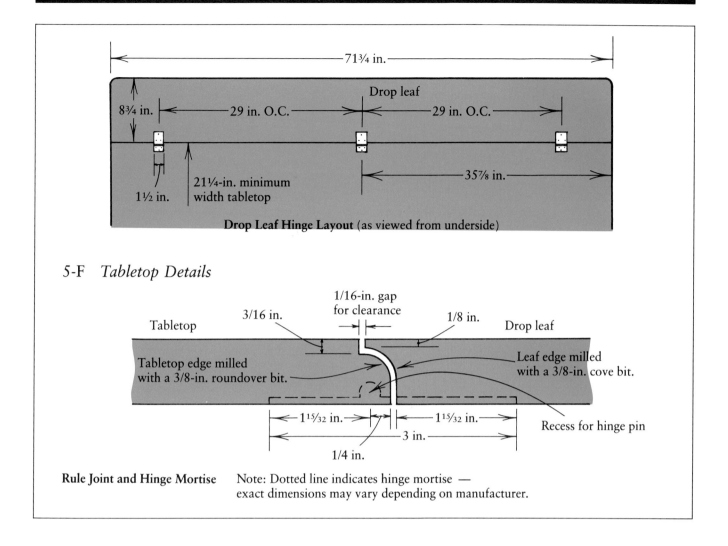

Drop Leaf Hinge Layout (as viewed from underside)

5-F *Tabletop Details*

Rule Joint and Hinge Mortise   Note: Dotted line indicates hinge mortise —
exact dimensions may vary depending on manufacturer.

jointer set for a 1/32-in. cut, I joint the sawed edge straight and
square. The finished top should be at least 21¼ in. wide (*drawing
5-A*). A little wider would be fine.

The tabletop is too large to square up on the table saw, so I
square up the ends with my circular saw. I clamp a straightedge
clamp across the work and guide the base of the saw against the
clamp for a straight cut. The top on my table measures 71¾ in. long
from end to end. I clean up the end grain with my random orbit
sander.

Milling the Rule Joint

My harvest table, like nearly every drop-leaf table I've ever seen, has
a "rule joint" milled along the edges where the leaves meet the top
(*drawing 5-F*). The rule joint provides support for the edge of the
leaf so it won't sag below the fixed part of the top.

In the days before power tools, craftsmen cut rule joints with
wooden planes — one to form the cove on the edge of the leaf, and
another to cut the corresponding "ovalo" profile on the edge of the
top. I use a router for milling the rule joint, but the principle's still

5-22 I mill the rule joint, where the top and leaves meet, with a router and 2 bits. Here I cut the rounded edge on the top with a 3/8-in. roundover bit. I make the cut in 2 passes, setting the bit to cut a 3/16-in. shoulder above the roundover on the second pass.

5-23 To mill the corresponding cove on the leaves, I place the leaf upside down on the bench and mill the cove with a 3/8-in. cove bit. It takes 3 passes to remove all the wood. The final pass leaves a 1/8-in.-wide shoulder underneath the cove.

the same: 2 separate bits — a 3/8-in.-radius roundover bit for the top and a 3/8-in.-radius cove bit for the leaves.

First, I mill the rounded edge on the top (*photo 5-22*). I mount a 3/8-in. roundover bit in my router and mill the edge in 2 passes. The first pass just rounds off the top edge. I lower the bit for the second pass, and set it to cut a 3/16-in. shoulder above the roundover (*drawing 5-F*). To cut the cove on the edges of the leaves, I exchange the roundover bit for a 3/8-in.-radius coving bit. I place the table leaf upside down on the bench and rout the cove in 3 passes, lowering the bit a little for each pass (*photo 5-23*). The final pass leaves a 1/8-in. shoulder at the bottom of the cove (*drawing 5-F*).

Routing the Hinge Mortises

Now I'm ready to cut the mortises for the drop-leaf hinges. Drop-leaf hinges are a special type of hinge with one leaf shorter than the other. The short leaf attaches to the fixed part of the top and the longer leaf screws to the drop leaf (*drawing 5-F*). I could cut these mortises by hand with a utility knife and a chisel, but since there are 12 identical mortises to cut on the harvest table I thought it worthwhile to make a jig so I could cut the mortises with a router.

The mortising jig is easy to make. It's just a piece of 3/4-in. plywood with a rectangular cutout in one edge (*photo 5-24*). Wooden strips tacked to this edge of the jig act as an edge guide to align the jig with the edge of the stock.

To use the jig, I lay out a centerline for every hinge mortise on the table. I slide the jig up against the edge of the table, line up the centerline on the cutout with my layout mark, and clamp the jig in place. I set up my router with a 5/8-in. O.D. guide collar and a 1/2-in.-diameter straight bit and set the depth of cut to the thickness of the hinge leaf. Then I rout the hinge mortise, guiding the collar around the inside of the cutout. The cutout in the jig is 1/16 in. larger all around than the mortise I need to cut to account for the difference between the radius of the router bit and the radius of the guide collar.

5-24 I rout the 12 hinge mortises with a homemade hinge template and a router. The notch in the template is 1/16 in. larger all around than the mortise to account for the difference between the radius of the guide collar and the radius of the router bit. I set the depth of cut to the thickness of the hinge and ride the collar around the notch.

The router bit leaves rounded corners, and I square these up with a corner chisel, a little device that has a spring-loaded, right-angle blade (*photo 5-25*). I align the device in the corner of the mortise and give it a tap with a hammer. It cuts a square corner, and I simply lift out the waste with a chisel. Squaring the corners with a chisel is slower, but would work just as well.

In order for the hinges to fit properly in the fixed part of the top, I also need to mill grooves to recess the hinge pins (*drawing 5-F*). To do this, I use my router, which I set up with a 1/4-in. roundnose bit and a fence. I position the fence so the center of the groove will be located 1/4 in from the edge of the top, as shown in drawing 5-F. I make a modified "plunge cut" by pivoting the router on the end of the fence to lower the spinning bit into the wood. When the base is flat on the wood, I mill the groove, stopping the router at the end of the cut (*photo 5-26*). All 6 mortises in the fixed part of the top get the same treatment. I square up the ends of the grooves with a 1/4-in. chisel so the hinge pins will fit and the hinge will sit flush in the mortise.

At this point, I drill pilot holes for the hinge screws and install all the hinges to fasten the leaves and the top together.

Attaching the Top

Now I'm ready to fasten the top to the base. I place the base on its side on my bench. With a 3/16-in.-diameter drill bit, I drill a hole through each corner block. I rock the bit from side to side to elongate the slot parallel to the short rails. These elongated holes will allow the screws to move as the fixed part of the top expands and contracts across the grain.

Now I place the base upside down on the top and measure around the edges to make sure it's centered. I install a screw through

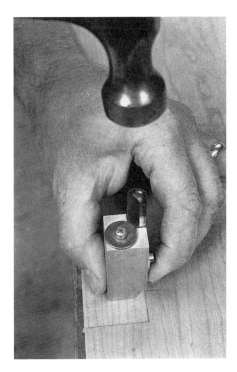

5-25 I square up the corners of the hinge mortises with a corner chisel. A tap with a hammer and the corner is squared.

5-26 Each mortise in the fixed part of the top needs a groove to recess the hinge pin. I cut these grooves with a 1/4-in. roundnose bit and a fence on my router.

5-27 I round off the top edges of the table with a 1/4-in.-radius roundover bit in my router.

each corner block to fasten the top to the base with 1⅝ in. bugle-head screws.

With the table back on its feet and the leaves up, I round the 4 corners with my belt sander. Then I round off the top edge with a 1/4-in.-radius roundover bit in my router (*drawing 5-A and photo 5-27*).

And Now for the Finish

I finished my harvest table with Danish oil, an attractive, natural-looking finish that will get darker and richer with age. I tinted the oil by adding some wild-cherry stain for a rich, reddish brown color that looks great on cherry. I can control the color by the amount of stain I add to the oil.

First, I flip the table upside down so I can finish the underside. It's important to finish both sides of the top and leaves so that both sides absorb and release moisture evenly. The top is likely to warp or cup if you finish only one side.

I brush a coat of oil on the underside of the top and leaves and on all surfaces of the rails, legs, and spinners. I let the oil soak in for a few minutes, then wipe off the excess with a rag. I apply a second coat with a rag. After a few minutes, I wipe off the excess oil with a clean rag.

The top of the table gets a similar treatment. First, I brush on some oil, let it soak for a few minutes, then wipe off the excess with a clean rag. I apply the second coat with a rag instead of a brush. I spread an even coat of oil on the wood and then rub in the oil with some 600-grit wet-and-dry sandpaper. This smooths the surface and forces more oil into the pores of the wood. When the oil starts to feel tacky, I stop sanding and wipe off the excess with a rag. Then I buff the surface with a clean rag to bring up a shine. Then I repeat this process for 4 more coats — 6 coats in all.

The undersides of the leaves will show when they're down, so I used the same finishing technique here that I used on the top. Same for the outside of the rails, which will show when the leaves are up. The finish looks better and better with each coat of oil.

That about does it for the harvest table. Maybe someday I'll find time to make some matching chairs to go with it.

SIX

Shaker Wood Box

PROJECT PLANNER

Time: 2 days
Special hardware and tools:
(2) 2-in. brass-plated butt hinges
(2) 3½-in. turned Shaker pegs
Thickness planer (optional)
Bench-top biscuit joiner (optional)
Wood:
(1) 6-ft 1 × 8 select pine
(1) 10-ft 1 × 6 select pine
Cut 1 × 8 into 2 pieces 35 in. long.
Cut 1 × 6 into 4 pieces 20 in. long.
Glue up 2 panels for wood-box
sides. Edge glue one piece of 1 × 8
next to 2 pieces of 1 × 6 for each
panel. Make ledge from leftover
1 × 6.
(2) 12-ft 1 × 6s select pine
Cut 12 pieces 23½ in. long. Glue
up 4 panels to make front, bottom,
and 2 back panels. Edge glue 3
pieces to make each panel.
(1) 6-ft 1 × 8 select pine
Cut 3 pieces 23½ in. long for
kindling-box front, bottom, and lid.

THE Shakers didn't invent the wood stove — Ben Franklin gets credit for that. But the Shakers had a knack for improving things, and the wood stove didn't escape their attention. They designed an efficient little cast-iron stove that throws a lot of heat with only a small amount of wood. I found one of these small, rectangular stoves in the schoolroom at The Shaker Village in Pleasant Hill, Kentucky. In the corner, next to the stove, stands the old, red-painted wood box that once held the fuel for the schoolroom fire. It has a small, lidded compartment at the top to store kindling, and a turned wooden peg on each side to hold tools for the fire. It's nicked and dinged from years of hard use, but the wood box is still as serviceable as the day it was made.

Except for the color, my version of the schoolroom wood box is a close copy of the original. It's made of pine, just like the old one, and finished with authentic, old-fashioned milk paint. More on that subject later.

As usual, gluing up panels is the first order of business. The wood box requires 6 of them: 2 for the back, a pair for the sides, one for the bottom, and one for the front. I bought some nice 1 × 6 and 1 × 8 select-pine boards for the wood box. The Project Planner explains how I cut up the boards to make the panels.

Some Pointers on Panels

A couple of tips about gluing up panels: Wood, as it comes from the lumberyard, is irregular stuff. The edges aren't straight and the thickness can vary a little from board to board. When you glue boards together edge to edge, any difference in thickness will really show up in the finished panel. The boards won't be even and you'll have to spend a lot of time with a belt sander or a plane to get a flat, smooth surface on both sides of the panel.

A thickness planer can save a lot of work. A planer will make the boards uniform in thickness and cut down the time you spend sanding or planing. Providing, that is, that you align the boards carefully when you glue them together. If the boards slip around when you

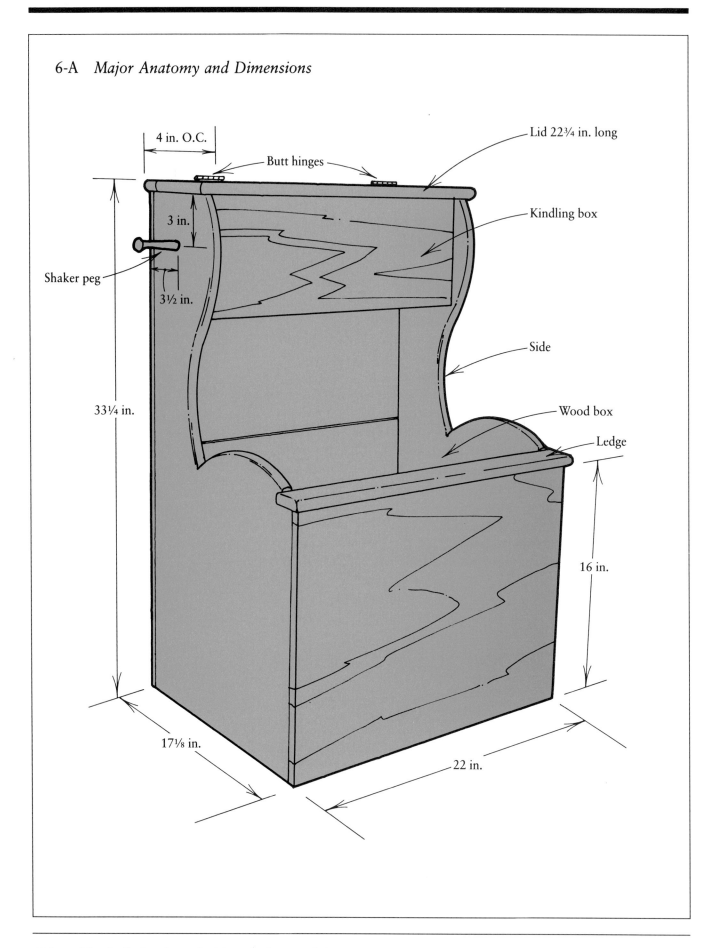

Lid 22¾ in. long

Butt hinges

4 in. O.C.

Kindling box

3 in.

Shaker peg

3½ in.

Side

Wood box

33¼ in.

Ledge

16 in.

17⅛ in.

22 in.

put on the clamps, you'll still have to do some sanding to smooth up the panel. One reason I like to use biscuits for edge joining is that the biscuits keep the boards aligned and can almost eliminate this alignment problem if you're careful when cutting the biscuit slots.

One thing to remember about a thickness planer: It will make a board thinner, but it won't flatten a board that's twisted or cupped. I make it a point to buy the flattest boards I can find.

I planed all the boards for the wood-box panels with my portable thickness planer (*photo 6-1*). The boards were a little thicker than 3/4 in. to start, so I ended up with a full 3/4-in. thickness after planing. (Measurements in the drawings are based on 3/4-in.-thick boards. Had the boards planed out thinner, I would have had to modify some dimensions.)

Once the boards are uniformly thick, I cut the pieces I need for the panels to length and lay them out on my bench. First I look at the growth rings on the ends of each board. I alternate the curve of the rings on adjacent boards — up, down, up, down. This orientation helps to minimize the effect of cupping over the width of the finished panel.

The next thing I look for is an attractive grain match on the surface of the panel. If necessary, I'll rearrange the boards until I'm happy with the grain. So that the boards will stay in the same order, I mark them with a pencil to code them. A single line across one joint, 2 lines across the next joint, and so on.

I want true, square edges for my glue joints, so I joint all the mating edges on my jointer so the boards fit together perfectly, without any gaps at the joints.

With the jointed boards aligned edge to edge, I draw pencil lines across each joint to mark where the biscuits will go. I like to space

6-1 Before I glued up the panels for the wood box, I ran the boards through my thickness planer so the thickness was uniform. This step saves sanding time later when smoothing the panels.

6-2 A bench-top biscuit joiner leaves both hands free to hold the work. A foot pedal activates the mechanism to plunge the cutter into the wood. Here I'm cutting biscuit slots in the boards for the wood box panels.

6-3 After arranging the boards the way I want them, and cutting all the biscuit slots, I stand the boards on edge and spread glue on all mating edges. The squeeze bottle at left is handy for getting glue into the biscuit slots.

6-4 When I clamp up the panel, I use just enough pressure to squeeze a little glue out of the joint. I let the glue squeeze-out dry on the wood.

6-5 I think a paint scraper is the best tool for scraping off the dry, excess glue.

them about 9 or 10 in. apart. To cut the slots, I line up the pencil marks with the index mark on my biscuit joiner and plunge the blade into the wood. It takes only a second or two to cut each slot.

For the wood box, I tried out my new bench-top biscuit joiner (*photo 6-2*). It cuts the same kind of half-moon–shaped slot as my hand-held biscuit joiner, but it leaves both hands free to hold the work. A foot pedal activates the mechanism to plunge the blade into the work.

The glue comes next. I like to use yellow carpenter's glue (aliphatic resin) for indoor furniture projects. I stand the boards on edge (*photo 6-3*) and spread glue on both mating edges. Then, with a small brush, I spread glue in the biscuit slots as well as on each biscuit just before I'm about to insert it in the slot. Glue swells the biscuits and makes the joint difficult to adjust. The idea is to get the glue on the biscuits and the joint assembled as quickly as possible.

When I put on the clamps, I use just enough pressure to squeeze a little glue out of the joint (*photo 6-4*). If the clamps are too tight, all the glue will squeeze out of the joint, creating a weak, or "starved," glue joint. I don't bother to wipe off the excess glue because I don't want to smear it into the wood. I prefer to scrape it off later, with a paint scraper, after the glue has dried (*photo 6-5*). Why scrape instead of sand? Sanding glue gums up a sanding belt or disk in no time, rendering it useless. I think a scraper is the best way to remove the dried glue.

Milling the Side Panels

After sanding the panels with my random orbit sander (*photo 6-6*), I'm ready to size them. Let's start with the 2 side panels. First, I joint the long edge of each side panel on the jointer. Then, I set the table saw rip fence $15\frac{7}{8}$ in. from the blade to rip the front edge of each panel.

The next step is to square up the bottom edge of each side panel. I use my homemade panel cutter to crosscut the bottom. Then I

6-6 I usually sand panels smooth with a belt sander, but because I planed these boards before glue-up, the panel faces are very even. My random orbit sander can handle what little smoothing there is to do.

6-B *Side Layout and Dadoes*

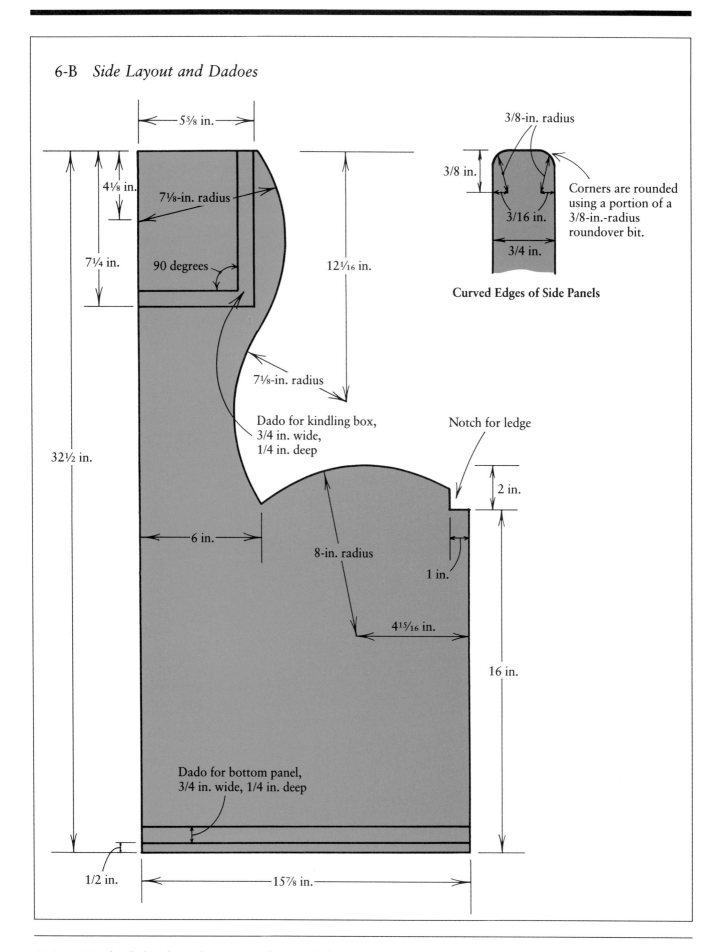

5⅝ in.

4⅛ in.

7⅛-in. radius

90 degrees

7¼ in.

12¹/₁₆ in.

7⅛-in. radius

Dado for kindling box,
3/4 in. wide,
1/4 in. deep

32½ in.

6 in.

8-in. radius

Notch for ledge

2 in.

1 in.

4¹⁵/₁₆ in.

16 in.

Dado for bottom panel,
3/4 in. wide, 1/4 in. deep

1/2 in.

15⅞ in.

3/8-in. radius

3/8 in.

3/16 in.

3/4 in.

Corners are rounded
using a portion of a
3/8-in.-radius
roundover bit.

Curved Edges of Side Panels

measure off the length of the panel — 32½ in. — and trim off the top of each one. I use the panel cutter to make this cut as well.

The sides of the wood box have some decorative curves that must be laid out with a large compass to the radii shown in drawing 6-B. I often draw arcs and cutouts right on the wood itself, but for complex curves like these I prefer to do the layout work on a large sheet of posterboard and cut out the shape to make a template.

I clamp both side panels together between the dogs on my workbench and make sure the back and bottom edges of the panels are nice and even. Then I trace around the template with a pencil to mark the curved profile on the wood (*photo 6-7*). I make the cut with my jigsaw, cutting both side panels at the same time (*photo 6-8*). I smooth up the edges with a drum sander chucked in my drill press. So that the curves are identical, I clamp the 2 side panels together and sand them both at the same time (*photo 6-9*). The drum sander can't get into the little corner where the 2 curves meet, so I clean up that corner with a rasp (*photo 6-10*).

6-7 To mark out the curves on the sides of the wood box, I first make a posterboard template. I clamp both sides together with the back and bottom edges aligned and trace around the template with a pencil to transfer the curves to the wood.

6-8 I make the cut with my jigsaw, cutting through both side panels at the same time so the sides are identical.

6-9 With a drum sander in my drill press, I smooth up the curved edges. I clamp the sides together and sand both edges at once.

6-10 The drum sander can't get into the little corner where the 2 curves meet, so I smooth up this area with a rasp.

6-11 Routing the L-shaped dado (*see drawing* 6-C) for the kindling-box bottom and front is a 2-step process that requires 2 templates, a 5/8-in. O.D. guide collar, and a 1/2-in.-diameter bit. First, I clamp the larger template to the work and guide the router around the template. The guide collar follows the template to cut a 1/2-in.-wide dado.

With the edges smooth and even, I'm ready to round off the corners with my router (*drawing 6-B, detail*). I use a 3/8-in. roundover bit, but I only expose part of the cutting edge because I only want a slight roundover. The router bit won't fit into the little corner where the 2 curves meet, so once again my rasp comes to the rescue for rounding the corners.

Kindling-Box Dadoes

The front and bottom of the kindling box are let into 1/4-in. by 3/4-in. dadoes in the side panels (*drawing 6-B and 6-C*). I mill these dadoes with a router, a guide collar with a 5/8-in. outside diameter, and a 1/2-in.-diameter straight bit. The 1/2-in.-diameter bit requires 2 passes to cut the 3/4-in.-diameter dado. It's an extra step, but I have the advantage of being able to fine-tune the width of the dado as necessary to match the thickness of the piece that fits into it. This wouldn't be possible if I milled the dado in one pass with a 3/4-in.-diameter bit.

The procedure I use calls for making 2 template blocks from pieces of 3/4-in.-thick scrap. One template block measures 5$\frac{1}{16}$ in. by 6$\frac{11}{16}$ in. The other measures 4$\frac{13}{16}$ in. by 6$\frac{7}{16}$ in. I mark the larger template block "1" and the smaller one "2" so I don't get them mixed up.

With the side panel clamped to my bench, I clamp block number "1" to the top of the panel so its edges are flush with the top and back edge of the panel. Then, with my router set for a 1/4-in.-deep cut, I guide the router around the corner of the block to cut an L-shaped dado as shown in drawings 6-B and 6-C. I have to keep the guide collar firmly against the edge of the block or the router will wander off and ruin the work (*photo 6-11*).

After the first cut, I clamp the smaller block number "2" in place and make a second pass to widen the dado to 3/4 in. (*photo 6-12*). The router cuts a curve on the outside corner when it swings around the corner of the first template block. I square up this corner with a chisel to complete the dadoes for the kindling-box front and bottom (*photo 6-13*).

The bottom of the wood box sits in dadoes in the side panels (*drawings 6-B and 6-D*). I mill these dadoes on the table saw with my stack dado set for a cut that's 3/4 in. wide and 1/4 in. deep. I set

6-12 Next, I clamp the smaller template to the work and make a second pass with the router, widening the dado to 3/4 in.

6-13 The outside corner of the dado is rounded where the router swings around the corner of the first template. It doesn't take long to square up this corner with a chisel.

6-C Back and Side Joinery

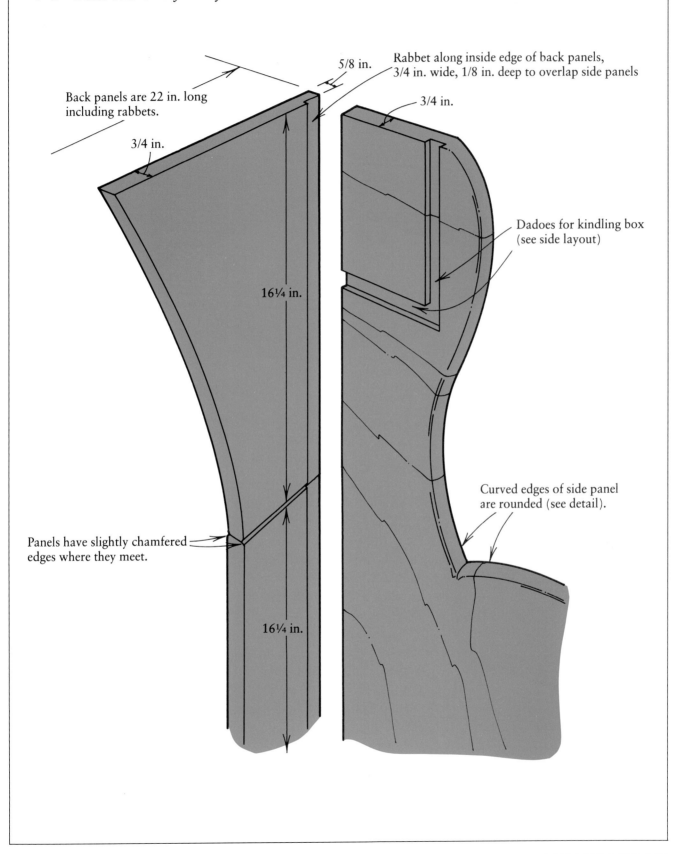

Back panels are 22 in. long including rabbets.

5/8 in.

Rabbet along inside edge of back panels, 3/4 in. wide, 1/8 in. deep to overlap side panels

3/4 in.

3/4 in.

16¼ in.

Dadoes for kindling box (see side layout)

Curved edges of side panel are rounded (see detail).

Panels have slightly chamfered edges where they meet.

16¼ in.

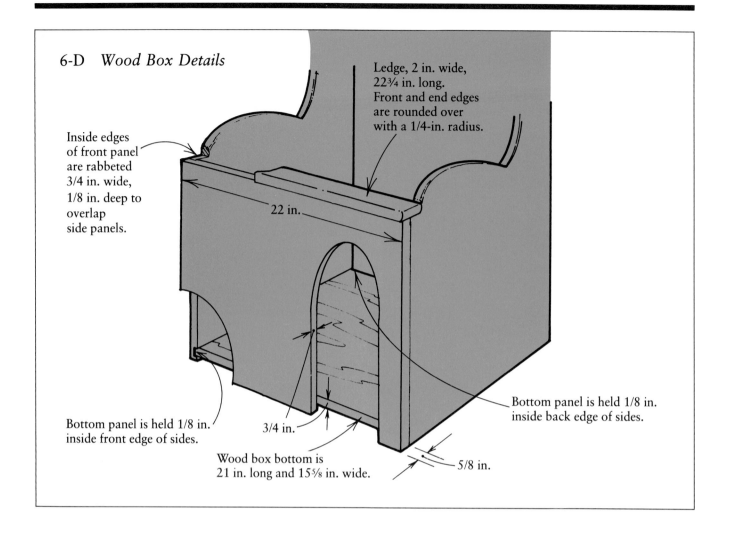

6-D Wood Box Details

Inside edges
of front panel
are rabbeted
3/4 in. wide,
1/8 in. deep to
overlap
side panels.

Ledge, 2 in. wide,
22¾ in. long.
Front and end edges
are rounded over
with a 1/4-in. radius.

22 in.

Bottom panel is held 1/8 in.
inside back edge of sides.

Bottom panel is held 1/8 in.
inside front edge of sides.

3/4 in.

Wood box bottom is
21 in. long and 15⅝ in. wide.

5/8 in.

the rip fence 1/2 in. away from the blade to locate the dadoes 1/2 in. up from the bottom edge of the side panel. Then I mill the dado in each side.

Now I can size the bottom panel. As usual, I joint one long edge square and rip the panel to its finished width of 15⅝ in. (*drawing 6-D*). Then, with my panel cutter, I crosscut one end square, measure and mark off the length (21 in.), and crosscut the panel to length.

With the bottom panel complete, I turn my attention to the front and bottom of the kindling box. I joint and rip them to width and cut them to length with my panel cutter.

Before I can size the front and back panels for the wood box, I have to do a little subassembly (*photo 6-14*). But first, I finish sand the inside of the side panels, the bottom panel, and the front of the kindling box. I sand both sides of the kindling-box bottom. Then I glue and nail the bottom panel to the sides with four 4d finish nails in each side. The front and back edges of the bottom panel are recessed 1/8 in. from the edges of the side panel to account for shallow rabbets in the front and back panels (*drawings 6-C and 6-D*).

Now I'm ready to install the front of the kindling box. A couple of nails secure the piece in its dadoes. I don't glue this joint because the side panel grain runs 90 degrees to the grain of the box front. The nails allow the box front to expand and contract in the dado. The bottom of the kindling box goes in next. I glue and nail it to the side panels as well as to the front of the kindling box.

With that part of the subassembly completed I can now measure across the front and back of the wood box to get accurate measurements for the front panel and the 2 panels that make up the back. The front panel is 16 in. wide by 22 in. long and each back panel is 16¼ in. wide by 22 in. long (*drawings 6-A and 6-B*).

Front and Back Panels

With the front and back panels cut to size, the next step is to mill the shallow rabbets for the corner joints (*drawings 6-C and 6-D*). I attach a wooden auxiliary fence to my table saw rip fence. Then I set my dado head for a rabbet 3/4 in. wide and 1/8 in. deep and mill the rabbets on the front and back panels.

After finish sanding the inside surface, I'm ready to install the front. No glue at the corner joints, just a few 4d finish nails to hold the front panel in place.

There's one more thing to do before I nail on the back. The joint where the 2 back panels meet will open up when the panels shrink. Instead of trying to hide this joint, I decided to "celebrate" it by chamfering the edges to draw your eye right to it (*drawing 6-C*). With a block plane, I mill a 45-degree chamfer on each edge where the back panels meet (*photo 6-15*). Then I finish sand the insides of the back panels and nail on the back, without any glue.

6-14 Before I can size the front and back panels, I have to assemble the bottom to the sides and install the kindling-box front and bottom. Then I put on the other side panel and nail it all together.

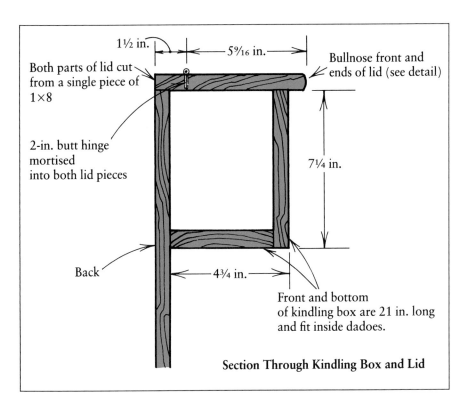

1½ in.
5⁹⁄₁₆ in.

Both parts of lid cut from a single piece of 1×8

Bullnose front and ends of lid (see detail)

2-in. butt hinge mortised into both lid pieces

7¼ in.

Back

4¾ in.

Front and bottom of kindling box are 21 in. long and fit inside dadoes.

Section Through Kindling Box and Lid

6-15 To decorate the joint where the 2 back panels meet, I chamfer each edge with a block plane.

6-16 I have to cut a notch in each side panel to accept the 2-in.-wide ledge that protects the top of the front panel. Two cuts with a backsaw is all it takes.

Bullnose Detail

1/2-in. radius

3/4 in.

Mill bullnose using a portion of a 1/2-in.-radius roundover bit.

Before I go any further, I smooth up the edges of the back and front panels with my random orbit sander.

The Ledge

A little ledge covers the top edge of the front panel to protect it from being banged up by logs (*drawings 6-A and 6-D*). It's just a 2-in.-wide strip, 22¾ in. long. I have to notch the side panels to receive the ledge, removing a little bit of wood at the top front corners (*drawing 6-B*). I do this with my backsaw, making 2 cuts for each notch — the first one horizontal, the second vertical (*photo 6-16*).

With a 1/4-in. roundover bit in my router, I round over the front edges and the ends of the ledge. Then I nail the ledge in place with 4d finish nails.

Kindling-Box Lid

The lid of the kindling box has 2 parts — a hinged section that opens and closes and a narrow fixed section at the back that's nailed to the sides and back of the box. I cut both parts from the same piece of wood — a 23½-in.-long piece of 1 × 8 (*drawing 6-A, detail*).

First I joint one edge of the stock, rip it on the table saw to a width of 7³⁄₁₆ in., and trim it to a length of 22¾ in. Then, on my router table, I rout a bullnose profile on both ends and along the front edge. I use a 1/2-in.-radius roundover bit partially set above the router table and rout the ends of the stock first, before routing the edge. This reduces the chance of tearing out the grain at the corners.

With the bullnose complete, I rip the stock into 2 pieces to make the 2 parts of the lid assembly — one piece 1½ in. wide and one piece approximately 5⁹⁄₁₆ in. wide (*drawing 6-A, detail*). I set my rip fence 1½ in. "strong" from the blade and make the cut with the square edge of the stock (not the bullnose edge) against the fence (*photo 6-17*). Then I joint the sawed edges of each piece on the jointer.

Routing the Hinge Mortises

Mortising the hinges comes next. I cut these with a router, a 5/8-in. O.D. guide collar, and a 1/2-in.-diameter straight bit. I made a hinge template from a piece of 3/4-in. plywood with some strips on the front to align the template with the face of the board to be mortised. I cut a rectangular notch in the template, 1/16 in. larger all around than the hinge mortise I need to cut (*photo 6-18*). That's to take into account the difference between the radius of the guide collar and the radius of my router bit. The guide collar rides around the inside of the notch to cut the mortise (*photo 6-19*).

I mortise both parts of the lid — 4 hinge mortises in all. First, I lay out a centerline for each mortise. Then I position the template on the edge of the stock where I want to cut the mortise and line up the centerline on the template's notch with the centerline marked on the lid. I set the depth of cut for the thickness of the hinge and rout the mortise. I reposition the template to rout the second hinge mortise. The router bit leaves rounded corners, and I have to square these up with a chisel so the hinge will fit. When the mortises are complete, I install the 2 brass-plated butt hinges and nail the lid assembly to the wood box with 4d finish nails through the fixed, rear piece of the lid.

One more thing before I put on the paint. I drill a 1/2-in.-diameter hole 5/8 in. deep into each side of the wood box and glue in a 3½-in.-long Shaker peg for hanging the tools (*drawing 6-A*).

A Milk-Paint Finish

To prepare the wood box for painting, I finish sand the entire outside of the box. Then I fill the nail holes with a bit of glazing compound. I like to use glazing compound because it won't shrink and fall out of the holes. I painted my wood box with blue, old-fashioned milk paint for an authentic-looking finish.

Today's modern paints are very different from the paints that the Shakers used back in the 1800s. In those days, paints were made from natural materials — linseed oil, iron oxide, lead, lime, and similar ingredients. Some paints contained milk, which is where the term "milk paint" originated.

The milk paint I used is sold as a powder that must be mixed with water before it can be applied. It's made from milk, lime, clay, and earth pigment (for the color). The instructions that come with the paint call for wiping the wood with a damp rag to remove any loose dust. Then I brush on the first coat with a disposable foam brush. The milk paint is runny, and doesn't seem to cover well at first. As the paint dries, it turns opaque and develops a chalky look. Interesting stuff. When the first coat is dry, I put on a second coat.

The milk-paint finish looks old and original. It doesn't cover the glazing compound in the nail holes very well, but that just adds to the rustic effect. Now, all I have to do is split a few logs and load up the wood box.

6-17 After routing the bullnose on the front and ends of the kindling-box lid, I rip the lid into 2 pieces — one piece 1½ in. wide and one piece approximately 5⁹⁄₁₆ in. wide. I set my rip fence 1½ in. "strong" from the blade to make the cut.

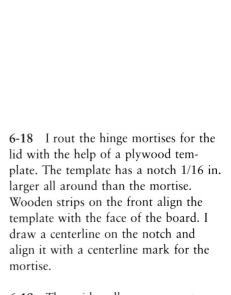

6-18 I rout the hinge mortises for the lid with the help of a plywood template. The template has a notch 1/16 in. larger all around than the mortise. Wooden strips on the front align the template with the face of the board. I draw a centerline on the notch and align it with a centerline mark for the mortise.

6-19 The guide collar on my router rides around the notch to cut the hinge mortise. The depth of cut matches the thickness of the hinge.

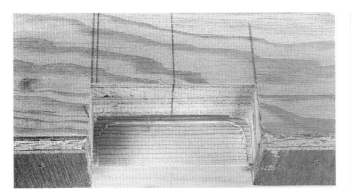

SEVEN

Library Table

PROJECT PLANNER

Time: 2 days
Special hardware and tools:
(4) 3/4-in.-diameter cherry Shaker knobs
Wood:
(1) 5-ft 8/4 × 4 cherry
Rip in half and cut into 4 pieces 30 in. long for legs.
(1) 4-ft 1 × 8 cherry
Cut according to instructions in text for front rail and drawer fronts.
(2) 10-ft 1 × 6 cherry
From one board, cut 2 pieces 12 in. long for end rails. Cut one piece 44 in. long for back rail. Edge glue remaining piece together with two 50-in. pieces cut from second board to make a panel approximately 16½ in. × 50 in. for top.
(1) 6-ft 1 × 4 pine
Cut into 6 equal pieces approximately 1 ft long. From 4 of these pieces, rip a lower drawer support and a drawer side guide. From the fifth piece, cut 2 upper drawer guides. From the sixth piece, rip and cut 4 corner blocks.
(1) 1/2-in. cabinet-grade, hardwood plywood
Cut one piece 18 in. × 20 in. and rip (along 18-in. length) and cut to dimensions in drawings to make drawer sides and backs.
(1) 1/4-in. cabinet-grade, hardwood plywood
Cut 2 pieces 12 in. × 14 in. for drawer bottoms.

H ERE'S a table that's just the right size to fit behind a sofa or in a hallway. I call it a library table, and I got the inspiration from an elegant, old walnut table I found in a New Orleans antique shop. It would function well as a telephone station with a lamp on it. I guess you could even use it as a desk — there's plenty of room to store writing supplies in the drawers.

Front Rail and Drawer Fronts

When I built this piece, I tried something that I'd never done before. I wanted the grain of the drawer fronts to match the grain of the table's front rail. So I decided to make the rail *and* the drawer fronts from a single piece of wood. Perhaps I should say that I *started* with a single piece of wood. The finished rail is actually made of 5 pieces, cut from the same board and glued back together as shown in drawing 7-B.

To make the rail and the drawer fronts, I start with a 4-ft length of 1 × 8 cherry. The first thing I do is joint one long edge of the board. Then I rip and joint the opposite edge to make both edges square and parallel.

Next, in the middle of the board, I lay out the 5¼-in. length of the center block (*drawing 7-B*). With a square, I extend these 2 layout lines across the entire width of the board so I can key all the pieces together later after I've cut them.

The next step is to rip the 2 long pieces at the top and bottom of the rail (*drawing 7-B and photo 7-1*). To cut the bottom piece, I set my table saw rip fence 1¼ in. "strong" (plus 1/32 in.) from the blade and make the cut. To cut the top piece, I set my rip fence 1 in. "strong" from the blade. Then I joint the edges to clean up the saw cuts (*photo 7-2*). So far, I've cut the original board into 3 pieces.

At this stage, I reassemble the 3 pieces as they came from the board and label them with a pencil so they don't get mixed up later. I number the drawer fronts "1" and "2" and draw arrows to indicate the top edge. I also mark the 2 long strips at the top and

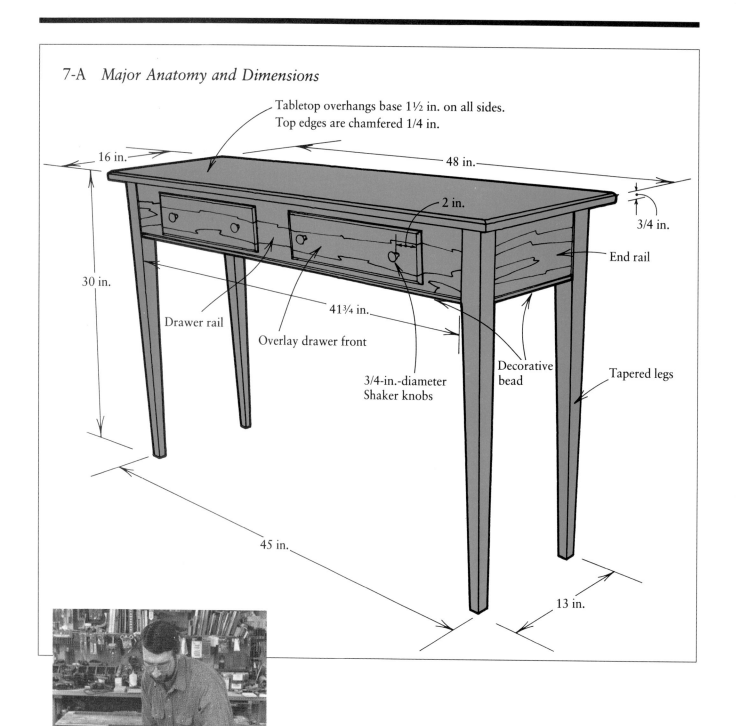

7-A Major Anatomy and Dimensions

Tabletop overhangs base 1½ in. on all sides.
Top edges are chamfered 1/4 in.

16 in.

48 in.

2 in.

3/4 in.

End rail

30 in.

Drawer rail

41¾ in.

Overlay drawer front

3/4-in.-diameter
Shaker knobs

Decorative
bead

Tapered legs

45 in.

13 in.

7-1 The front rail and the drawer fronts are all made from one board, cut apart, then glued back together. Here I'm ripping the 1¼-in.-wide strip for the bottom of the rail. After this, I'll rip a 1-in.-wide strip from the other side of the board.

7-B Drawer Rail Cut-up and Assembly

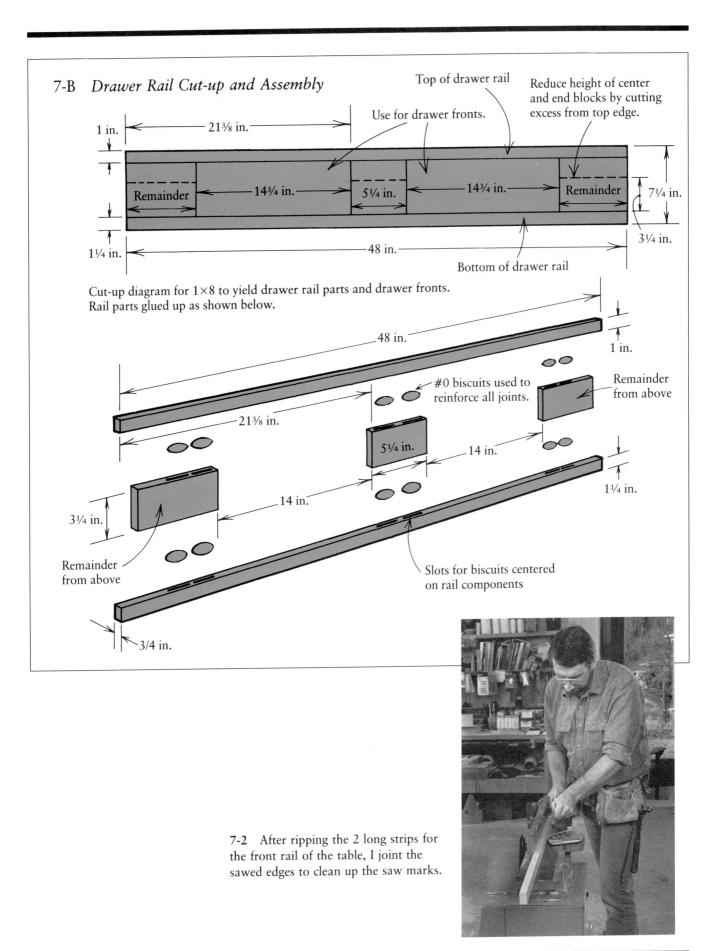

Top of drawer rail

Use for drawer fronts.

Reduce height of center and end blocks by cutting excess from top edge.

1 in.

21⅜ in.

Remainder — 14¾ in. — 5¼ in. — 14¾ in. — Remainder

7¼ in.

1¼ in. ← 48 in. →

3¼ in.

Bottom of drawer rail

Cut-up diagram for 1×8 to yield drawer rail parts and drawer fronts.
Rail parts glued up as shown below.

48 in.

1 in.

21⅜ in.

#0 biscuits used to reinforce all joints.

Remainder from above

5¼ in.   14 in.

1¼ in.

3¼ in.

14 in.

Remainder from above

Slots for biscuits centered on rail components

3/4 in.

7-2 After ripping the 2 long strips for the front rail of the table, I joint the sawed edges to clean up the saw marks.

7-3 I make 2 crosscuts to saw out the 5¼-in. block in the middle of the rail. I cut the 2 layout lines I marked previously across the width of the board.

7-4 To reduce the height of the drawer openings in the front rail, I reduce the width of the 3 blocks to 3¼ in., ripping the wood from the top edges.

bottom of the rail so I can reassemble all the pieces in the same order later.

Now, on my radial-arm saw, I make 2 crosscuts to saw out the 5¼-in.-long block in the middle of the rail (*photo 7-3*). From the 2 long pieces that are left over after making these cuts, I'll make a couple of blanks for the drawer fronts. I'll cut these 14¾ in. long, a little longer than the finished length I'll need.

Holding my tape on the ends where the center block once was attached, I mark off 14¾ in. for each blank. Then I cut both drawer fronts to length on the radial-arm saw. The finished blanks measure approximately 4⅝ in. wide and 14¾ in. long.

I now have 7 pieces in all: a 1-in.-wide top strip, a 1¼-in.-wide bottom strip, two 4⅝-in. by 14¾-in. drawer-front blanks, one 4⅝-in. by 5¼-in. center block, and two 4⅝-in.-wide blocks approximately 6¼ in. long (*drawing 7-B*).

If I were planning to make flush drawer fronts I could glue the rail pieces back together right now. But my design calls for overlay drawer fronts, which overlap the drawer opening on all 4 sides. I have to reduce the size of the drawer openings in order to make them smaller than the drawer fronts.

I reduce the height of the drawer openings by ripping wood from the top edges of the three 4⅝-in.-wide blocks. I set my rip fence 3¼ in. from the blade and rip the 3 blocks, making sure I cut off the tops of the blocks, not the bottoms (*photo 7-4*). The missing wood will break up the grain pattern when the rail is glued back together, but you won't really notice it at the top of the rail.

With all 3 blocks ripped and put in the right location between the long strips, I'm ready to lay out the length of the drawer openings. I want to make these drawer openings 14 in. long, so I hold my tape on one of the center-block layout lines I drew earlier and mark off 14 in. along the top strip. Then I hold my tape on the other center-

7-5   So the ends of the biscuits won't stick into the drawer openings, I place the biscuits where I want them and make a pencil mark at the center of the biscuit as a guideline for cutting the slot.

7-6   Then I cut the slots with my biscuit joiner, lining up the index mark on the joiner with the marks on the wood.

block layout line and mark off 14 in. in the opposite direction. With a square, I transfer these marks to the bottom strip, first making sure to even up the ends of the top and bottom strips.

Now I'm just about ready to glue the pieces of the rail back together again. To reinforce the joints between the blocks and the 2 strips, I install 2 biscuits in each joint. So that the biscuits don't stick into the drawer openings, I take extra care in marking and cutting the slots. Instead of just marking a pencil line for the slot by sight, as I usually do, I place a biscuit where I want it and make a pencil mark at the center of the biscuit (*photo 7-5*). This way I can be sure to keep the ends of the biscuit well away from the drawer openings. With the slots all marked out, I cut them with my biscuit joiner, lining up the index mark on the joiner with the slot-layout marks on the wood (*photo 7-6*).

Now let's glue up the rail. I glue and clamp the blocks between the long strips one at a time, starting with one of the end blocks first (*photo 7-7*). I brush glue on the edges of the block and the strips and

7-7   To glue the front rail back together, I glue and clamp the blocks between the long strips one at a time.

pop in the biscuits. Then I put the block in between the 2 strips, make sure that the layout marks are properly aligned, and clamp the joint tight. Next, I glue and clamp in the center block, and then the last end block, spreading the 2 strips apart to fit the blocks in between.

That about does it for the front rail. I set the assembly aside for a while and turn my attention to the top.

Gluing Up the Top

The top of the library table is glued up from three 50-in. lengths of 1×6 cherry (see Project Planner). As usual, I joint both edges of each board to make them straight and square. Then I cut biscuit slots every 9 or 10 in. along the mating edges. I spread glue on the edges, a little on the biscuits, and clamp the boards together. Three pipe clamps does it, and I alternate the clamps — bottom, top, bottom — to keep the top from bowing as I tighten up the clamps.

When the glue is dry, I take off the clamps and scrape off the excess glue with my paint scraper. Then I true up the faces of the panel with my belt sander.

Now it's time for me to square up the top and cut it to length. I rip and joint the top on my table saw to its finished width of 16 in. Then, with my homemade panel cutter, I square up one end of the top on the table saw. I measure off the finished 48-in. length of the top and crosscut it to length with my panel cutter. I smooth up the end grain with my random orbit sander and set the top aside to work on the legs.

Making the Legs

The legs of the library table are tapered for a light and graceful look. The taper begins 1 in. below the rail and extends all the way to the floor. Only the inside edges of the legs are tapered — the outer edges are straight from top to bottom. Mortise-and-tenon joints connect the legs to the rails.

The first thing to do is to make the leg blanks. I start with a 5-ft length of 8/4 cherry (2 in. thick) that's a full 4 in. wide. I square up one long edge on the jointer and rip the board in half on my table saw. I set the rip fence approximately 1⅞ in. from the blade and make the cut with the jointed edge against the fence. I square up 2 adjacent sides of each blank by running them over the jointer. Then I plane the blanks on my thickness planer, taking them down to 1⅝ in. square. Finally, I square up one end of each blank on my power miter box and cut the 4 legs to a length of 29¼ in. (*drawing 7-C*).

Cutting the mortises is the next step, but before I lay out these joints, I take a moment to study the grain of the legs. I want the surface grain to show on the front of the legs, not the edge grain. So when I lay out the mortises, I'm careful to make sure that the surface grain faces the front of the table.

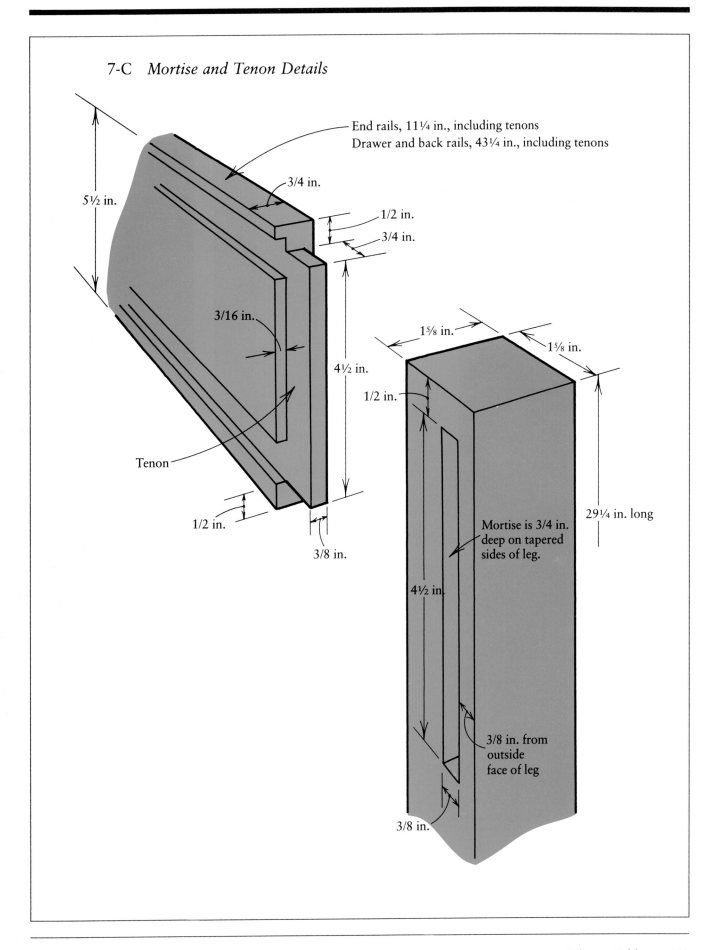

7-C *Mortise and Tenon Details*

End rails, 11¼ in., including tenons
Drawer and back rails, 43¼ in., including tenons

5½ in.

3/4 in.

1/2 in.

3/4 in.

3/16 in.

4½ in.

Tenon

1/2 in.

3/8 in.

1⅝ in.

1⅝ in.

1/2 in.

29¼ in. long

Mortise is 3/4 in. deep on tapered sides of leg.

4½ in.

3/8 in. from outside face of leg

3/8 in.

7-8 I cut the mortises in the legs with the hollow-chisel mortising attachment for my drill press. I use a 3/8-in. bit and set my depth stop for a 3/4-in.-deep cut.

With a square, a rule, and a pencil, I lay out the mortises at the tops of the legs (*drawing 7-C*). The mortises are 3/8 in. wide, 4½ in. long, and 3/4 in. deep. I cut the mortises on the drill press with my hollow-chisel mortising attachment and a 3/8-in. mortising bit. The bit consists of a 3/8-in. square hollow chisel with a drill bit inside. As you plunge the bit down into the wood, the drill removes most of the wood and the chisel squares up the hole. Each hole is only 3/8 in. square. I make repeated holes to cut the length of each mortise (*photo 7-8*).

Tapering the Legs

With the mortises taken care of, I'm ready to taper the legs. On the leg blanks, I measure 6½ in. down from the top ends and mark a line across the 2 tapered sides (the sides with the mortises). This line marks the starting point for the taper (*drawing 7-D*).

I rip the taper on my table saw with the help of my homemade tapering jig. You can buy commercially made tapering jigs made of metal, but they're simple enough to make out of wood (*photo 7-9*).

My tapering jig consists of 2 long pieces of oak, about 30 in. long and 3⅛ in. wide. The pieces are hinged at one end like a V. At the other end, I've installed an adjustment bar that allows me to cut a variety of tapers by adjusting the spread of the V. The adjustment bar is just a piece of oak measuring 1½ in. by 9½ in. with a 1/4-in.-wide by 7-in.-long slot down the middle. One end of the adjustment bar is screwed permanently to one of the long pieces. A bolt in the other long piece sticks up through the slot. A wing nut on the bolt tightens down on the adjustment bar to lock the setting. A stop block is screwed to the side of the piece with the bolt (*photo 7-9*).

To set up the jig, I first draw the taper on one of the leg blanks with a pencil, making sure the taper goes on one of the mortised sides. The taper runs straight from the starting-point line to the bottom of the leg, leaving 7/8 in. remaining at the bottom end (*drawing 7-D*). Then I place the marked leg blank in the jig with the bottom end of the leg against the tapering jig's stop. With the side of the jig positioned against the rip fence, I adjust the opening of the jig until the taper line on the leg is parallel to the rip fence. I check by measuring from the line to the fence at both ends of the layout line. When the layout line is parallel to the fence, I lock the jig's adjustment nut. Then I position the rip fence so the blade will cut to the layout line. The settings stay the same for all tapers.

With the setup complete, I taper 2 adjacent sides of each leg, keeping the side of the jig firmly against the rip fence for each cut (*photo 7-9*). So I don't taper the wrong side by mistake, I cut the first taper on each leg with one mortise facing the blade and the other mortise facing down. For the second taper, I turn the leg clockwise 90 degrees so one mortise faces up and the other mortise faces the blade. When the cuts are complete, I smooth up the saw cuts on the jointer, with the top end of the leg leading the cut (*photo 7-10*).

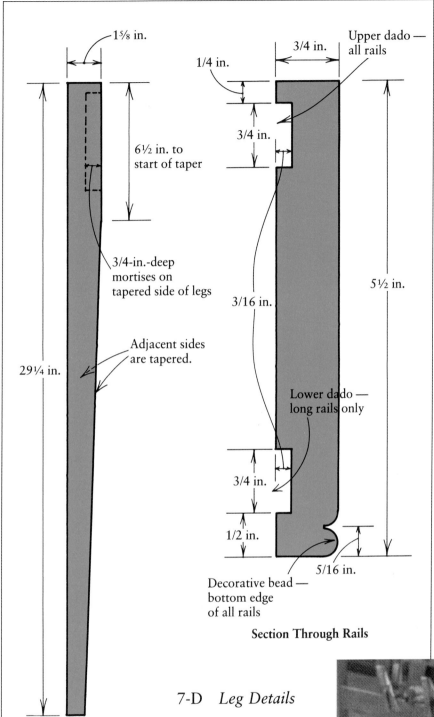

1⁵⁄₈ in.

3/4 in.

1/4 in.

Upper dado — all rails

3/4 in.

6½ in. to start of taper

3/4-in.-deep mortises on tapered side of legs

3/16 in.

Adjacent sides are tapered.

29¼ in.

5½ in.

Lower dado — long rails only

3/4 in.

1/2 in.

5/16 in.

Decorative bead — bottom edge of all rails

Section Through Rails

7-D   *Leg Details*

7/8 in.

7-9   I use my homemade tapering jig to taper the legs. I keep the bottom end of the leg against the jig's stop and keep the jig tight against the rip fence throughout the cut. The taper starts 6½ in. below the top end of the leg.

7-10   After tapering the legs on the table saw, I clean up the tapers by jointing the legs.

Making the Rails

Now I'm going to turn my attention back to the front rail. I take off the clamps, scrape off the excess glue with my scraper, and sand the rail smooth with my random orbit sander.

Before I cut the front rail to length, I mark a centerline across the width of the rail's center block. Then I mark off 21⅝ in. on each side of this centerline to lay out the overall length of the rail. The finished rail should be 43¼ in. long. This measurement takes into account the 3/4-in.-long tenons on the ends of the rail. I double-check my measurements before cutting the ends of the rail to length on the radial-arm saw.

I cut the other 3 rails from a piece of 1 × 6 cherry (see Project Planner). I rip and joint each piece to a width of 5½ in. and cut all the rails to length. The 2 short end rails are 11¼ in. long, including the tenons. The back rail is the same length as the front rail — 43¼ in., including the tenons.

With the rails all cut, I'm ready to make the tenons. For the library table, I'm going to make the tenons a little differently than I usually do. In most cases, I cut the shoulders with the rail lying flat on the table saw. Then I cut the cheeks with my table saw tenoning jig, standing the rails on end for the cheek cuts. Because the rail tenons are so short — only 3/4 in. long — I can cut both the shoulders and the cheeks in just one pass with my stack dado head (*drawing 7-C*).

I set up my table saw with a 3/4-in.-wide stack dado head and screw an auxiliary wooden fence to my rip fence to protect it from hitting the blade (*photo 7-11*). Then I set the blade height to 3/16 in. and adjust the rip fence so it's aligned with the side of the cutter. With the workpiece against my miter gauge, I butt the end of the rail against the rip fence, then move the stock forward into the blade. I don't believe that a gauge block is necessary for this procedure because the cut is open at one end. The blade can't bind in the cut as it could with a dado cut, so there's little risk of kickback with a stack

7-11 With a 3/4-in. dado head on the table saw, I can cut the rail-tenon shoulders and cheeks at the same time. First I cut one side, then I flip the rail over and cut the other. A wooden auxiliary fence protects the rip fence from the cutter.

7-12 After cutting the shoulders, I raise the dado head to a 1/2-in. height and cut the top and bottom of each tenon. I stand the rail on end against the miter gauge.

dado head. With a wobble dado head, however, I would use a gauge block for this setup — just to play it safe.

I cut a sample tenon in some scrap stock as thick as my rail, and I test the fit of the sample in one of the leg mortises. I cut one side first, then I flip it over and cut the other side. The resulting tenon should be 3/8 in. thick. I make any necessary adjustments, and then I mill the tenons on all 4 rails.

Without changing anything else, I raise the blade 1/2 in. above the table and cut the top and bottom of each tenon. I stand the rail on edge and support the face against the miter gauge to make the cuts (*photo 7-12*). That takes care of the tenons.

While the dado head is still in the saw, there are a couple more cuts I want to make. At the top of each rail is a shallow 3/4-in. groove that houses 4 corner blocks and the ends of the upper drawer guides (*drawings 7-C, 7-D, and 7-E*). There's another 3/4-in. groove near the bottom edge of the front and back rail. The ends of the 4 lower drawer guides fit into this groove (*drawing 7-E*).

To mill these grooves, I adjust the dado head (which is already set for a 3/4-in. width) to a height of 3/16 in. To set up for the top groove, I position the fence so it's exactly 1 in. from the *far* side of the dado head. Then I mill the groove along the top, inside edge of all 4 rails. When I mill the front rail, I double-check to make sure that I've got the top of the rail against the rip fence. It's easy to make a mistake.

To cut the lower groove in the front and back rails, I move the fence over so it's 1¼ in. from the far side of the blade. Then I mill the lower groove in these 2 long rails only. For this second groove, I want the bottom edge of the rails against the fence.

There's one more milling operation to perform on the rails. I run a decorative 5/16-in.-diameter bead along the bottom outside edges of all 4 rails (*drawing 7-D*). I do this on my router table with a beading bit. To keep the rails tightly up against the router-table fence, I clamp a homemade feather board against the table (*photo 7-13*). A feather board is nothing more than a scrap piece of wood with one end cut at an angle and some rip cuts made to create fingers, like the teeth of a comb. I mill the bead on all 4 rails, holding the stock flat against the fence and making sure that the bottom of the rail faces down. I feed the wood from right to left, against the rotation of the bit.

With the beading complete, I finish sand all the rails and legs with my random orbit sander.

Drawer Guides and Corner Blocks

There are a few more pieces to make before I can assemble the base of the table. I need 4 drawer supports, 4 drawer side guides, 2 upper drawer guides, and the 4 corner blocks that will hold down the top (*drawing 7-E*). To make these pieces, I start with a piece of 1 × 4 pine (see Project Planner and drawing 7-E). On the power miter box

7-13 With a beading bit in my router table, I mill a decorative bead along the bottom edge of each rail. The home-made feather board clamped to the table holds the rail tight against the fence.

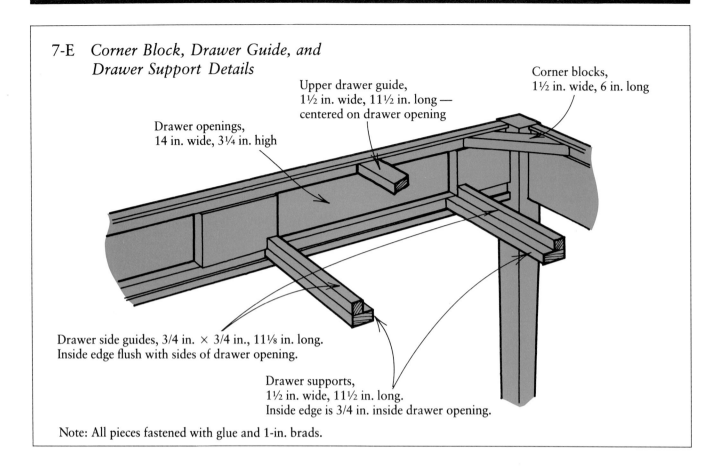

7-E *Corner Block, Drawer Guide, and Drawer Support Details*

Drawer openings, 14 in. wide, 3¼ in. high

Upper drawer guide, 1½ in. wide, 11½ in. long — centered on drawer opening

Corner blocks, 1½ in. wide, 6 in. long

Drawer side guides, 3/4 in. × 3/4 in., 11⅛ in. long. Inside edge flush with sides of drawer opening.

Drawer supports, 1½ in. wide, 11½ in. long. Inside edge is 3/4 in. inside drawer opening.

Note: All pieces fastened with glue and 1-in. brads.

and table saw, I cut the parts according to the Project Planner. I square off one end of each piece on my power miter box and trim all the pieces to length. The corner blocks have angled cuts on the ends, so I swing my miter box around to 45 degrees to make these end cuts.

Putting It All Together

Now it's time for a little assembly. I start by gluing the legs to the front and back rail. I brush some glue on the tenons and put a little more in the mortises. Then I assemble the joints and clamp them together with a long pipe clamp.

While the long rails are still in the clamps, I glue in the 2 short rails and clamp these joints tight (*photo 7-14*). At this stage, I find it easiest to work with the table upside down on my bench. To make sure the table is square, I measure diagonally across the frame, from corner to corner. Both diagonal measurements should be exactly the same. If they aren't, the frame isn't square. In that case I loosen the clamps a little and move it back into square. Then I retighten the clamps and check the diagonals again to be sure.

While the table is still upside down, I glue the 2 upper drawer guides into their grooves. Each guide is centered directly above the drawer opening and square to the rails. I brush some glue in the grooves and on the ends of a guide. I slip it into its groove and fas-

7-14 While the 2 long assemblies are still in the clamps, I glue in the short rails and check the assembly for square.

7-15 While the table's upside down on my bench, the 2 upper drawer guides get glued and toenailed into the top groove in the front and back rails. I position the guides directly above the center of each drawer opening. A clamp pulls the rails together while I nail in the drawer guides.

ten it in place with some 1-in. brads, toenailing through the drawer guide into the groove (*photo 7-15*). I repeat the procedure to install the other upper drawer guide. I use a clamp, as necessary, to pull the 2 rails together while I nail in the guides.

Now, with the clamps still in place across the legs, I flip the table over and set it on its feet on the floor to finish the assembly. The lower drawer supports are the next pieces to install. These supports are 1½ in. wide. The centerline of these pieces must line up with the side of the drawer openings (*drawing 7-E and photo 7-16*). I glue the 4 drawer supports into the lower groove in the front and back rails. Then I toenail them into the grooves with a few 1-in. brads.

A 3/4-in.-square piece goes on top of each drawer support. These are the drawer side guides, which keep the drawers from moving side to side as they're opened and closed (*drawing 7-E*). I glue and nail these to the lower drawer supports, aligning them so the edge of the side guide is flush with the outer edge of the drawer support (*photo 7-17*). If I had to nail these with a hammer instead of my pneumatic nailer, I'd probably nail these side guides to the drawer supports before I installed the drawer supports.

7-16 The lower drawer supports get glued and nailed into the bottom groove in the front and back rails. Note that the centerline of the drawer support is lined up with the side of the drawer opening.

7-17 A 3/4-in.-square drawer side support gets nailed to the top of each lower drawer support. These keep the drawer from moving sideways.

7-18 Corner blocks for fastening the top get glued and nailed into the grooves in the rails.

7-19 As I drill the holes for the screws that hold the top, I rock the drill to elongate the holes parallel to the short rails of the table. These slots will allow the screws to move as the top expands and contracts in width.

The corner blocks go in next. They fit into the top groove at each corner of the table and are simply glued and nailed in the groove (*drawing 7-E and photo 7-18*).

Before I can attach the top, I have to drill screw holes in the corner blocks and the 2 upper drawer guides. Each corner block gets one hole, and each drawer guide gets 2 — one at each end. As I drill the 3/16-in.-diameter holes, I rock the bit from side to side to elongate the holes parallel to the short rails (*photo 7-19*). These elongated holes will allow the screws to move as the top expands and contracts across the grain with seasonal changes in humidity. If the screws weren't free to move, the top would be likely to split.

Now I can put on the top. I place the top upside down on my bench and carefully position the base of the table on top of it. I measure carefully all around to make sure the top is centered and square. Then I fasten the top with eight 1⅝-in. bugle-head screws.

With the table back on the floor, I chamfer the corners of the top with my router and a chamfering bit. I run the chamfer around all 4 sides of the top. I smooth up this edge with some sandpaper and finish sand the top with my random orbit sander.

Making the Drawers

As I mentioned before, the library table has overlay drawers. In other words, the drawer front overlaps the drawer opening on all sides. I decided to keep things simple by making all the joints for the drawer on the table saw. I made a rabbeted lock joint between the drawer front and the sides (*drawing 7-G*). It's a simple joint to cut on the table saw, and it's strong. As shown in the drawing, a tab on the drawer front fits into a dado cut in the side.

I make the backs, sides, and bottoms of the drawers from a cabinet-grade hardwood plywood known as "Baltic birch" ply. It comes in 5-ft by 5-ft sheets and has 9 plies instead of 5, or 7, like most plywood. It's a very stable material. The sides and the backs are made from 1/2-in.-thick plywood — the bottoms are only 1/4 in. thick (see Project Planner). I rip and crosscut the sides and the backs to the dimensions shown in drawing 7-F. Then I cut out two 12-in. by 14-in. pieces of 1/4-in. plywood. Using my panel cutter on the table saw, I trim the bottoms to 11⅛ in. by 13³⁄₁₆.

Next, I size the drawer fronts. The blanks that I cut earlier are 4⅝ in. wide and 15 in. long. I want to make them 1/2 in. longer than the drawer openings and 5/8 in. wider than the drawer openings. First I rip them to width. I set my table saw rip fence 3⅞ in. "strong" from the blade and rip the drawer fronts to width, being sure to remove the excess material from the top of the drawer-front blank. Then I clean up the sawn edges on the jointer. Finally, I crosscut the drawer fronts on my radial-arm saw to a length of 14½ in.

With the drawer fronts cut to size, I'm ready to rabbet the edges where they'll overlap the drawer opening (*drawings 7-F and 7-G*). I could mill this rabbet on the table saw with my dado head, but I'll do it with a router and a 3/8 in. rabbeting bit instead (*photo 7-20*). I mill the rabbet in 2 passes since there's too much wood to remove with one pass.

I need to cut a dado at the back end of each drawer side to secure the back of the drawer (*drawing 7-F*). I set up my table saw with a 1/2-in. dado head and a gauge block clamped to the fence. Then I mill a 1/4-in.-deep by 1/2-in.-wide dado at the back end of each side-piece (*photo 7-21*).

7-20 The drawer fronts have a 3/8-in. rabbet on all inside edges. I mill this with a router and a 3/8-in. rabbeting bit. I make the cut in 2 passes.

7-21 The sides of the drawer get a 1/2-in.-wide dado at one end to house the drawer back. I butt the end of the stock against a gauge block to locate the cut before moving it into the blade.

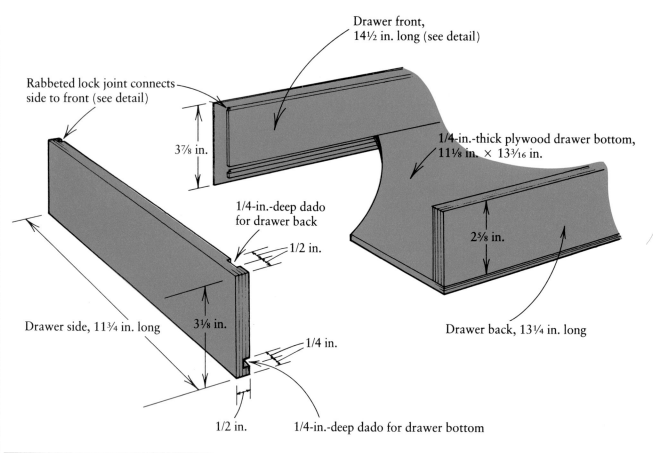

Drawer front,
14½ in. long (see detail)

Rabbeted lock joint connects
side to front (see detail)

3⅞ in.

1/4-in.-thick plywood drawer bottom,
11⅛ in. × 13³⁄₁₆ in.

1/4-in.-deep dado
for drawer back

1/2 in.

Drawer side, 11¾ in. long

3⅛ in.

1/4 in.

2⅝ in.

Drawer back, 13¼ in. long

1/2 in.

1/4-in.-deep dado for drawer bottom

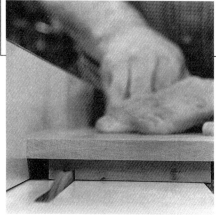

7-22 The drawer fronts and drawer sides get a 1/4-in. groove for the drawer bottom. After grooving the drawer sides, I move the fence 3/8 in. farther away from the blade to mill the grooves in the drawer fronts.

Next, I change the dado head to a 1/4-in. width and mill 1/4-in. by 1/4-in. grooves on the inside of the sidepieces and the bottom edge of the drawer fronts to accept the plywood drawer bottoms (*drawings 7-F and 7-G*). I mill the side grooves first, then move the rip fence 3/8 in. farther from the dado head to cut the groove in the drawer front (*photo 7-22*).

Cutting the Rabbeted Lock Joint

All I need to cut the rabbeted lock joint in the drawer fronts and sides is a regular table saw blade and my rip fence. First, I make the small tab on the drawer front (*drawing 7-G*). It takes 3 cuts to complete the tab.

For the first cut, I raise the blade to a height of 7/8 in. Then I position the rip fence 3/8 in. from the blade. I stand the drawer front

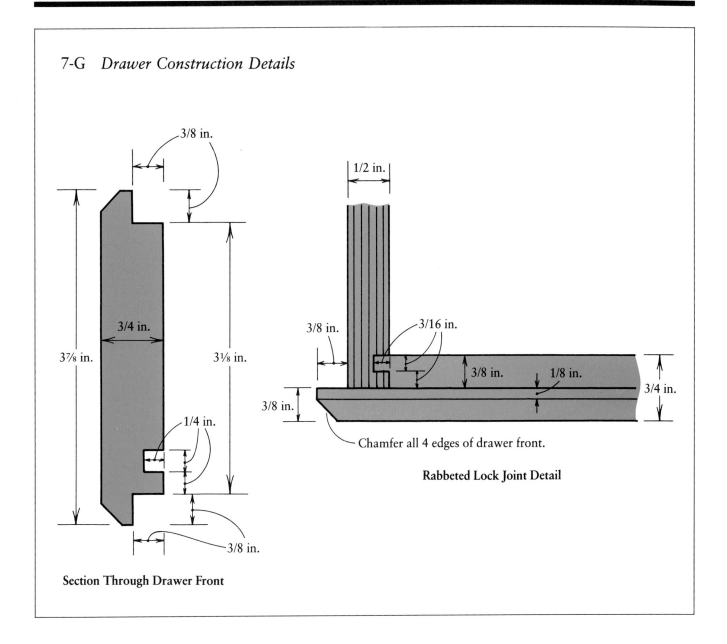

7-G *Drawer Construction Details*

3/8 in.

3/4 in.

3⅞ in.

3⅛ in.

1/4 in.

3/8 in.

1/2 in.

3/8 in.

3/16 in.

3/8 in.

1/8 in.

3/4 in.

Chamfer all 4 edges of drawer front.

Rabbeted Lock Joint Detail

Section Through Drawer Front

on end and make a rip cut, keeping the front side of the drawer front against the fence.

For the second cut, I bump the rip fence away from the blade by about 1/16 in. I make the second cut just as I made the first, with the stock on end and the front of the drawer front against the fence (*photo 7-23*).

For the third and final cut, I position the rip fence 11/16 in. from the *far* side of the blade and lower the blade height to 5/16 in. I make this third cut with the drawer front lying flat on the table, face-up, using the miter gauge to support the piece (*photo 7-24*). This third and final cut trims the little tab to a 3/16-in. length.

The dadoes in the drawer sides come next. Because the blade cuts a kerf only 1/8 in. wide, it will take me 2 cuts to get the 3/16-in. width I need. For the first cut, I raise the blade to a 3/16-in. height

7-23 The rabbeted lock joint for the drawers can be made entirely on the table saw. Here, I'm making the second of three cuts that form the tab on the drawer front that fits into a dado in the drawer side. The front of the drawer front is against the fence.

7-24 The third cut is made with the drawer front lying flat on the table. It trims off the tab to a 3/16-in. length.

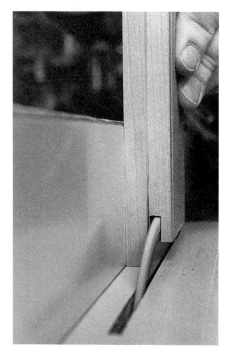

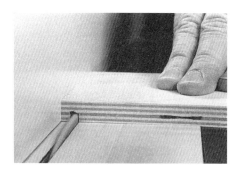

7-25 The tab on the drawer fronts fits into a 3/16-in. by 3/16-in. dado in the sides of the drawer. The saw blade cuts a 1/8-in.-wide kerf, so I have to make 2 passes for a 3/16-in.-wide dado.

and set the fence 3/16 in. from the blade. I make a crosscut in the front ends of the drawer sides and also make a cut in a piece of scrap so I can cut a sample dado.

For the second cut, I bump the rip fence about 1/32 in. farther away from the blade and make a second cut in the piece of scrap to form a dado that's 3/16 in. wide (*photo 7-25*). I test the fit of the drawer-front tab in the sample dado. When the setting's right, I make the second cut in each drawer front to complete the dadoes. That's all there is to making the rabbeted lock joint.

For a decorative touch, I chamfer the edges of the drawer fronts. I could do this with my router table and the chamfering bit that I used for the tabletop, but I decided to use my jointer instead. I tilt the fence to a 45-degree angle and chamfer the edges and ends of the drawer fronts (*photo 7-26*). Four passes through on each edge (depth of cut set at 1/32 in.) gives me the look I want. I joint the ends of the drawer front first, then the 2 long edges.

After finish sanding the drawer fronts inside and out. I'm ready to assemble the drawers. I glue the rabbeted lock joints together and shoot a few brads through the sides to secure the joint. I glue and nail the drawer back in place. The bottom of the drawer gets slipped into the grooves (no glue here), and I fasten the bottom to the lower edge of the drawer back with a few brads.

The drawer knobs are the last thing to add. I drill two 1/4-in.-diameter holes in each drawer front and glue in the knobs (*drawing 7-A*).

7-26 I chamfer the edges of the drawer fronts by tilting my jointer fence 45 degrees. With the jointer set for a 1/32-in. cut, it takes 4 passes to chamfer each edge.

A New Kind of Oil Finish

I chose a Danish oil finish for my library table. Most Danish oils contain solvents that emit vapors which may be harmful to breathe. Also, used rags soaked in oil are a fire hazard because they can combust spontaneously. (Never leave oil-soaked rags in your home or workshop!) The Danish oil that I used for my table is a water-based formulation. It's nonflammable and has no odor. It comes in a plastic bottle and I just squeeze a little on a rag and rub it into the wood with a circular motion. Then I even it out by rubbing straight with the grain. It's possible to buy this oil with pigment in it, but I chose a clear finish. Cherry will darken with age, all on its own. I apply 2 or 3 coats of the water-based Danish oil. It dries fast, so I can recoat every half hour.

One nice thing about oil-finished cherry, the older it gets, the better it will look. I have a feeling that this table's going to be in my family for a long, long time.

EIGHT

Corner Cupboard

PROJECT PLANNER

Time: 4–5 days
Special hardware and tools:
(8) 4-in. Colonial-style, steel "H" hinges
(2) 3-in. Colonial-style bar latches
(2) small barrel bolts or elbow catches
(12) plastic flush-mount panel-retaining buttons and screws for glass panels
(2) 9¼-in. × 38½-in. double-strength glass
Wood:
(1) sheet 4×8, 3/4-in.-thick MDO (medium-density overlay) plywood.
Cut 2 pieces 15¼ in. × 96 in. Each piece makes 3 shelves — 6 shelves total.
(2) sheets 4×8, 1/2-in.-thick MDO plywood
Cut 2 pieces 18 in. × 96 in. for angled back sidepieces. Cut one piece 13³⁄₁₆ in. × 96 in. for back piece.
(1) 14-ft 1×10 select pine
Cut 2 pieces 8 in. × 80 in. for front sides. Use reminder to make 5 edging strips for shelves.
(1) 8-ft 1×6 select pine
Cut 3 pieces 31 in. long. Two of these are for top and bottom rails. Rip third piece to 3-in. width for center rail. Use remainder to make one edging strip for shelf.
(2) 14-ft 1×6s select pine
From each board cut one piece 43½ in. long and rip in half for upper-door stiles (4 total); one piece 24¾ in. long and rip in half for lower-door stiles (4 total); one piece 11½ in. long and rip in half for lower-door rails (4 total); one piece 11½ in. long for upper-door rails (2 total); one piece 11½ in long and rip in half for narrow upper-door rails (2 total). Cut 2 pieces 5½ in. × 20 in. (4 total) and edge glue together in pairs to make 2 lower-door panels.

THIS handsome corner cupboard was inspired by an early-nineteenth-century corner cupboard in the Parsonage at Old Sturbridge Village in Sturbridge, Massachusetts. It's just the thing for displaying some heirloom china and will look really great in a dining room or living room. It sure was a big hit in my house the day I brought it home from the shop.

The outside of the cupboard is made of clear select pine (see Project Planner). I made the shelves, back sides, and back of the cupboard from a special type of plywood called MDO (medium-density overlay) board. MDO board has a laminated core just like regular plywood, but there's a thin layer of paper bonded to both sides of the sheet. This paper surface is very smooth — perfect for painting. MDO board is also very durable. In fact, it's so durable that it's used to make road signs.

Cutting the Back Pieces

The first thing I do is cut the 2 back sides and the back of the cupboard from 1/2-in. MDO board (see *drawing 8-B* and Project Planner). I do this on my table saw. To cut the back sides, I set my rip fence 18 in. from the blade. To cut the back piece, I set the fence 13³⁄₁₆ in. from the blade. If you don't have extension tables on your saw, as I do, a couple of auxiliary roller stands on the infeed and outfeed sides of the saw will help to support the 8-ft-long pieces where they hang over the saw table. I often use my workbench, which is about the same height as the saw and positioned behind it, to support the end of a very long piece.

Next, I cut these 3 pieces to length. The 2 back sidepieces are too wide to cut on my radial-arm saw so I cut these to length on the table saw with my shop-built panel cutter (*photo 8-1*). All 3 pieces for the back of the cupboard are 76 in. long.

Making the Shelves

Now I'm ready to make the shelves. The cupboard has 6 identical shelves (including the "ceiling"), and I cut them all from 3/4-in.

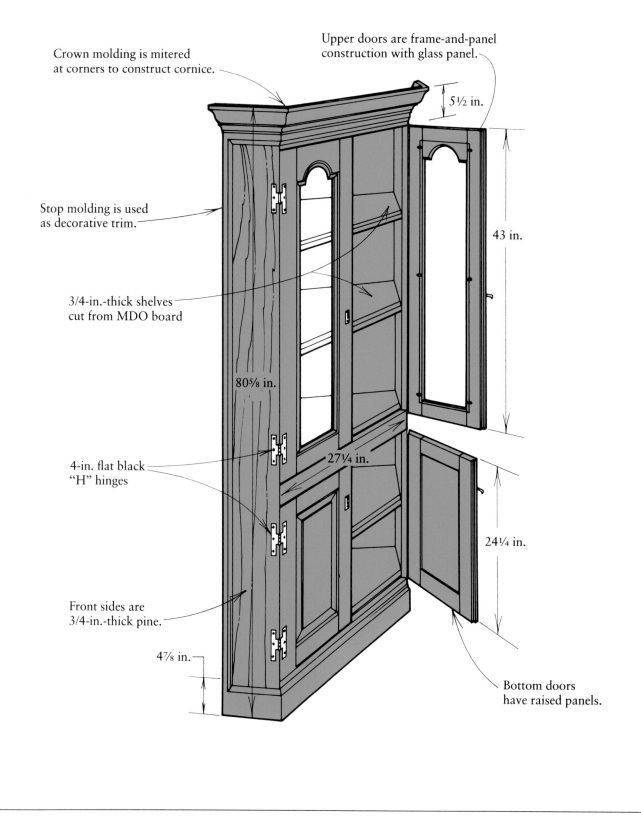

Crown molding is mitered at corners to construct cornice.

Upper doors are frame-and-panel construction with glass panel.

5½ in.

Stop molding is used as decorative trim.

43 in.

3/4-in.-thick shelves cut from MDO board

80⅝ in.

4-in. flat black "H" hinges

27¼ in.

Front sides are 3/4-in.-thick pine.

24¼ in.

4⅞ in.

Bottom doors have raised panels.

Cornice Construction

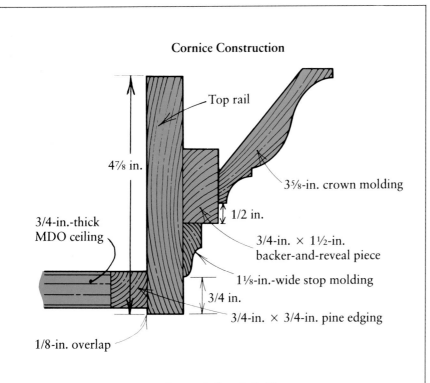

Top rail

4⅞ in.

3⅝-in. crown molding

1/2 in.

3/4-in.-thick MDO ceiling

3/4-in. × 1½-in. backer-and-reveal piece

1⅛-in.-wide stop molding

3/4 in.

3/4-in. × 3/4-in. pine edging

1/8-in. overlap

Center Rail and Shelf

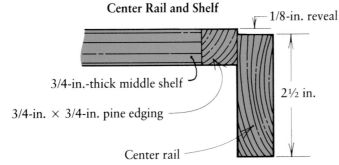

1/8-in. reveal

3/4-in.-thick middle shelf

3/4-in. × 3/4-in. pine edging

2½ in.

Center rail

Base Details

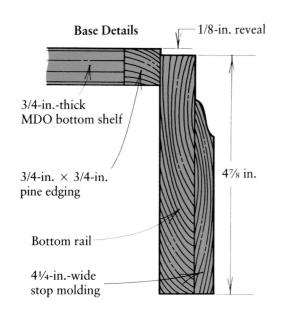

1/8-in. reveal

3/4-in.-thick MDO bottom shelf

3/4-in. × 3/4-in. pine edging

4⅞ in.

Bottom rail

4¼-in.-wide stop molding

(1) 4-ft 1 × 2 pine
Joint one edge for cornice backer and reveal piece.

(1) 4-ft length, 3/8 in. × 4¼ in. pine window-stop molding
Cut and fit to carcass for base molding.

(1) 16-ft length, 3/8-in. × 1⁵⁄₁₆-in. pine window-stop molding
Cut 2 pieces approximately 74 in. long and rip to 1⅛-in. width for decorative trim on front sides. Rip remaining piece to 1⅛-in. width and cut and fit to carcass for cornice molding.

(1) 5-ft length, 9/16-in. × 3⅝-in. pine crown molding
Cut and fit to carcass for cornice.

8-B *Cupboard Cross Section*

Back edge of shelf measures
13 in.

45-degree-angle dado

Back sides are
1/2-in.-thick MDO board

1⅛-in.-wide stop molding

16⅛ in.

Dado, 1/4-in. deep, 1/2-in. wide

18 in.

1/2-in.-thick MDO back,
13³⁄₁₆ in. wide

16 in.

26¹¹⁄₁₆ in.

6⁷⁄₁₆ in.

7⅝ in.

Front side

Double-strength glass

3/4-in. × 3/4-in. pine lip

Stile edges are rabbeted
to overlap at cupboard center.

Door and front side edges
are beveled at 22½-degree angles.

Plan View at Top-Shelf Level

8-1 The 2 back sides of the cabinet are too wide to cut on my radial-arm saw, so I cut these to length on the table saw with my panel cutter.

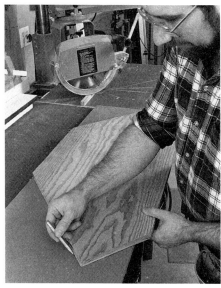

8-2 I make a plywood template in the shape of the shelves to ensure that all 6 shelves are exactly the same. I align the back edge of the template with the edge of the MDO board and trace around the template with a pencil.

MDO board. Because I want all the shelves to be identical, I first make a plywood template in the shape of a shelf, and use this template to lay out the shelves. Using a template is the only way I know of to get shelves that are *exactly* the same size.

The template represents the shelf, the 3/4-in.-wide edging strip that goes on the front of the shelves, and the 3/4-in. width of the rails (*drawing 8-A, detail, and drawing 8-B*). I lay out the shape (*drawing 8-B*) on a piece of plywood and cut out the template on my radial arm saw. I double-check the measurements after cutting, to make sure the template is symmetrical.

Setting the template aside for the moment, I pick up a sheet of 3/4-in. MDO board and cut 2 pieces 15¼ in. wide and 8 ft long (see Project Planner). I can cut all 6 shelves from these 2 pieces of MDO board.

To lay out a shelf, I place the template on the right-hand end of the MDO board and align the back edge of the template with the edge of the MDO board. Then I trace around the template with a sharp pencil (*photo 8-2*).

I cut out the shelf on my radial-arm saw. First, I pivot the saw arm 45 degrees to the right, place the back edge of the shelf against the fence, and make a 45-degree cut on the back, right-hand side of the shelf (*photo 8-3 and drawing 8-B*). Then I swing the saw around 45 degrees to the left and cut the back, left-hand side of the shelf.

After both back sides are cut, I flip the shelf around so the front edge faces the fence. With the saw blade still swung to the left, I make the short, 45-degree cut on the front side of the shelf (*drawing 8-B*). Then I swing the saw back 45 degrees to the right and cut the other short front side of the shelf. I repeat this entire procedure to

8-3   I cut out the shelves on my radial-arm saw. I pivot the saw carriage 45 degrees to the right and cut the long angled side of the shelf. Then I swing the saw around 45 degrees to the left to cut the other angled side.

cut each shelf. When the shelves are all cut out, I check each one against the template just to make sure they're all exactly the same.

If you don't have extension tables for your radial-arm saw, as I do, it will be difficult to support the long piece of MDO board on the saw. You can use a circular saw to rough cut the shelves, a little oversize, from the long piece, then cut to the layout line on the radial-arm saw.

Milling Dadoes in the Back Sides

The next thing I want to do is mill a 1/2-in-wide, 45-degree dado in the 2 back sidepieces into which the back of the cupboard will fit (*drawing 8-B*). I do this on the table saw with a stack dado head set for a 1/2-in.-wide cut and tilted to 45 degrees. (If you must mill this dado with a wobble dado head, you need to first make a wooden insert for the saw table with an extra-wide slot so the dado head fits when it's tilted. The slot in the metal table saw insert — even the wide-slotted one designed for use with a dado head — isn't wide enough to accommodate a wobble dado head when it's tilted at a 45-degree angle.)

With the dado head tilted 45 degrees, I raise the cutter about 3/8 in. above the table and make a test cut in some 1/2-in.-thick scrap. Then I adjust the height until there's only about 1/8 in. of material remaining above the top corner of the dado. It looks like there's not much material left, but the joint will be strong enough when the back's glued in place.

Once the height of the cutter is adjusted, I have to position the rip fence to locate the dado. Getting it right is a trial-and-error proce-dure that requires a few sample cuts. The distance from the *front* edge of the back sidepiece to the *front* edge of the dado (front being the front of the cupboard) is the same as the long, angled side of the shelf template (in this case, 16⅛ in.) plus an extra 1/4 in. to account for the 1/4-in.-deep dado in the front sidepiece (*drawing 8-B*).

Using one of the 18-in.-wide MDO-board cutoffs as a test piece, I mark a line 16⅜ in. from one edge as a guide. Then I position the table saw rip fence approximately 16⅜ in. from the dado head and cut a sample, adjusting the fence as necessary, until the cut is right on the line. When the setting is right, I mill the angled dado on each back sidepiece, making sure to hold the MDO board right against the table at all times (*photo 8-4*). Both sides are cut at the same setting.

Spacing the Shelves

The next thing to do is to draw some layout lines to locate the shelves in the carcass. On the insides of the 2 back sidepieces and the back piece, I draw lines to mark the *tops* of the bottom shelf and the middle shelf (*drawing 8-C*). On the outsides of all 3 of these pieces, I draw lines to mark the *center* of all 6 shelves. These centerlines serve as guidelines for screwing the shelves in place.

8-4 The back of the cupboard fits into 1/2-in.-wide angled dadoes in the back sidepieces. I use a stack dado-head cutter set for a 1/2-in.-wide cut and I tilt the dado head 45 degrees.

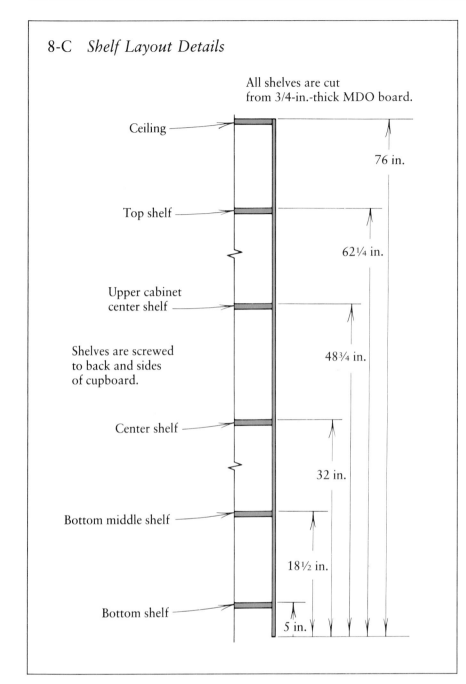

8-C *Shelf Layout Details*

All shelves are cut
from 3/4-in.-thick MDO board.

Ceiling

Top shelf

Upper cabinet
center shelf

Shelves are screwed
to back and sides
of cupboard.

Center shelf

Bottom middle shelf

Bottom shelf

76 in.

62¼ in.

48¾ in.

32 in.

18½ in.

5 in.

8-5   To assemble the carcass, I set up 2 sawhorses with a sheet of plywood on top. Pipe clamps (at left) keep the angled side from sliding off on the floor. I slip scrap pieces of 1/2-in. MDO board in the sidepiece dado and align the inside corner with the corner of the bottom shelf. Then I drill and install a drywall screw through the sidepiece into the shelf. I install the ceiling shelf next, and then the middle shelf. Each shelf gets 4 screws along the side.

Assembling the Carcass

Now for a little assembly. The corner cupboard carcass is a very clumsy piece to put together. To make things manageable during this first assembly procedure, I set up 2 sawhorses with a sheet of plywood on top (*photo 8-5*). I clamp a couple of pipe clamps to the ends of the sawhorses to keep the back sides from sliding off onto the floor during assembly (*photo 8-5*).

For this first assembly step I need the 2 back sidepieces, the back, 3 shelves, and 2 of the pieces of 1/2-in. MDO board that I cut off from the back sidepieces.

8-6 The back goes on next. I glue it into the dado in the sidepiece and screw it to the backs of the shelves.

I place one of the back sidepieces on my makeshift assembly bench with the back side facing up and the front edge against the 2 pipe clamps. Then I tip the back edge up and slip the bottom shelf under one end and the "ceiling" shelf underneath the opposite end (*drawing 8-C*). When I lower the sidepiece down again, it holds these 2 shelves (very precariously) in a vertical position. It might be necessary to use a couple of extra clamps to keep the shelves from falling over.

Now I want to get everything perfectly aligned. Working at the bottom end of the carcass, I take the piece of scrap MDO board and slip it into the dado in the sidepiece. This scrap MDO board simulates the back of the cupboard. I slip the other piece of MDO board into the dado at the top of the cabinet (*photo 8-5*). Then I tap the sidepiece and the "back" until the inside corner, where these 2 pieces meet, aligns perfectly with the back corner of the shelf. Then I tap the bottom shelf to align it with its layout line. When everything's lined up, I use a combination drill and countersink to drill a pilot hole through the back of the sidepiece into the shelf. Then I install a 1¼-in. drywall screw to hold the shelf in place (*photo 8-5*). Then I install 3 more screws along the side, making sure that the shelf is lined up with its layout line. I predrill and countersink all the screw holes before installing the screws.

I repeat the procedure to align and install the ceiling shelf next, then the center shelf. Each shelf gets 4 screws along the side.

The back of the cupboard goes on next. I spread glue along one edge and slip it into the dado. When it's seated in the dado, I make sure the ends are lined up with the ends of the sidepiece and screw the back to the rear edges of the shelves — 3 screws into each shelf — making sure the shelves are aligned with their layout lines (*photo 8-6*). Then I reinforce the glued dado with some 1-in. brads.

Once the back is installed, I spread glue on the opposite edge of the back and put the other sidepiece in place with glue and some brads in the dado. I screw this sidepiece to the shelves with 4 screws in each shelf. Now I can stand the carcass upright on the floor to install the other 3 shelves.

I find scrap pine spacers helpful for positioning the 3 intermediate shelves. I cut the spacers to a length equal to the distance between the shelves (*drawing 8-C*) and stand them on end — 4 to a shelf. I clamp 2 spacers to the front edges of the back sides, as shown in photo 8-7, and lean 2 more spacers against the back of the cupboard. Then I place the shelf on top. The spacers ensure that the shelves will be parallel, and they hold the shelf steady while I screw it in place through the back of the cupboard.

With all 6 shelves installed, the next thing to do is to dress up the front edges of the shelves with some 3/4-in. by 3/4-in. pine edging strips (see Project Planner). The ends of these strips must be cut at a 45-degree angle (*drawing 8-B*). Since they're all the same length, I set the stop on my power-miter-box fence, swing the blade 45 degrees to the left, and cut 6 pieces. I attach the strips to the shelves with glue and some 4d finish nails (*photo 8-8*). I set the nails with a nail set.

The two front sides of the cupboard are ripped from the remainder of the 1 × 10 (see Project Planner). I rip these pieces to an 8-in. width and joint one long edge. Then I square up one end of each piece on my radial-arm saw, measure off 76 in., and crosscut the other end to length.

The doors will be hung from these 2 sidepieces, so I have to bevel the inside edges at a 22½-degree angle (*drawing 8-B*). I set my table

8-7 Spacers make it easy to nstall the intermediate shelves. The length equals the distance between shelves. I clamp the outer 2 spacers to the carcass and stand 2 more against the back. I place the shelf on top and screw it in place through the back and the back sidepieces.

8-8 The front exposed edge of the MDO board shelves gets covered with a 3/4-in. by 3/4-in. pine strip. I cut the ends of the strip at 45 degrees and glue and nail the strips in place.

8-9 The front sides of the cupboard have a 22½-degree bevel on their front edges. I rip this bevel on the table saw, tilting the saw blade 22½ degrees. Note that the rip fence is positioned to the left side of the blade.

8-10 I have to mill a 1/4-in.-deep by 1/2-in.-wide dado on the back side of each sidepiece to receive the edge of the back sidepiece. I use a dado-head set for a 1/2-in.-wide cut.

saw rip fence to the left of the blade and tilt the blade 22½ degrees. Then I position the fence so the finished piece is 7⅝ in. "strong" on its widest face (the side that faces up on the table saw). When the fence is properly positioned, I rip the bevel on the inside edge of both front sidepieces, keeping the jointed edge against the rip fence (*photo 8-9*). A roller stand on the outfeed end of the table saw will help to support the board when it comes off the saw. Then I tilt my jointer fence 22½ degrees and joint the beveled edge to remove any saw marks.

Next, I have to mill a 1/4-in.-deep by 1/2-in.-wide dado in each sidepiece to house the end of the back sidepiece (*drawing 8-B*). To locate this dado, I lay the carcass on its back and hold one of the front sidepieces in position on the carcass. I line up the inside corner of the beveled edge with the corners of the pine trim strips on the shelves. When they're lined up, I note where the edge of the back sidepiece meets the front sidepiece and mark the dado location on the top end of the front piece (*drawing 8-B*).

Now I'm ready to mill the dadoes. I set up my dado head for a 1/2-in.-wide cut that's 1/4 in. deep, and position the table saw rip fence to cup the dado on the location I've just marked. I double-check to make sure I'm cutting the dado on the *back* side of the front piece, then mill the dadoes on both pieces (*photo 8-10*).

Now I'm ready to install the front sidepieces. I spread glue along the short angled sides of the shelves and nail the front sidepiece to the edges of the shelves with some 4d finish nails. Then I install the second front sidepiece in the same way (*photo 8-11*) and set all the nails with a nail set.

Next, I make the 3 rails across the front of the cupboard (*drawing 8-A*). I cut these from 1 × 6 pine (see Project Planner). I joint one long edge of each rail and rip them to width 1/32 in. "strong." Then I joint the sawed edge to remove the extra 1/32 in. of material. The top and bottom rail are both 4⅞ in. wide. The center rail is 2½ in. wide.

The ends of these rails must be beveled to 22½ degrees to fit tightly against the beveled edges of the front sidepieces. I do this on the table saw. I bevel one end and cut the other end slightly longer than I need. I cut the rails approximately 27⁵⁄₁₆ in. long, and then I trim off just a little, as necessary, to get a perfect fit. When the rails are cut to length, I glue and nail them to the front sidepieces and the edges of the shelves. As shown in the details for drawing 8-A, the edges of the rails are set 1/8 in. below the shelves.

Making the Doors

I need to make 2 different-style doors for the corner cupboard — raised-panel doors for the bottom and frame-and-panel doors with glass panels for the top (*drawings 8-A, 8-D; and 8-E*). All 4 doors are joined with mortise-and-tenon joints.

I cut the frame parts for all 4 doors from 1 × 6 pine (see Project

Planner). I joint and rip each piece 1/32 in. "strong" and joint the sawed edge to trim the pieces to width. Except for the 5-in.-wide top rails on the upper doors, all frame parts are 2½ in. wide (*drawings 8-D and 8-E*).

Next, I trim the frame parts to length (*drawings 8-A, 8-D, and 8-E*). First, I square up one end on my power miter box. To determine the length of the stiles, I measure between the rails on the cupboard and cut the stiles about 1/4 in. shorter than the opening height (in this case, 43 in. for the upper-door stiles and 24¼ in. for the lower-door stiles). The upper- and lower-door rails are 11¼ in. long (including the tenons). I set a stop on my miter-box fence to make sure that corresponding pieces are exactly the same length.

With the frame parts all cut to size, I'm ready to mill a bead on the inside edges of the stiles and rails (*drawings 8-D and 8-E*). I set up my router table with a 1/4-in.-radius roundover bit and a fence (*photo 8-12*). I hold a straightedge across the fence to make sure that the fence is tangent to the edge of the pilot bearing on the router bit. Then I mill a bead on the edge of all 16 door-frame parts, holding the stock flat on the table, with the best side facing down.

The panel in the lower doors fits into a 1/4-in. by 1/4-in. groove in the stiles and rails (*drawing 8-D*). I mill this groove on the table saw with a dado head set for a 1/4-in.-wide cut. I set the rip fence 1/8 in. from the blade and mill the groove in the bottom-door stiles and rails, keeping the beaded side facing away from the fence.

Mortises and Tenons

Cutting the mortises is the next step. The mortises are "blind"; that is, they don't go all the way through the stiles. The mortises in both upper and lower doors are 1/4 in. wide. I set up the hollow-chisel mortising attachment on my drill press with a 1/4-in. chisel. With a pencil, a square, and a rule, I lay out the mortises on the stiles for the upper and lower doors (*drawings 8-D and 8-E*). Then I set the mortising chisel for a 1⁵/₁₆-in.-deep mortise (measured from the edge of the rail) and mill the mortises in all 8 stiles (*photo 8-13*).

The tenons come next. The decorative beading complicates things a little and adds a couple of extra steps to the tenon-making process, but the procedure isn't very difficult.

First, I mill the tenon shoulders and cheeks on the front side of all 8 door rails. To do this, I mount a dado head on the table saw, set for a 3/4-in.-wide cut. I raise the dado head to a height of 3/8 in. above the table.

To ensure that the tenons will all be the same length, I clamp a wooden gauge block to the rip fence, slightly forward of the dado head (that is, toward the operator). I place a rail against the miter-gauge head and slide the rail to my right until the end butts against the gauge block. Then I move the miter gauge and rail forward toward the dado head to make the shoulder cut. When the rail contacts the cutter, the end should no longer be touching the gauge

8-11 I nail the 2 front sidepieces to the edges of the shelves with 4d finish nails.

8-12 Both the upper and lower doors have a decorative bead around the inside of the frame. I mill this bead along one edge of all the stiles and rails using a 1/4-in.-radius roundover bit in the router table.

8-D *Lower-Door Details*

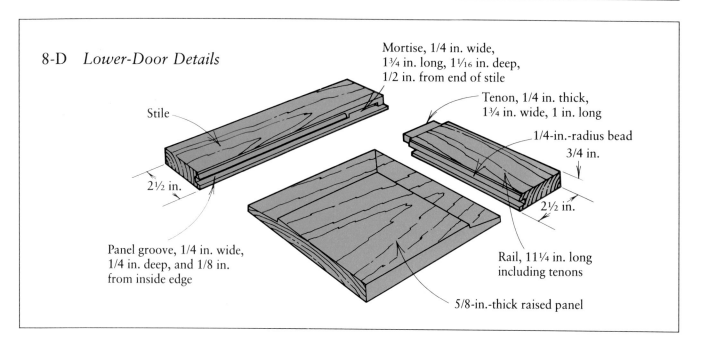

Mortise, 1/4 in. wide,
1¾ in. long, 1¹/₁₆ in. deep,
1/2 in. from end of stile

Stile

Tenon, 1/4 in. thick,
1¾ in. wide, 1 in. long

1/4-in.-radius bead

3/4 in.

2½ in.

2½ in.

Panel groove, 1/4 in. wide,
1/4 in. deep, and 1/8 in.
from inside edge

Rail, 11¼ in. long
including tenons

5/8-in.-thick raised panel

8-E *Upper-Door Details*

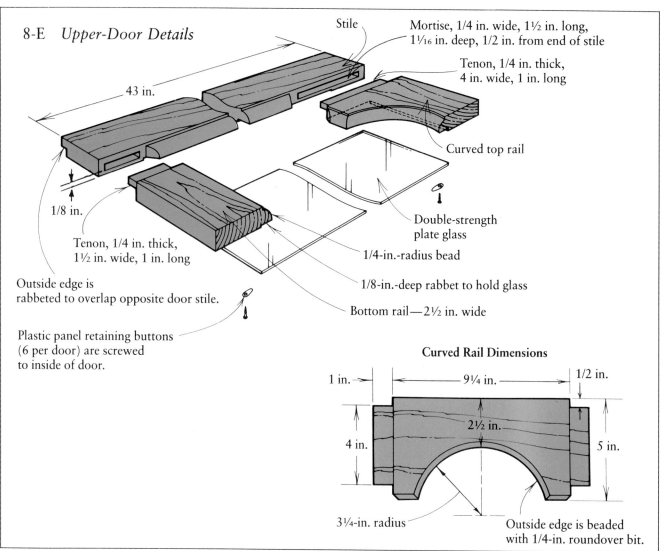

Stile

Mortise, 1/4 in. wide, 1½ in. long,
1¹/₁₆ in. deep, 1/2 in. from end of stile

Tenon, 1/4 in. thick,
4 in. wide, 1 in. long

43 in.

Curved top rail

1/8 in.

Double-strength
plate glass

Tenon, 1/4 in. thick,
1½ in. wide, 1 in. long

1/4-in.-radius bead

1/8-in.-deep rabbet to hold glass

Outside edge is
rabbeted to overlap opposite door stile.

Bottom rail—2½ in. wide

Plastic panel retaining buttons
(6 per door) are screwed
to inside of door.

Curved Rail Dimensions

1 in.

9¼ in.

1/2 in.

2½ in.

4 in.

5 in.

3¼-in. radius

Outside edge is beaded
with 1/4-in. roundover bit.

block. I set the fence for a 1-in.-long tenon and move the rip fence to adjust the length of the tenon. I cut a sample to test the setting.

I make the first cut with the rail end against the gauge block — this cut forms the tenon shoulder. Then I complete the rest of the cheek by making a second crosscut, moving the rail away from the fence for the second cut (*photo 8-14*).

Now, with my rip fence and gauge block in the same position, I lower the height of the dado head to 1/8 in. and cut the back side of my sample. The resulting tenon should be exactly 1/4 in. thick. I test the fit of this sample tenon in a mortise and adjust the height of the dado head, as necessary, to get a nice slip fit. When I've got the adjustments just right, I cut the shoulders and cheeks on the back sides of the upper-door rails only, making 2 passes to complete each cheek (*photo 8-15*).

Without moving the fence or the gauge block, I raise the dado head 1/2 in. above the table to make the cut that forms the top edge of the top-rail tenons and the bottom edge of the bottom-rail tenons (*drawings 8-D and 8-E*). I stand the rails on edge against the miter gauge, making sure that the beaded edge faces up. Then I cut the shoulder on all 16 tenons, making sure to keep the beaded edge of the rail facing up. It takes 2 passes to complete each tenon (*photo 8-16*). The upper-door rails have an additional shoulder on the

8-13 I cut all the mortises for both upper and lower doors with a 1/4-in. hollow-chisel mortising bit in my drill press. The mortises are all 1⁵⁄₁₆ in. deep. Here I'm mortising a stile for the lower door.

8-14 The first step in making the door-frame tenons is to mill the shoulder and tenon cheek on the front sides of the rails. I set my dado head for a 3/4-in.-wide cut and a 3/8-in. height. Then I clamp a gauge block to the fence to determine the length of the tenon. I butt the end of the rail against the gauge block and push it forward with the miter gauge to cut the shoulder. I move the rail and make a second pass (shown here) to complete the tenon cheek.

8-15 With the front cheeks complete, I lower the blade to 1/8 in. Without moving the fence or the gauge block, I cut the back shoulders and cheeks on the upper-door rails only, taking 2 passes to complete each cheek.

8-16 I cut the tenon shoulders on the outer edges of the rails by raising the dado head to a height of 1/2 in. It takes 2 passes to complete each cut. The fence and the gauge block haven't been moved.

8-17 The upper-door rails have 1/2-in. shoulders on both the top and the bottom of each tenon.

8-18 and 8-19 The shoulder on the back side of the lower-door rails is offset from the front shoulder by 1/4 in. To make this cut, I set the dado head 1/8 in. above the table and move the fence (gauge block still in place) 1/4 in. farther away from the blade. The first cut forms the shoulder (*8-18*). I move the rail away from the fence and make a second pass to complete the cheek (*8-19*).

beaded-edge side of the tenons. With the blade at the same setting, I cut that shoulder on each upper-door tenon (*photo 8-17 and drawing 8-E*).

The shoulder cut on the back side of the lower-door rails is offset from the front shoulder by 1/4 in. (*drawing 8-D*). To make this cut, I move the rip fence 1/4 in. farther away from the blade and lower the blade height to 1/8 in. Then I cut the back shoulders and cheeks on the lower-door rails, using the miter gauge and gauge block just as I did for the other cheek cuts (*photos 8-18 and 8-19*). The resulting tenon should be 1/4 in. thick.

Mitering the Door Molding

The next thing I want to do is to miter the inside corners of the rails and stiles, so that the beaded molding will meet at a miter when the door frames are assembled. I miter all the rails first. I tilt the table saw blade 45 degrees and raise the blade 1/4 in. above the table. Then I stand a rail on edge against the miter gauge head (beaded edge down) and position the rip fence and guide block so that the outer corner of the miter will fall directly on the point where the tenon shoulder intersects with the shoulder of the bead (*photo 8-20*). Then I miter the bead on both ends of each rail.

Next, without changing the blade setting, I miter the bead on the upper-door stiles. To mark the outer corner of the miter, I insert a

8-20 On the table saw, I miter the bead on all the rails and the stiles for the upper doors so the beaded molding will meet at a miter when the doors are assembled. With a gauge block to locate the cut, I tilt the saw blade 45 degrees and adjust the height so the outside corner of the miter falls on the point where the tenon shoulder intersects the shoulder of the bead. Here I'm cutting a miter on one of the lower-door rails.

8-21 The upper-door stiles also get mitered on the table saw. I reposition the fence and guide block to position the cut. Here I'm mitering the bottom end of one of the upper-door stiles.

top rail and a bottom rail into one of the stiles and use a square and a pencil to mark where the outer corner of the miter needs to be located on the stile. Then I position the rip fence and gauge block so the outer corner of the miter falls right on this pencil line (*photo 8-21*). First I cut the miter at the bottom ends of the stiles, then I reposition the fence to cut the miter at the top ends.

I also have to miter the bead on the lower-door stiles, but I have to cut these miters by hand (I'll explain how a little later on). I can't use the table saw procedure to miter the lower-door stiles because I don't want to cut through the 1/8-in. section on the back side of the panel groove (*drawing 8-D*).

Before I can assemble the lower-door frames, I have to cut away a section of the bead on the end of each stile. I insert a rail tenon into one of the stiles and use a square and a pencil to mark the stile where it meets the shoulder of the bead on the rail. I want to remove the bead on the stile from this point to the end of the stile (*drawing 8-D*). I do this on the router table.

I set up my router table with a 1/2-in.-diameter straight bit. I raise

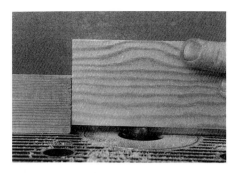

8-22 Before I can assemble the door frames, I have to rout away a section of the bead where it would interfere with the rails. For the lower-door stiles, I rout off only the bead. For the upper-door stiles, I rout away the entire width of the frame from the miter to the end of the stile. A stop block clamped to the router-table fence stops the cut at the layout line. Here I'm routing off the bead on a lower-door stile.

8-23 After routing off the bead on the lower-door stiles, I have to miter the corner of the bead with a utility knife to match the miter on the rail.

the bit 1/4 in. above the table and position the router-table fence so the bit completely removes the bead without disturbing the 1/8-in.-thick section on the back side of the panel groove. I cut a sample in a piece of scrap and clamp a stop block to the router-table fence to stop the cut at the line I've marked on the stile. When the setting's right, I rout away the bead on both ends of all 4 lower-door stiles (*photo 8-22*). I'll leave this setup as is for now. I'll need it again for the upper-door stiles.

Now I can almost assemble the lower-door frames. Before the joints will go together completely, however, I have to cut a 45-degree miter on the stile bead. I assemble the joints as far as I can, then miter the bead with a sharp utility knife (*photo 8-23*).

The upper-door stiles, too, need to have wood removed from the ends before the joints can be assembled. I cut away this wood on the router table, which is still set up from removing the beads on the lower-door stiles. The main difference here is that I'm not just removing the bead — I'm routing off the entire 3/4-in. thickness of the stile between the miter cut (which I made earlier on the table saw) and the end of the stile (*drawing 8-E*).

For the bottom ends of the upper-door stiles, I can use the same stop-block setup I used to rout off the bead on the lower-door stiles. Since I have to remove a longer section of wood from the top ends of the stiles, however, I have to reposition the stop block to rout away the wood from the top ends.

I make this cut in 2 passes, taking half of the stile's thickness in each pass. Here's my procedure: First, I make one pass on the bottom ends of all 4 stiles. Then, I reposition the fence to make the second pass on the bottom ends of 4 stiles. To cut the two ends, I repeat the process, after first moving the stop block to account for the longer cut I have to make.

Cutting the Upper-Door Arches

To lay out the decorative arches in the top rails of the upper doors, I make a cardboard template with a 3¼-in. radius, as shown in drawing 8-E. Then I trace the curve on each door rail and cut out the curves on my band saw. I use a drum sander in my drill press to smooth up the curves.

I want to continue the decorative bead around the insides of the arches, and I'll do this on my router table, which I set up again for beading the arches. I take off the fence and set the height of the roundover bit the same as it was earlier for beading the stiles and rails. I mill a bead around the inside of each arch, guiding the stock against the pilot bearing and feeding from right to left, against the rotation of the bit (*photo 8-24*).

Lower-Door Panels

In the planning stages for this project, I glued up 2 blanks for the lower-door panels (see Project Planner). Now, I scrape off the excess glue with my paint scraper and belt sand one side of each panel smooth and flat. Then I run the panels through my thickness planer to take them down to a 5/8-in. thickness (*drawing 8-D*).

With the frames for the lower door loosely fitted, I'm ready to cut the door panels to final size. The bead on the inside of the stiles and rails is 1/4 in. wide — the same as the depth of the panel groove. I measure across the frame, from bead shoulder to bead shoulder, and cut the panel about 1/8 in. narrower in width and about 1/16 in. shorter in height than these measurements. The panel will expand and contract in width, and this leaves a little room to allow for expansion. I use my panel cutter on the table saw to cut the ends of the panel to length.

In other chapters of this book I've shown several different ways to raise a panel. For this project, I raised the panels on my radial-arm saw with a panel-raising molding head. This cutter spins in a horizontal plane, so after I install the cutter on my saw, I tilt the motor so the arbor points straight down. Then I fit the accessory guard over the cutter.

I raise the panels in 2 passes, lowering the molding head for the second pass. I feed the panels into the cutter from right to left, guiding the edge of the panel along the radial-arm-saw fence (*photo 8-25*). I always cut both ends of the panel first, to avoid tearout at the corners.

Assembling the Doors

At last, I'm ready to assemble the doors. Before I spread glue on the joints, however, I do a dry run to make sure that everything fits. If I have to, I make any necessary adjustments before I put things together for keeps.

Starting with one of the lower doors, I spread glue on the tenons and a little in the mortises. The panel doesn't get any glue — it must be free to "float" in the groove. With the panel in place, I assemble the frame and tap the joints together with my shot-filled mallet. Then I put on some clamps to pull the joints tight and set the door aside to dry. I repeat the procedure for the other lower door. Next, I put glue on the joints of the upper-door frames and clamp them together to dry.

Routing Rabbets for the Glass

When the glue is dry, I scrape off the excess with my paint scraper. Now I'm ready to rout a 1/8-in.-deep by 5/16-in.-wide rabbet around the door-frame opening on the back of each upper door. The glass door panels fit into these rabbets (*drawings 8-A and 8-E*). Because the glass is square at the top, and not rounded to fit the arch, I have to rout out additional material at the top of each door to accommodate the glass (*drawing 8-A*). Here's the way I do it.

First, I measure in 2³⁄₁₆ in. from the outside edges of the frame to locate the edges of the rabbet (including the top edge of the routed-

8-24 After sawing out and sanding the arch in the upper doors, I rout a bead around the inside of the arch using the 1/4-in.-radius roundover bit that I used for beading the stiles and rails. The setting's the same, but I remove the fence and guide the stock against the pilot bearing on the bit, feeding the stock from left to right against the rotation of the bit.

8-25 I raise the panels for the lower doors on the radial-arm saw with a panel-raising molding head.

8-26 The glass panel in each upper door fits into a 1/8-in.-deep rabbet routed around the inside of the frame. The glass is square at the top, so I also need to rout out an area above the arch. I make the straight, top cut with a fence on the router. Then I remove the fence and rout out the rest of the recess freehand.

8-27 On the table saw, I bevel the edge of each hinge stile to 22½ degrees, making sure to keep the door facing up on the table saw. Note that the fence is positioned to the left of the blade.

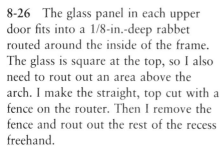

out area in the top rail). Then, with a square and a pencil, I mark where the outer corners of the rabbet will be.

Next, I set up my router with a fence and a 1/2-in.-diameter straight bit set for a 1/8-in. depth of cut. I adjust the fence so it's 2³⁄₁₆ in. from the bit. When I guide the fence along the stiles and rails, the bit mills a 5/16-in.-wide rabbet located 2³⁄₁₆ in. from the outer edges of the door frame. Along the top rail, the bit mills a 1/2-in.-wide groove that defines the top edge of the routed-out area for the glass. I stop the cut when the bit touches the corner marks. I mill the rabbets on both doors. Then I remove the fence and rout out the rest of the material in the top rail freehand (*photo 8-26*). Finally, I square up the corners with a chisel.

Both the upper and lower doors overlap where they meet in the middle of the cabinet. I need to cut a 3/8-in. by 3/8-in. rabbet along the fronts of the left-hand doors and on the backs of the right-hand doors (*drawings 8-A, 8-B, and 8-E.*). I do this with a 3/8-in. rabbeting bit in my router, guiding the pilot bearing along the edge of the stile.

The doors require one more milling operation, and that's to rip a 22½-degree bevel on the hinge stile of all 4 doors (*drawing 8-B*). I position the table saw rip fence to the left of the blade and tilt the blade 22½ degrees to the right. Then I position the rip fence to give me a 13¾-in.-wide door, measured from the long point of the bevel, including the entire 3/8-in. width of the rabbet. I rip the beveled edge on the hinge stile of all 4 doors (*photo 8-27*), making sure to keep the fronts of the doors facing up when I make the cut. Then I tilt my jointer fence 22½ degrees and joint the beveled edge. Now I can finish sand the doors with my random orbit sander and put them aside.

Applying the Molding

The corner cupboard has decorative moldings along the sides, bottom, and top (see Project Planner and *drawings 8-A and 8-B*). The molding at the bottom is standard 4¼-in. stop molding available at most lumberyards and home centers (see Project Planner). The side moldings, too, are standard lumberyard window-stop moldings. The cornice at the top of the cupboard is a composite molding built up from several different stock shapes, including a piece of 3⅝-in. crown molding (*drawing 8-A, cornice construction detail*).

I install the base molding first, cutting and fitting the long front piece to the carcass (*drawing 8-A*). The ends are all mitered at 22½ degrees, and I cut these angles on my table saw before nailing the molding in place. The short end pieces on the sides of the cupboard get a 22½-degree miter on the front end and a square cut on the back. Before nailing them in place with 1-in. brads, I make a 45-degree angle cut on the back corner of each piece for the narrow vertical molding on the sides of the carcass (*photo 8-28 and drawing 8-A*).

Then I cut and fit the vertical window-stop moldings on the sides of the case and across the top (*drawings 8-A and 8-B*). The side moldings get 45-degree miters on both ends before I nail them in place (*photo 8-28*). Then I fit the window-stop molding around the top of the cupboard. The 2 short sidepieces at the top also get a 45-degree miter cut on the corners to match the miters on the vertical side moldings. Next, I cut, fit, and nail the band of 3/4-in. by 1½-in. flat stock that forms a backer-and-reveal piece above the narrow molding at the top of the cupboard (*drawing 8-A, cornice construction detail*).

The crown molding is the last piece of molding to go on the cupboard (*drawing 8-A, cornice construction detail*). Cutting crown molding is a little bit tricky. The thing to remember is that you always put crown molding *upside down* in the miter box.

On my power-miter-box table, I clamp a straightedge parallel to the miter-box fence. I position this fence so that the 2 flat edges of the crown molding are flat against both the fence and the table of the miter box at the same time (*photo 8-29*).

First, I'll cut the long piece of crown molding across the front of the cupboard. With the crown molding upside down in the miter box, I swing the blade 22½ degrees to the right and cut the right-hand end of the molding (this will be the left-hand end when the molding's installed). Then I put the molding in position against the backer-and-reveal piece, line up the angled cut with the end of the backer-and-reveal piece, and mark the bottom edge of the crown molding at the opposite end of the backer-and-reveal piece. With the molding back in the miter box, upside down as before, I swing the saw 22½ degrees to the left and cut the left-hand end of the molding (this will be the right-hand end when the molding's installed).

8-28 The vertical molding along the side of the cabinet is standard pine window stop. The top and bottom are mitered to 45 degrees to fit the molding at the top and bottom of the cupboard.

8-29 The trick to cutting crown molding is to place it upside down in the miter box. I clamp a straightedge to the miter-box table, parallel to the fence. I position this straightedge so that the 2 flat edges of the crown molding are flat against both the fence and the table of the miter box at the same time. I pivot the blade to 22½ degrees to cut the ends.

I nail the crown molding to the backer-and-reveal piece with 4d finish nails. The 2 short return moldings on the sides of the cupboard have 22½-degree miters in front and square cuts at their back ends. These pieces, too, are placed in the miter box upside down. When they're cut, I put some glue on the miters and nail them in place, setting all the nails as I go.

With my sander, I finish sand the cupboard and clean off all the dust. At this point, I make a final inspection and set any nails that I might have missed. I also install the hinges and doors at this point (*photo 8-30*). This gives me a chance to make any necessary adjustments so the doors will fit properly. Then I remove the hinges for finishing.

Painting, Staining, and Finishing

The inside of the corner cupboard gets painted. First, I brush on a coat of oil-based primer. When the primer is dry, I sand it lightly with 220-grit sandpaper. Next, I apply 2 coats of oil-based enamel, sanding lightly between coats. The color I chose is a "Wedgewood" blue. It looks really nice.

I stain the outside of the corner cupboard with a wild cherry–colored oil-base stain. I brush on the stain and allow it to soak into the wood. Then I rub off the excess with a rag. When the stain is thoroughly dry, I brush on the first of 2 coats of satin polyurethane. I sand the first coat lightly, when dry, with 220- (or finer) grit paper. Then I fill all the nail holes with a colored putty stick before applying the second coat of polyurethane.

Installing the Glass and Hardware

When the paint is dry, I install the 2 glass panels in the backs of the upper doors and secure them in place with the plastic panel-retaining

8-30 The doors swing on 4-in. H hinges screwed to the door stiles and the front sidepieces. I install the hinges and doors to fine-tune the fit, if necessary, then I remove them for finishing.

buttons — 6 to a door (*drawing 8-A*). Then I reinstall the hinges and put on the latches, and the barrel bolts or elbow catches (*drawing 8-A*). The barrel bolts (or elbow catches) go on the bottoms of the left-hand doors.

That about does it. You know, when I stand back and look at it, this corner cupboard looks pretty good.

NINE

Cricket Table

PROJECT PLANNER

Time: 2 days
Special hardware and tools:
Skip-tooth band saw blade, 1 in. wide, 4 teeth per inch
Thickness planer
Wood:
(1) 2½-ft 10/4 × 8 red oak
Rip and plane into 3 pieces 2¼ in. × 2 in. for legs. Cut to length according to instructions in text.
(1) 6-ft 1 × 6 red oak
Rip and joint into 2 pieces 2¼ in. wide. Cut 3 pieces 23 in. long for shelf rails. Cut 3 pieces 19 in. long for top rails.
(1) 3-ft 1 × 6 red oak
Resaw, along the 3/4-in.-thickness, into 2 pieces approximately 11/32 in. thick. Plane both pieces to a 5/16-in. thickness. Cut and fit for shelf.
(1) 10-ft 1 × 8 red oak
Cut 4 pieces 29½ in. long and edge glue together to make a blank approximately 29 in. × 29½ in. for tabletop.
(1) 1-ft 1 × 3 pine
Cut according to instructions in text for corner blocks.
(1) 16-in.-long, 3/8-in.-diameter oak dowel
Cut 12 pieces 1 in. long as pins for mortise-and-tenon joints.

WHILE browsing through my favorite antique shop one day I came across an unusual 3-legged table. It had a round top on a triangular base with a small shelf underneath. The owner called it a cricket table. It was used, so he told me, to serve refreshments at cricket matches — the English ball game that's kind of like baseball. Judging from its weathered look, this table was mostly used outdoors. The 3-leg design makes sense on an outdoor table — it will be steady on uneven ground.

One thing really intrigued me about this cricket table. At first I thought the top was off center. But from another vantage point, the top looked just fine. That had me stumped for a minute. Then I figured it out. The base of the table is an equilateral triangle — all sides are equal. When I looked straight on from any point of the triangle, the top was perfectly centered. If I looked perpendicular to any side of the triangle, the top was centered. But if I turned the table just a little bit, the top looked like it was hanging way too far off to one side. It was just an optical illusion caused by the triangular base. The top really was centered on the base. For me, this unusual feature just adds to the charm of the piece.

I really liked this little cricket table, and I decided to build one for my office. The top was just the right size for a TV, and my answering machine would fit on the small shelf below. I decided to make it of red oak, so I headed on down to my local hardwood dealer to buy the wood that I needed to build it (see Project Planner).

Gluing the Top

Now to get started. The first thing I'll do is glue up a panel to make the top. I was lucky to find a nice 10-ft-long 1 × 8 without any defects. I can make the entire top from this board (see Project Planner). This way, I'll get a better color and grain match than if I had to use 2 different boards.

From the 10-ft 1 × 8, I cut 4 pieces 29½ in. long. Then I lay the boards edge to edge on my bench. First, I look at the growth rings

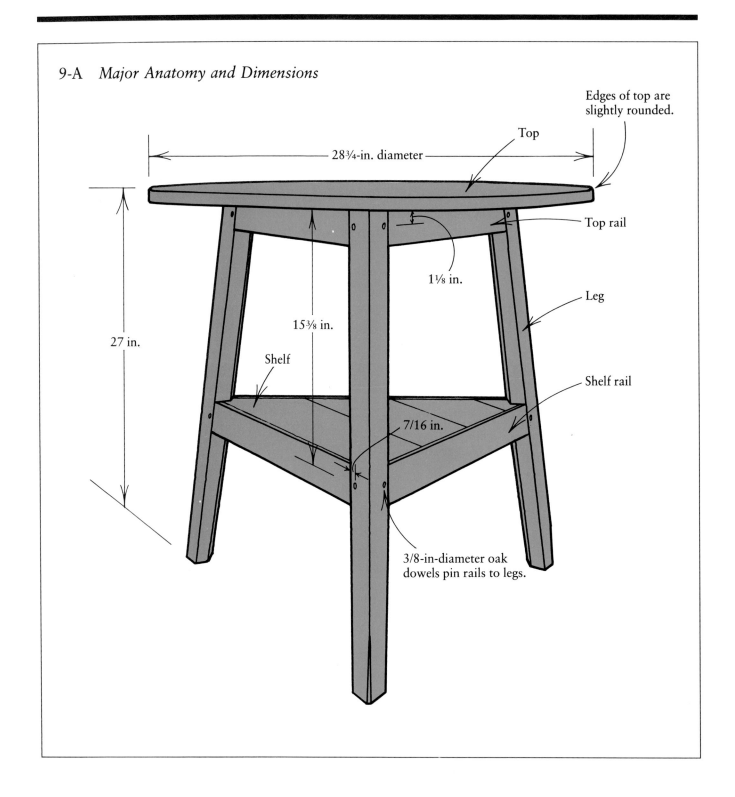

Top

Edges of top are
slightly rounded.

28¾-in. diameter

Top rail

1⅛ in.

Leg

15⅜ in.

27 in.

Shelf

Shelf rail

7/16 in.

3/8-in-diameter oak
dowels pin rails to legs.

on the ends of the boards. I alternate the rings in adjacent boards —
up, down, up, down. This minimizes cupping in the finished tabletop. Then I rearrange the boards, if necessary, for the best color and
figure match, checking to make sure that the growth rings still alternate. When I'm satisfied, I mark the joints with a pencil. I make one
"witness mark" across the first joint, 2 across the second, 3 across
the third. These pencil marks will allow me to reassemble the boards

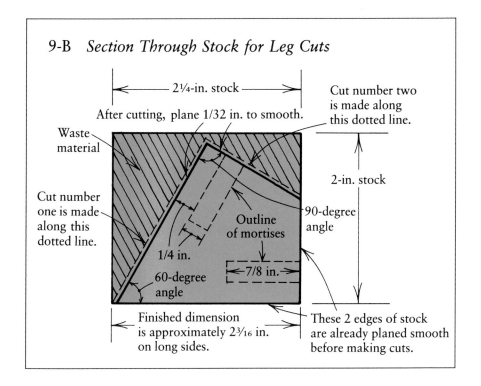

9-B *Section Through Stock for Leg Cuts*

2¼-in. stock

Cut number two is made along this dotted line.

After cutting, plane 1/32 in. to smooth.

Waste material

2-in. stock

Cut number one is made along this dotted line.

90-degree angle

Outline of mortises

1/4 in.

7/8 in.

60-degree angle

Finished dimension is approximately 2³⁄₁₆ in. on long sides.

These 2 edges of stock are already planed smooth before making cuts.

in the same order. Now I can joint the long edges of these 4 boards on the jointer so the joints will be nice and tight.

Now I'm ready to mark slots for some biscuits, which will reinforce the joints and make it easier to align the boards. The top of the table will be a 28¾-in.-diameter circle (*drawing 9-A*), and I don't want any biscuits near the circumference of the circle or I'm likely to cut into them when I saw out the top. To make sure, I mark the approximate center of the top and hold my tape on this point. Then I measure off 29 in. from the center point to each of the joint lines, one by one, and mark approximately where the edge of the top will fall on the joints. I come back about 2½ in. from this point to mark the center for my outermost biscuit slot. Then I mark the other biscuit slots about 8 in. apart along each joint. I cut the slots with my biscuit joiner, lining up the joiner's index mark with the pencil marks on the wood.

With the biscuit slots cut, I spread glue on the edges of the boards and brush some in the biscuit slots. A little glue on the biscuits and I pop them in place and assemble the joints. I close up the joints with clamps and put on just enough pressure to squeeze some glue from each joint. Now I'll set the top aside to dry while I work on the legs.

Making the Legs

The legs of the cricket table have 4 angled sides (*drawing 9-B*). The outer corner is a 60-degree angle. The 2 side corners are both 90 degree angles. The angle of the inner corner is 120 degrees. I rip these angled sides on the table saw with a sharp, ripping blade. Oak is tough stuff, and it takes lots of power to rip a 2-in.-thick piece. The

9-1 The legs of the cricket table have 4 angled sides. Here, I make the first of 2 angled rip cuts. I tilt the saw blade 30 degrees and position the rip fence 2¼ in. away from the bottom of the blade. The cut forms the 60-degree outer corner of the leg.

9-2 The second and last angled cut is at 90 degrees to the first angled cut. I keep the blade tilted 30 degrees and position the fence 1¼ in. "strong" to the left (operator's viewpoint) of the blade. I keep the long outer corner of the leg pointing up toward the top of the fence.

9-3 After ripping the second angled cut, I smooth up the sawed faces on my jointer. Here I'm jointing the inside face of the leg.

9-4 I cut the ends of the legs on my radial-arm saw, with the blade tilted 7½ degrees. For the angle to be correct, the leg must be oriented with the long outer corner pointing straight down and the inner corner pointing straight up. To support the leg in this position, I hold it against an accessory fence that has one face ripped at a 30-degree angle.

motor will run cooler (and therefore be less likely to trip the circuit breaker) if you use the right blade and feed the stock slowly. This is especially important on home-shop table saws with motors of less than 1 HP. A thin-kerf blade will put less strain on the saw than a conventional saw blade with the same number of teeth.

First, I rip and plane 3 leg blanks that are 2 in. by 2¼ in. by 30 in. long (see Project Planner). With these blanks all squared up, I'm ready to make the first of 2 angled rip cuts. This cut will form the 60-degree outer corner of the leg (*drawing 9-B*). I tilt the table saw blade 30 degrees and position the rip fence 2¼ in. away from the blade (measured at the very bottom of the blade). Since the leg blanks are 2¼ in. wide, I use one of these blanks as a gauge to position the fence. Then I make the first angled rip cut on all 3 legs (*photo 9-1*). This cut forms the 60-degree outer corner of the leg.

Now the second angled cut will be 90 degrees to the cut I just made (*drawing 9-B*). I keep the saw blade tilted to 30 degrees, but I move the rip fence 1¼ in. "strong" to the *left* of the blade (measured at the bottom of the blade). When the setup is right, I rip the second angled cut on all 3 legs, keeping the long, outer corner of the leg pointing up toward the top edge of the rip fence (*photo 9-2*). After ripping all 3 legs, I true up the sawed faces on the jointer (*photo 9-3*). The finished legs should measure approximately 2³⁄₁₆ in. on each long side (*drawing 9-C*).

The legs of the cricket table splay out at a slight angle — 7½ degrees, to be exact (*drawing 9-A*). That means that the tops and bottoms of the legs — as well as the mortises and tenons for the top rails and shelf rails, must all be cut at this 7½-degree angle.

I cut the legs to length on my radial-arm saw. The shape of the leg makes things a little tricky. I can't just put the leg up against the saw fence and make the cut — the angle won't be right. For the angle to be correct, the leg must be oriented with the long outer corner facing straight down and the inner corner facing straight up (*drawing 9-C*). To support the leg in this position, I made an accessory for the saw fence. It's just a piece of scrap wood, about 18 in. long, with one face ripped at a 30-degree angle. I place this angled piece up against the saw fence with the 30-degree angle pointing up. Then I support the leg against this accessory fence with the long point facing down.

To make the cut, I tilt my radial-arm saw blade counterclockwise 7½ degrees and put the angled accessory fence against the fence to the left of the blade. I put a leg against the accessory fence, long point down, and cut off the right-hand end of the leg (*photo 9-4*). I cut the other 2 legs in the same way.

Now the length of my legs is 26½ in. from long point to short point. I measure the legs and mark the length. Then I slide my accessory fence to the right of the blade, position a leg against it, and cut the opposite end of the leg. The procedure's the same for the other 2 legs.

9-C   Leg Details

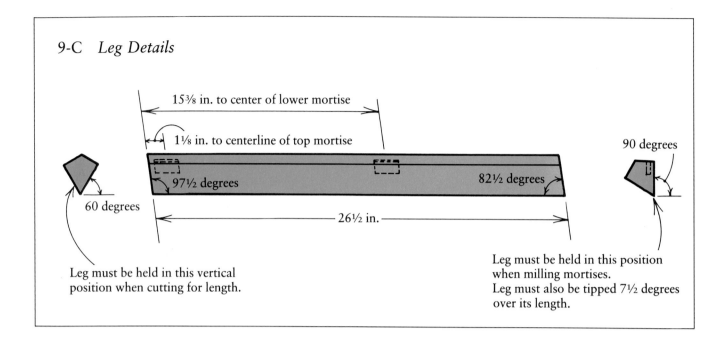

15⅜ in. to center of lower mortise

1⅛ in. to centerline of top mortise

97½ degrees

82½ degrees

90 degrees

60 degrees

26½ in.

Leg must be held in this vertical position when cutting for length.

Leg must be held in this position when milling mortises.
Leg must also be tipped 7½ degrees over its length.

Angled Mortises

Now that the legs have been cut to size, the next thing to do is to lay out and cut the 1/4-in.-wide by 1½-in.-long mortises for the top rails and shelf rails. The center of each top-rail mortise is located 1⅛ in. from the top of the leg (*drawing 9-C*). The center of each shelf-rail mortise is located 15⅜ in. from the top of the leg. Once I've marked these centerlines, I lay out the lengths of the mortises with a pencil and square. The mortises are located 1/4 in. from the outside face of the leg, and I lay out the width on the stock (*drawing 9-B*).

With the mortises laid out, I'm ready to cut them. As usual, I do this on my drill press with a hollow-chisel mortising attachment and a 1/4-in. chisel. Now remember, these mortises must be angled 7½ degrees (*drawing 9-C*). This angle, combined with the shape of the leg, makes the setup a little bit tricky. I had to make a special jig with a 7½-degree taper to position the leg at the proper angle under the mortising bit (*photos 9-5 and 9-6 and drawing 9-C*). The jig is simple, just a 7½-degree scrap-wood wedge screwed to the fence of the mortising jig.

With the high end of the wedge to the left, I position a leg on the jig with the top end facing left, the long outer corner facing down, and one long face of the leg flat against the mortising jig's fence (*drawing 9-B*). Holding the leg against the jig's fence, I move the mortising-attachment fence around on the drill-press table (the jig and the leg move along with it) to line up the mortise layout lines under the bit. Then I tighten the wing nuts that lock the mortising-attachment fence to the table. Next, I place a long piece of wood up against the front of the leg and clamp it across the drill-press table (*photo 9-5*). This piece will keep the leg from flopping over from the downward pressure of the mortising chisel.

9-5 I cut the angled leg mortises with a hollow-chisel mortising attachment and a 1/4-in. chisel. To hold the leg at the proper angle, I make a jig consisting of a 7½-degree wedge screwed to the mortising jig's fence. This jig screws to the front of the mortising attachment's fence. With the high end of the wedge to the left, I position a leg on the jig with the top end facing left, the long outer corner facing down, and one long face of the leg flat against the jig's 1 × 4 fence. Then I clamp a long piece of wood up against the front of the leg to keep the leg from flopping over. With this setup, I cut 2 mortises on one face of each leg.

9-7 With the wedge reversed, I reclamp the long piece of wood against the front of the leg and cut the mortises on the adjacent face of all 3 legs.

9-6 To mortise the adjacent face, I unscrew the 7½-degree wedge and reverse it on the fence of the mortising jig. Note that the end of the wedge should be even with or extend past the edge of the table.

Now I set the bit for a 7/8-in.-deep mortise (*drawing 9-B*). I double-check my setup to make sure that the vertical travel of the mortising chisel is parallel to the top end of the leg. When everything's right, I cut the top-rail and shelf-rail mortises on one face of each leg (*photo 9-5*).

With the first set of mortises cut, I have to modify my setup a little bit to cut the mortises on the adjacent face of each leg. I simply unscrew the 7½-degree wedge and reverse it on the fence. This time, I position the leg so the top end faces right (*photo 9-6*). Then I cut the mortises on the adjacent face of each leg (*photo 9-7*).

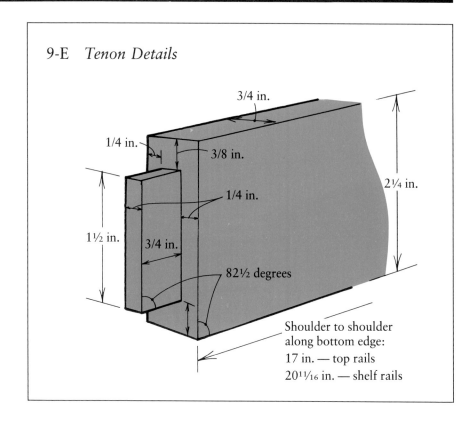

9-E *Tenon Details*

3/4 in.

1/4 in.

3/8 in.

1/4 in.

1½ in.

3/4 in.

2¼ in.

82½ degrees

Shoulder to shoulder along bottom edge:
17 in. — top rails
20¹¹/₁₆ in. — shelf rails

Rails and Tenons

Now it's time to start working on the rails. I rip, joint, and crosscut the 3 top rails and 3 shelf rails from a 6-ft-long 1×6 board (see Project Planner).

The rails all have tenons to fit into the leg mortises. The angle of the tenon shoulders, as well as the ends of the tenons themselves, is 7½ degrees (*drawing 9-E*). I swing the blade on my power miter box 7½ degrees to the left and cut one angled end of each rail. The top rails, including the tenons, are 18½ in. long, measured along the bottom edge. The shelf rails measure 22³/₁₆ in. along the bottom edge, including the tenons. I mark off the lengths on the bottoms of the rails and cut each one to length (*drawing 9-E*). I also make an angled cut on the end of some scrap to use as a stop block when I cut the tenons on the radial-arm saw.

With the rails all cut to length, I'm ready to start making the tenons (*drawing 9-E*). I mount a stack dado head on the radial-arm saw arbor, set up for a 3/4-in.-wide cut. Then I swing the saw arm 7½ degrees to the left and, with the power off, pull the saw forward a little to position my stop block. I butt the 7½-degree angled end of the stop block up against the right side of the dado head and clamp it to the saw table. Now, when I cut the tenons, I can simply butt the end of the rail against the end of the setup block and cut a tenon that's exactly 3/4 in. long. With this setup, I'll be able to cut one cheek on each tenon. I have to modify the setup to cut the opposite cheek.

I adjust the height of the dado head to remove exactly 1/4 in. of wood. Then I mill one cheek on each tenon (*photo 9-8*). To set up for cutting the opposite cheek, I swing the saw 7½ degrees to the right, flip over the stop block, and reset it for length — still to the right of the blade. I cut a sample tenon to check the setting and test the fit in one of the mortises. After making any necessary adjustments, I cut the opposite cheek on each rail tenon (*photo 9-9*).

I make the rip cuts that form the tops and bottoms of the tenons (*drawing 9-E*) on my band saw, setting the fence 3/8 in. from the right side of the blade (*photo 9-10*). Then I cut the top and bottom shoulders by hand with a dovetailing saw. That takes care of the tenons.

The tops of the shelf rails must be beveled so they'll be flush with the shelf. I do this on the jointer. I tilt the fence 4 degrees and bevel the top edges of the 3 shelf rails. With the jointer fence tilted toward the table, I hold the inner face of the rail against the fence, top edge down (*photo 9-11*). Some jointer fences tilt *away* from the table only. In this case, I'd hold the outer face of the rail against the fence.

9-8 After cutting the rails to length, I mill the angled tenons on the radial-arm saw with a stack dado head set for a 3/4-in.-wide cut. I clamp an angled stop block to determine the length of the tenon. To cut the first cheek, I swing the saw 7½ degrees to the left and remove 1/4 in. of wood to form one shoulder and cheek of each tenon.

9-9 For the second tenon cheek, I flip the angled stop block over and swing the saw 7½ degrees to the right. Then I cut the opposite shoulder and cheek of each tenon.

9-10 After cutting the tenon cheeks, I make the rip cuts that form the top and bottom of each tenon on the band saw.

9-11 I bevel the tops of the rails so they're flush with the shelf. I tilt my jointer fence 4 degrees and hold the inner face of the rail against the fence, top edge down.

9-12 I mill a 5/16-in. by 5/16-in. angled rabbet in the tops of the shelf rails to recess the shelf boards. It takes 2 cuts to complete this rabbet. For the first cut (shown here) I tilt the blade 4 degrees and position the rip fence 1^{15}/$_{16}$ in. from the blade. I keep the inside facedown on the table.

9-13 To complete the rabbet, I make a second cut with the rip fence 3/8 in. from the blade. I raise the blade just a hair, and hold the rail with the top edge down and the outside face against the rip fence.

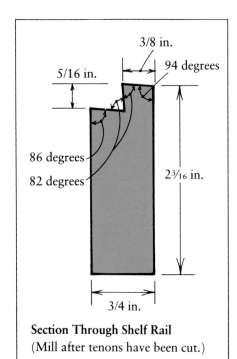

Section Through Shelf Rail
(Mill after tenons have been cut.)

Rabbeting the Shelf Rails

There's just one more milling operation on the shelf rails. I have to mill a 5/16-in. by 5/16-in. rabbet to recess the boards for the shelf. This rabbet, too, needs to be angled. I mill the rabbet on the table saw with a regular saw blade in place on the arbor.

It takes 2 cuts to complete the rabbet. First, I tilt the blade 4 degrees and position the rip fence 1^{15}/$_{16}$ in. from the blade (measured at the bottom of the blade). With the bottom edge of the rail against the fence and the inside facedown on the table. I rip a cut along the top inside edge of all 3 rails (*photo 9-12*).

For the second cut, which completes the rabbet. I leave the saw at the same angle but I move the fence closer — 3/8 in. from the blade. Then I raise the blade slightly and make the cuts. I hold the top edge of the rail down on the table, and the outside face against the rip fence (*photo 9-13*).

Tapering the Legs

The 2 inside faces of the leg, where the rails join, are tapered at the bottom. The taper starts at a point about 1 in. below where the bottom edge of the shelf rail joins the leg and tapers in 3/16 in. at the bottom of the leg (*drawing 9-D*). This taper makes the table look light on its feet and gives it a little more elegance.

There are several different ways I could mill these tapers: I could belt-sand them, hand plane them, or cut them on the jointer. This time I think I'll use my stationary belt sander instead. I mark off the ends of the taper and hold the leg vertically against the sanding belt and sand to the lines with an 80-grit belt (*photo 9-14*).

Each leg gets 2 additional tapers (*drawing 9-D*). On the sharp, 60-degree outer corner, I sand a 1/8-in. taper starting at a point 3 in. up from the bottom of the leg. On the inside, 120-degree, corner, I sand a 1/8-in. taper starting at a point 8 in. up from the bottom of the leg.

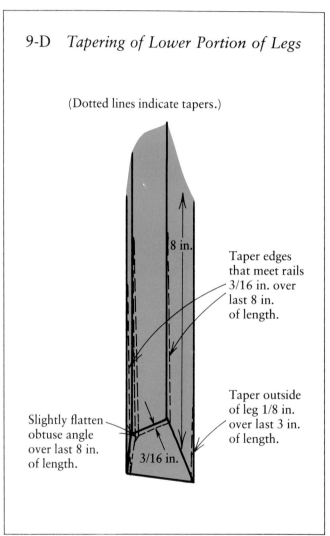

9-D *Tapering of Lower Portion of Legs*

(Dotted lines indicate tapers.)

8 in.

Taper edges that meet rails 3/16 in. over last 8 in. of length.

Taper outside of leg 1/8 in. over last 3 in. of length.

Slightly flatten obtuse angle over last 8 in. of length.

3/16 in.

9-14 I sand the taper at the bottoms of the legs by holding the leg against my stationary belt sander. Note that the bottom of the leg is supported against the sander table.

9-15 To assemble the base, I start by gluing 2 legs and 2 rails together. Angled clamping blocks make it easier to clamp this angled assembly. Once the clamps are in place, I drill a 3/8-in.-diameter hole in each joint and pin the joint with a 3/8-in.-diameter dowel.

Assembling the Base

After finish sanding the legs and rails, it's time for some assembly. The base is kind of tricky to put together because of all the angles. First thing I do is cut 2 scrap-wood wedges, about 18 in. long with a slight taper. These will come in handy as clamping blocks when I clamp the base together. They'll prevent the clamps from marring the edges of the legs and keep the clamps from sliding off the angled faces of the legs.

Let's start with 2 legs, one shelf rail, and one top rail. I brush glue in the mortises and on the tenons and slip the tenons into their mortises. Now I put the clamping blocks against the outsides of the legs and put 2 clamps across the legs to close up the joints (*photo 9-15*).

With the clamps in place, I'm ready to drill holes for the oak dowels that pin the joints (*drawing 9-A*). I install a 3/8-in. diameter brad-point bit in my drill. The holes will be 3/4 in. to 7/8 in. deep, and I put a piece of tape on the bit as a depth stop. I drill a hole in each joint. The holes in the top rail are centered 1⅛ in. down from the top of the leg and 7/16 in. in from the joint. The holes in the shelf rail are centered 15⅜ in. from the top of the leg. When the holes are drilled, I brush glue in the hole and tap in a 3/8-in. oak dowel. With the dowel pins in place, I can take off the clamps.

Now I can put on a couple more rails. Glue on the tenons, glue in the mortises, and 2 more rails go in place. With a clamping block against the leg, I put a clamp on each rail to pull the rail tight into its mortise. Then I drill holes for the dowels and glue the dowels in place (*photo 9-16*). I can take off the clamps once the dowels are glued in.

I glue the last 2 rails in their mortises, but I don't clamp them or drill the dowel holes yet. I still have to put on the third leg, and it's easier if these other 2 rails are loose. I put glue on all the joints and finesse the rail tenons into the mortises of the third leg. Once they're started, a couple of taps with my shot-filled mallet (being careful not to damage the edge of the leg) drives the leg home. I clamp the joints to pull them tight while I drill and install the dowels.

When the glue is dry, I sand the dowels flush with my belt sander and smooth up the legs and rails with my random orbit sander.

Corner Blocks

In order to fasten the top to the base, I need to make some corner blocks. I cut these from a length of 1 × 3 pine (see Project Planner). The corner blocks measure 4¼ in. on their longest side (*drawing 9-F*). The sides of these corner blocks must be cut at a 60-degree angle to fit inside the rails. These side cuts must also be beveled to match the splay of the rails. I tilt the radial-arm saw blade 4 degrees and swing the arm 30 degrees to the left to cut these 3 corner blocks.

9-16 I glue in 2 more rails and pull them tight in their mortises with clamps. Then I drill holes for the dowel pins with a 3/8-in. brad-point bit. A piece of tape around the bit serves as a depth stop to keep me from drilling too deep.

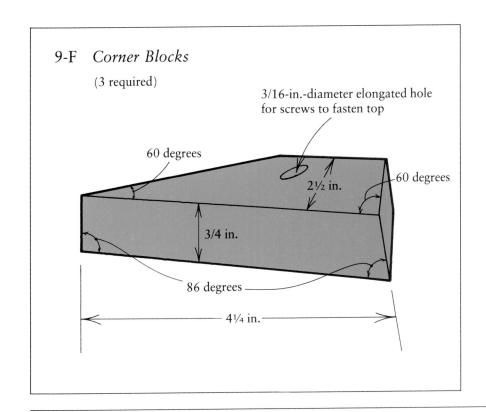

9-F   Corner Blocks

(3 required)

3/16-in.-diameter elongated hole for screws to fasten top

60 degrees

60 degrees

2½ in.

3/4 in.

86 degrees

4¼ in.

9-17 I cut out the top on the band saw with a shop-built circle-cutting jig. I measure off 14⅜ in. along the jig's centerline and drill a 1/4-in.-diameter hole for a pivot pin. The 1/4-in.-diameter pin fits into a hole drilled in the underside of the top.

9-18 I place the top blank over the jig and slip the hole in the underside over the 1/4-in.-diameter pin. Then I switch on the saw and rotate the top blank clockwise on the pin. The result? A perfect circle every time.

I cut one end of a block, then I flip the 1 × 3 over to cut the other end of the block. I repeat this procedure to cut all 3 blocks.

After cutting the blocks to size, I glue and nail them to the insides of the rails with two 4d nails in each block, setting the blocks 1/4 in. below the top edge of the rails. Next, I predrill a hole in each block for the screws that will fasten the top. I elongate these holes by rocking the drill back and forth. All 3 holes should be elongated in the same direction.

Sawing the Circular Top

Now it's time to get back to work on the top. I scrape the excess glue from the panel with my paint scraper and sand the joints flush with my belt sander.

Next, on the least-attractive side of the panel, I measure in 14⅜ in. from one long edge and square a line across the panel (this line should run parallel to the grain). At the midpoint of this line, I drill a 1/4-in.-diameter hole about 3/8 in. deep to mark the center of the top. I'll use this hole as a pivot point for the circle-cutting jig on my band saw. This jig is just a piece of 3/4-in. MDO board (plywood would also work well) approximately 10 in. wide by 36 in. long. One end rests on the band saw table with the end just touching the blade (*photo 9-17*). MDO-board strips screwed to the underside of the jig allow me to secure this end of the jig to the band saw table. I support the other end of the jig with a roller stand.

A centerline runs down the length of the jig. Holding my tape on the band saw end of the jig, I measure off 14⅜ in. along this centerline and drill a 1/4-in.-diameter hole. I tap a short 1/4-in. dowel in the hole (no glue) to use as a pivot point for sawing the top (*photo 9-17*). The dowel should protrude no more than 3/8 in. above the surface of the jig.

At the band saw end of the circle-cutting jig, I align the centerline with the front edge of the blade. Then I put the top blank on the jig, placing the hole in the underside over the 1/4-in. pivot pin, and the long edge, from which I measured for the centerpoint, against the blade. To cut the circle, I turn on the saw and rotate the blank clockwise into the blade (*photo 9-18*). That's all there is to it. I get a perfect circle every time. Now I remove the top from the jig and smooth up the edge with my random orbit sander. Then I finish sand the entire top.

I ease the top and bottom edges of the top to soften the sharp corners. I use a 1/4-in.-radius roundover bit in my router. I only expose part of the bit because I only want to round the edge gently. I don't want a full quarter round. I guide the bit's pilot bearing against the edge to make the cuts.

Installing the Shelf

The shelf is made of 5/16-in.-thick oak boards that I cut and fit into the rabbets in the shelf rails (*drawing 9-G*). I could start with 3/4-in. stock and plane it down with my thickness planer, but that would waste a lot of wood. Instead, I start with a 3-ft-long piece of 1 × 6 and "resaw" it on my band saw. That is, I split the board down the middle to make 2 thinner boards. The procedure is easy.

I set up my band saw with a 1-in.-wide, 4-tooth-per-inch, skip-tooth blade (a 3/4-in. blade will also work, if that's the widest that will fit on your saw). I clamp a high auxiliary fence to the band saw table to support the board during the cut (*photo 9-19*).

I joint both edges of the 1 × 6 board and mark a centerline along one edge. Then I adjust the auxiliary rip fence so the blade will cut on this centerline. I support the board against the fence and feed the stock slowly into the blade (*photo 9-19*). If the blade starts to wander off the line, chances are that my fence isn't parallel or that I'm feeding too fast.

9-19 To minimize waste, I resaw the 5/16-in.-thick shelf boards from 1 × 6 stock. A high wooden fence, clamped to my band saw table, supports the board through the cut. I use a 1-in.-wide skip-tooth blade to ensure a straight cut.

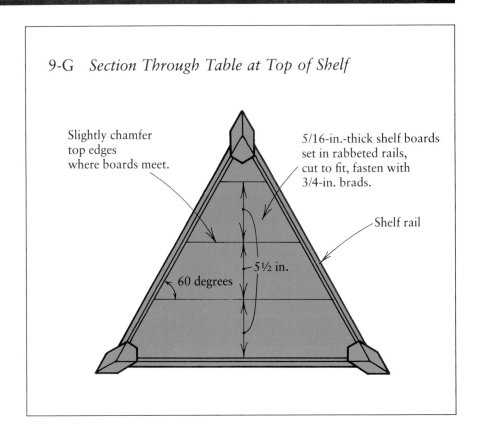

9-G *Section Through Table at Top of Shelf*

Slightly chamfer
top edges
where boards meet.

5/16-in.-thick shelf boards
set in rabbeted rails,
cut to fit, fasten with
3/4-in. brads.

Shelf rail

5½ in.

60 degrees

9-20 Installing the shelf boards is a cut-and-fit procedure. The boards must be carefully notched at the corners to fit around the legs. I tack them in place with some 3/4-in. brads.

I end up with two 5½-in.-wide boards that are a little more than 5/16 in. thick. I plane off the band saw marks by running the boards through my thickness planer with the rough side up. One pass is all it takes to clean up the sawed face and take them down to a 5/16-in. thickness.

Installing the shelf boards comes next. I start at the base of the triangle and work my way up to the point, cutting and fitting the boards one at a time (*drawing 9-G*). I swing the blade 30 degrees to the side to cut the ends of the boards. I cut one end of a board, place that end in the rabbet, and mark where the other end needs to be cut. Then I cut the board to length. The first board needs to be notched at the corners to fit around the legs. So does the very last piece at the tip of the triangle. I carefully measure, mark, and cut these notches with a small backsaw. When all the boards are cut, I chamfer the top, mating edges with a block plane. Then I drop the boards into the rabbets (no glue) and tack them to the rails with 3/4-in. brads (*photo 9-20*).

Attaching the Top

Now I'm ready to put on the top. I place the top upside down on my bench and position the base upside down on the top. I center the base on the top and orient it so the grain of the top runs perpendicular to the length of the screw slots in the corner blocks. Then I screw it in place with three 1⅝-in. bugle-head screws (*photo 9-21*).

With the table back on its feet again, I give the top a good finish sanding with some 220-grit paper. The only thing left to do is to apply the finish.

Staining and Finishing

I wanted a "pickled" or "limed-oak" finish on my cricket table, so I chose an oil-base stain called "Silver Birch." It has a very slight green tint that will give me just the look I want.

I apply the stain with a brush and let it penetrate for a few minutes. Then I wipe the surface very lightly with a rag, leaving much of the pigment still on the surface. As usual, I make sure to get these oil-soaked rags out of the shop when I'm finished so there's no chance of fire from spontaneous combustion.

When the stain is completely dry (a couple of days, in this case, since I didn't wipe off all the stain), I brush on a coat of satin-finish polyurethane. When the first coat is dry, I sand it lightly with 220-grit sandpaper and brush on a second coat. You know, I really like that "Silver Birch" stain — I think it makes the oak look really nice.

That about does it. Judging from the response I've gotten from my family and friends, I'll probably be making a couple more cricket tables before too long.

9-21 I fasten the top to the base with three 1⅝-in. screws through the corner blocks. I elongate the screw holes in the corner blocks so the top can expand and contract across the grain.

TEN

Pie Safe

PROJECT PLANNER

Time: 5 days
Special hardware and tools:
(4) 3-ft-long adjustable shelf standards
(8) adjustable shelf clips
(6) 2-in. brass-plated butt hinges
(1) double-door magnetic catch
(6) 1¼-in.-diameter Shaker knobs
(6) 10¾-in. × 11⅞-in. "low-grade black tin" panels (I got my tin from Country Accents, P.O. Box 437, Montoursville, PA 17754; 717-478-4127).

Wood:
(1) 8-ft 1 × 12 select pine
Plane to 1/2-in. thickness and cut into 4 equal pieces approximately 2 ft long for side panels.
(1) 6-ft 1 × 10 select pine
Rip and joint 4 pieces 2 in. wide × 72 in. long. From each piece cut one piece 40 in. long for door stiles (4 required) and 2 pieces 12 in. long for door rails (8 required).
(2) 14-ft 1 × 6s select pine
Cut one 14-ft board into:
One piece 46 in. long. Rip and joint into one piece 4 in. wide for top and bottom side rails and one piece 1¼ in. wide for 3 cleats (2 for upper-drawer frame and one for fixed shelf).
Two pieces 60 in. long. From each piece rip and joint one piece 1⅞ in. wide for front side stile (2 required) and one piece 2⅝ in. wide for back side stile (2 required). Rip scrap into 5/16-in. × 5/16-in. strips to secure tin panels in doors.
Cut second 14-ft board into:
Four pieces 40 in. long. Rip one piece in half. Joint edges and glue 3½ boards together to make a panel approximately 18 in. × 40 in. for top. From remaining half board, rip one piece 3/8 in. wide for fixed-shelf edging. Then rip and joint 2 pieces 1 in. wide for adjustable-shelf edging.

BAKING day was a weekly ritual on the early American farm. The country housewife turned out enough bread and cakes, cookies and pies to last her family a week. These goodies were often stored in a pie safe — a ventilated cupboard with decorative pierced-tin panels that kept out the critters and allowed air to flow through so the baked goods wouldn't get moldy.

The pie safe shown here was inspired by an old one I found in an antique shop. It has two small drawers at the top and a single large drawer at the bottom. The tin-paneled doors hide a relatively deep storage compartment with 3 shelves. Two of these shelves can be adjusted up and down on metal shelf standards.

The pie safe is relatively easy to build since most of the joinery's done with biscuits. The punched-tin panels are great fun to make, although it takes quite a while to punch all those holes. There are 450 holes in each pineapple panel!

Side Frames and Panels

The sides of the pie safe feature frame-and-panel construction (*drawings 10-A and 10-B*). Each frame consists of 2 stiles and 3 rails joined with biscuits. Two solid-wood panels fit into grooves milled in the stiles and rails.

The first thing I do is make the frames for the sides. I rip and joint the frame rails and stiles to width (see Project Planner and *drawing 10-B*). Then I square up one end of each piece on my power miter box and cut the rails and stiles to length. The rails are all 10¾ in. long and the stiles are 59¼ in. long. One of the things I like about biscuit joinery is that I can cut the rails to their finished length — I don't have to allow any extra length for tenons.

With the frame parts cut to size, I lay them out on my bench and mark the outside face of each frame piece — the side that I'll see when the pie safe's assembled. Then I use a square and a pencil to

185

(2) 12-ft 1 × 6s select pine

Cut one 12-ft board into:

Three pieces 11 in. long for drawer frames and top-frame center-pieces. Rip and joint remainder into 2 pieces 2½ in. wide, then cut to 3-ft lengths for drawer frames and top-frame front and back pieces (6 required).

Cut second 12-ft board into:

One piece 25 in. long. Rip and joint to a 4⅞-in. width, then cut in half for upper-drawer backs (2 required). Rip and joint remainder 5⅜ in. wide and cut 2 pieces 13½ in. long for upper-drawer fronts, 4 pieces 14¼ in. long for upper-drawer sides, 2 pieces 12 in. long for upper-drawer-front backers.

(1)10-ft 1 × 6 select pine

Cut one piece 30 in. long. Rip and joint to a 4⅞-in. width for lower drawer back. Rip and joint remainder 5⅜ in. wide and cut: one piece 31 in. long for lower-drawer front, 2 pieces 14¼ in. long for lower-drawer sides, one piece 29½ in. long for lower-drawer-front backer.

(2) 8-ft 1 × 6s select pine

From one board, rip one strip 3 in. wide and cut into 6 pieces 12 in. long for drawer-frame and top-frame end pieces (6 required). Make cleat for fixed shelf from remaining 3-in.-wide piece. Rip one strip 1¼ in. wide and cut into 6 pieces 5½ in. long for side guides on drawer frames. From remainder of board, cut and rip: 2 pieces 1 in. × 16 in. for lower-drawer top guides, 2 pieces 1/2 in. × 15 in. for upper-drawer stops, one piece 1/2 in. × 32 in. for lower-drawer stop.

From second board, cut one piece 59¼ in. long. Rip and joint into 2 pieces 2⅝ in. wide for face-frame stiles. From remainder, cut one piece 5½ in. long and rip and joint to 4⅛ in. wide for stile between drawers. From remainder, rip and joint 2 pieces 1½ in. wide for face-frame rails and one piece 2 in. wide. Cut 2-in.-wide piece in half to make middle side rails (2 required).

(1) 3-ft × 4-ft, 3/4-in.-thick birch-veneer plywood

Cut into 3 pieces 15 in. × 36 in. for fixed and adjustable shelves.

(1) 4-ft × 8-ft, 1/4-in.-thick plywood

Cut one piece 35³⁄₁₆ in. × 57 in. for back. Cut one piece 13¼ in. × 29¹³⁄₁₆ in. for lower-drawer bottom. Cut 2 pieces 12⅜ in. × 13¼ in. for upper-drawer bottoms.

(1) 8-ft length, 5/8-in. × 3/4-in. pine scotia molding

Cut to fit for molding under front and sides of top.

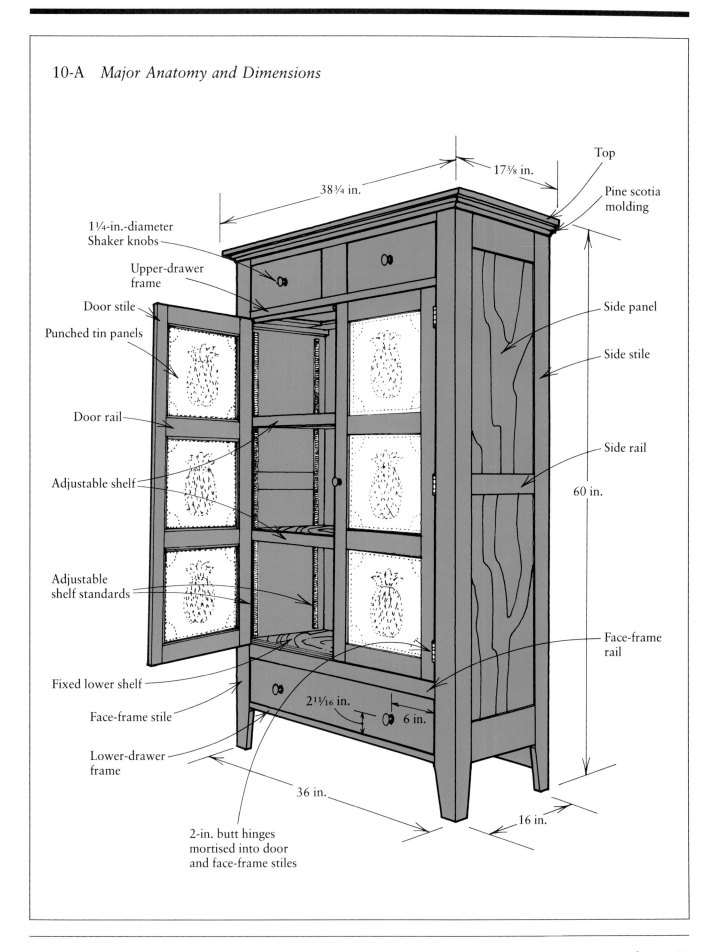

10-A *Major Anatomy and Dimensions*

1¼-in.-diameter
Shaker knobs

Upper-drawer
frame

Door stile

Punched tin panels

Door rail

Adjustable shelf

Adjustable
shelf standards

Fixed lower shelf

Face-frame stile

Lower-drawer
frame

2-in. butt hinges
mortised into door
and face-frame stiles

38¾ in.

17⅜ in.

Top

Pine scotia
molding

Side panel

Side stile

Side rail

60 in.

Face-frame
rail

2¹¹⁄₁₆ in.

6 in.

36 in.

16 in.

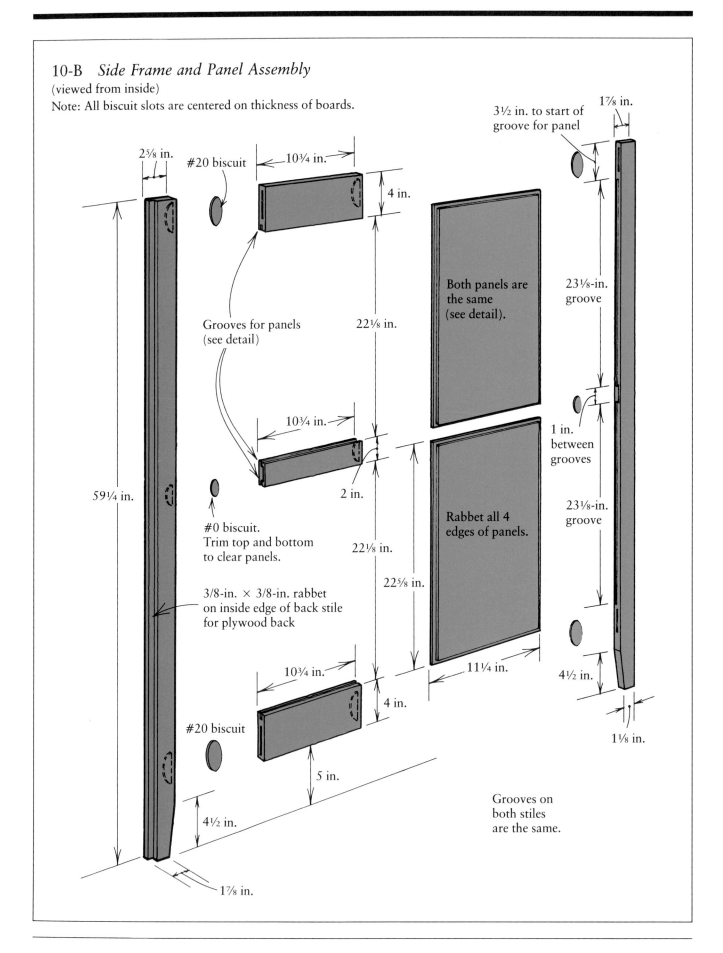

10-B Side Frame and Panel Assembly

(viewed from inside)

Note: All biscuit slots are centered on thickness of boards.

2⅝ in.

#20 biscuit

10¾ in.

4 in.

3½ in. to start of groove for panel

1⅞ in.

23⅛-in. groove

Grooves for panels (see detail)

Both panels are the same (see detail).

22⅛ in.

10¾ in.

1 in. between grooves

59¼ in.

2 in.

#0 biscuit. Trim top and bottom to clear panels.

Rabbet all 4 edges of panels.

23⅛-in. groove

22⅛ in.

3/8-in. × 3/8-in. rabbet on inside edge of back stile for plywood back

22⅝ in.

10¾ in.

11¼ in.

4½ in.

4 in.

1⅛ in.

#20 biscuit

5 in.

Grooves on both stiles are the same.

4½ in.

1⅞ in.

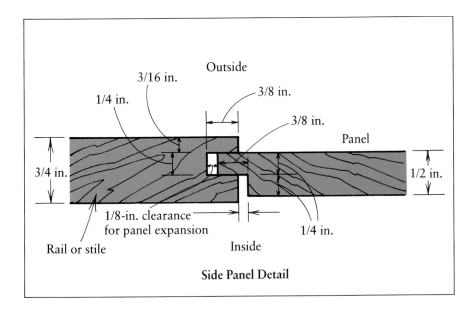

3/16 in.
1/4 in.
Outside
3/8 in.
3/8 in.
Panel
3/4 in.
1/2 in.
1/8-in. clearance
for panel expansion
1/4 in.
Rail or stile
Inside

Side Panel Detail

mark the locations of the rails on the stiles. I also draw a pencil line across each joint to mark the center of each biscuit slot.

Milling the Panel Grooves

The next step is to mill a panel groove 1/4 in. wide by 3/8 in. deep in the edges of the stiles and rails. As shown in the side panel detail above, the groove is held a little bit closer to the outside face of the frame so the panels won't stick out past the frame on the inside of the cabinet.

I mill the groove on my router table with a 1/4-in.-diameter straight bit. I set the bit for a 3/8-in.-deep cut and adjust the fence so that the edge of the groove will be 3/16 in. from the outside face. (I keep the inside face of the frame parts against the fence as I mill the grooves.) When the fence is properly adjusted, I clamp a feather board to the table to hold the stock tight against the fence during the cut. I mill a groove along both edges of the 2 narrow center rails (*photo 10-1*). Then I mill a groove on the inside edges of the top and bottom rails, feeding the stock from right to left (*drawing 10-B*).

Grooving the stiles is a little more complicated. I don't want a groove where my biscuits are going to go, so I can't mill a groove the full length of the stile. Instead, I mill 2 stopped grooves in each stile. The grooves are as long as the distance between rails plus an extra 1/2 in. on either end (*drawing 10-B*).

So I know where to start and stop the grooves, I stick a piece of masking tape in front of the router bit and make a pencil mark 1/4 in. from the bit on either side (*photo 10-2*). I align the rail layout lines I marked on the stile with these marks on the tape to locate the beginning and end of the groove.

Here's how I mill the grooves on the back right stile. To start the cut, I hold the stile against the router-table fence with the top-rail layout line over the right-hand mark on the tape. I make a "plunge

10-1 The side panels fit into grooves in the side frames. I mill these grooves on the router table with a 1/4-in. straight bit. The middle rail (shown) gets a groove along both edges. A feather board clamped to the table holds the stock tight against the fence.

10-2 To locate the beginnings and ends of the stopped grooves in the side-frame stiles, I stick some tape on the router table and make pencil marks 1/4 in. on either side of the bit. To start the cut, I hold the stile against the fence with the left-hand layout line over the right-hand mark on the tape. I make a "plunge cut" by lowering the stile on the spinning bit. Then I feed the stock from right to left.

10-3 When the right-hand layout line is over the left-hand mark on the tape, I stop the cut.

10-4 With my biscuit joiner, I cut biscuit slots in the side-frame stiles and rails. Here I'm slotting the end of the upper rail.

cut" by lowering the stile on the spinning bit (*photo 10-2*). Then I feed the stock from right to left, carefully lifting the stile up off the bit when the middle-rail layout line is over the left-hand mark on the tape (*photo 10-3*). I start the next groove with the second middle-rail layout line over the right-hand mark on the tape, feeding the stock from right to left until the bottom-rail layout line is over the left-hand tape mark. The principle is the same for all 4 stiles.

With all the panel grooves completed, I'm ready to cut the biscuit slots in the stiles and rails (*drawing 10-B*). With my biscuit joiner set for #20 biscuits, I cut slots in the upper and lower rails and matching slots in the stiles, lining up the index mark on the biscuit joiner with my biscuit marks on the stiles and rails (*photo 10-4*). The narrow middle rails need a tiny #0 biscuit, so I reset my biscuit joiner for a #0 slot. I cut biscuit slots in both ends of the middle rails and cut matching slots in the stiles.

Making the Panels

The 4 side panels come next. I run an 8-ft-long 1 × 12 through my thickness planer, taking it down to a 1/2-in. thickness. Then I cross-cut it into 4 equal pieces approximately 2 ft long (see Project Planner). I joint one edge of each panel blank straight and square, then rip each piece 11¼ in. wide. With a panel cutter on my table saw, I

10-5 In order for the 1/2-in.-thick side panels to fit into the frame grooves, I have to mill a rabbet around all 4 edges. The wooden fence screwed to the rip fence allows me to cover up part of the dado head to adjust the width of the rabbet.

10-6 I use a handsaw to taper the bottom ends of the stiles. I leave the layout line on the stock as I cut.

square up one end of each panel, measure off 22⅝ in., and cut the panels to length (*drawing 10-B*).

In order for the panels to fit in the frame grooves, I have to mill a rabbet around the edges of the panels (*side panel detail and photo 10-5*). I do this on the table saw. I set up my stack dado head for a 1/2-in.-wide cut and screw a wooden auxiliary fence to the table saw's rip fence. I raise the dado head 1/4 in. above the table and then move the wooden fence over the dado head, exposing only 3/8 in. of the cutter. Then I run a sample and make adjustments, if necessary, to mill a rabbet that's 3/8 in. wide and 1/4 in. deep. When the setting's right, I mill a rabbet on all 4 edges of each panel, making sure to keep the best-looking side of each panel facing up on the saw.

The bottoms of the stiles have a slight taper that's mostly for looks (*drawings 10-A and 10-B*). I lay out the tapers on the bottom ends of the stiles and make the cuts with a handsaw (*photo 10-6*). I leave the layout line on the stock when I cut. Next, with a block plane, I clean up the saw cuts, planing right to the line.

Now I finish sand both sides of the panels with my random orbit sander. It's easier to do this now, before the frames are assembled.

Assembling the Side Frames

Now I'm ready for some assembly. First, I nip the ends off four #0 biscuits and set them aside for the middle-rail joints (the biscuits are too long otherwise). Working on one side at a time, I place a stile edge-up on my bench and spread glue where the 3 rails will go. Some glue in the biscuit slots, a bit more on the biscuits, and I pop the biscuits into their slots in the stiles.

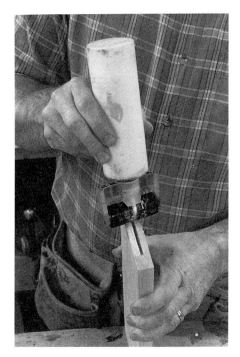

10-7 Speed is important when gluing up with biscuits. Work too slowly and the biscuits will swell from the glue, making alignment of the joints very difficult. Tools like this glue spreader help speed the process of spreading glue on stiles and rails.

Working quickly, before the glue sets, I roll glue on the rail ends (*photo 10-7*) and brush glue in the slots and slip the 3 rails in place on the stile. The panels come next and they slide into their grooves without any glue (*photo 10-8*). Next, I glue biscuits in the rail ends, spread some glue on the stile, and install the other stile. I make sure that the rails are aligned with my layout lines and then put a clamp across each joint (*photo 10-9*). I check the frames for square by measuring across the diagonals from corner to corner. If the frame is square, both diagonals will be exactly the same. If not, I loosen the clamps, tap the frame back into square, and retighten the clamps. I also wipe off any excess glue squeeze-out in the area of the panels, and I make sure the panels are centered on the inside. Then I put the other frame together and set them both aside to dry.

Drawer Frames and Top Frame

The sides of the pie safe are connected by 3 horizontal frames (*drawing 10-A*). The top frame (*drawing 10-C*) prevents the upper drawers from tipping out when they're opened. The top of the pie safe is also screwed to this frame. The 2, small upper drawers of the pie safe ride on the upper-drawer frame (*drawing 10-D*). The wide, lower drawer rides on the lower-drawer frame (*drawing 10-E*).

All 3 frames are cut from 1 × 6 pine (see Project Planner) and joined with biscuits. With the frame parts ripped and jointed to width, I square up one end of each piece on my power miter box and cut the frame parts to the lengths specified in drawings 10-C, 10-D, and 10-E.

I lay the frame parts out on the bench and mark the locations of the biscuit slots and the location of the rails. Then I cut the slots with my biscuit joiner and assemble the frames with biscuits, glue, and clamps. I set the 3 frames aside to dry while I work on the doors.

10-8 I put the side frames together with glue and biscuits and slip the panels into their grooves (no glue here). Then I put on the opposite stile.

10-9 When the side frame's assembled, I make sure the rails are aligned with my layout lines and then put a clamp across each joint.

10-C Top Frame

Note: All frame joints are reinforced with glue and biscuits.

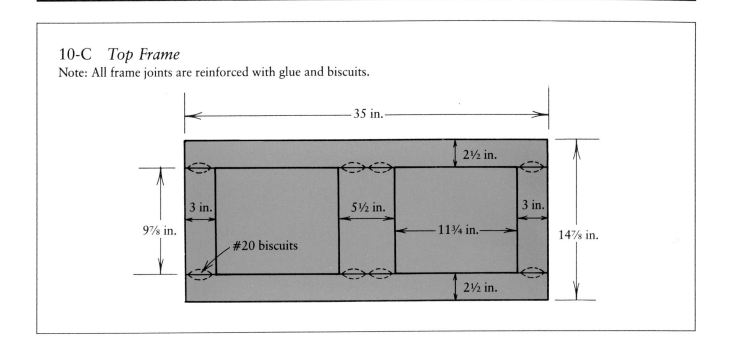

35 in.

9⅞ in.

3 in.

5½ in.

2½ in.

11¾ in.

3 in.

14⅞ in.

2½ in.

#20 biscuits

10-D Upper-Drawer Frame

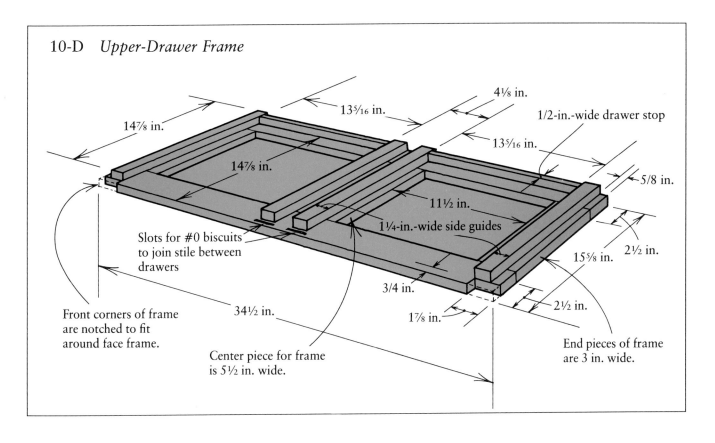

14⅞ in.

13⁵⁄₁₆ in.

4⅛ in.

1/2-in.-wide drawer stop

13⁵⁄₁₆ in.

5/8 in.

14⅞ in.

11½ in.

1¼-in.-wide side guides

2½ in.

Slots for #0 biscuits
to join stile between
drawers

3/4 in.

15⅝ in.

2½ in.

Front corners of frame
are notched to fit
around face frame.

34½ in.

Center piece for frame
is 5½ in. wide.

1⅞ in.

End pieces of frame
are 3 in. wide.

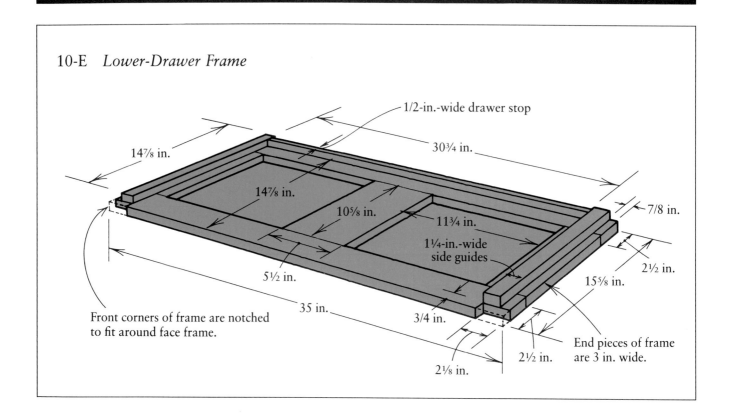

10-E *Lower-Drawer Frame*

1/2-in.-wide drawer stop

14⅞ in.

30¾ in.

14⅞ in.

10⅝ in.

11¾ in.

1¼-in.-wide side guides

7/8 in.

2½ in.

5½ in.

15⅝ in.

35 in.

3/4 in.

Front corners of frame are notched to fit around face frame.

2½ in.

End pieces of frame are 3 in. wide.

2⅛ in.

Door Frames

The doors of the pie safe consist of a frame with 2 stiles and 4 rails joined with biscuits (*drawing 10-F*). The frame parts are rabbeted for the tin panels after they're glued together.

I cut the stiles and rails from 1 × 10 pine (see Project Planner), then rip and joint them to width (*drawing 10-F*). Both the stiles and the rails are 2 in wide. Then, I square up one end of each piece on my power miter box and cut the parts to length. The stiles are all 38½ in. long and the rails are 11¼ in. long.

With the parts cut to size, I lay them out on my bench and draw a line across each joint to mark the centers of the biscuit slots and the location of the rails. Each joint gets a #0 biscuit, and I cut the slots with my biscuit joiner. I assemble the door frames with biscuits, glue, and clamps and check them for square by measuring the diagonals (*photo 10-10*). Then I set them aside to dry.

Punching the Tin Panels

While all the frames are drying in the clamps, I turn my attention to the tin panels. The "low-grade black tin" I bought for the panels had a few spots of rust scattered here and there — just the effect I want. The sheets of tin I bought are larger than I need, so the first order of business is to cut the individual panels to size — 10¾ in. high by 11⅞ in. wide. It's nearly impossible to make long straight cuts with a tin snips. The edges get ragged and the tin always curls. I figured out a better technique. I score the tin with a sharp utility knife by guid-

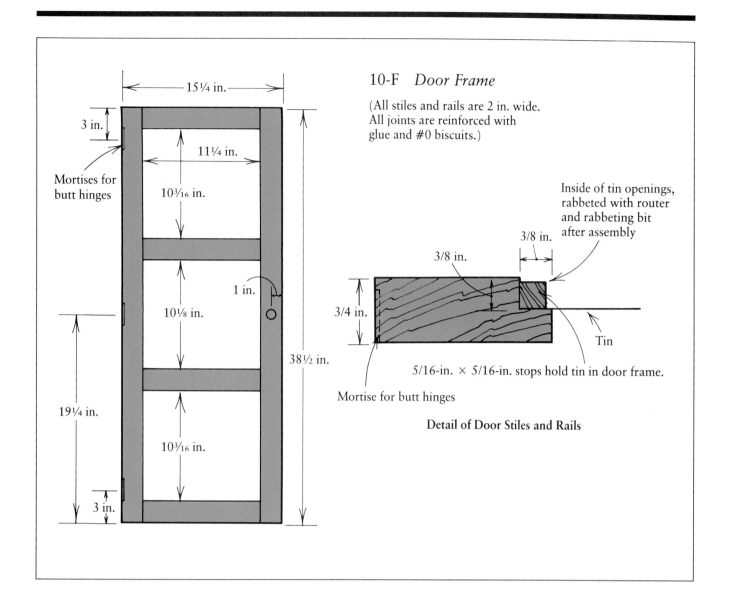

10-F *Door Frame*

(All stiles and rails are 2 in. wide. All joints are reinforced with glue and #0 biscuits.)

15¼ in.

3 in.

Mortises for butt hinges

11¼ in.

10³⁄₁₆ in.

10⅛ in.

1 in.

38½ in.

19¼ in.

10³⁄₁₆ in.

3 in.

Inside of tin openings, rabbeted with router and rabbeting bit after assembly

3/8 in.

3/8 in.

3/4 in.

Tin

Mortise for butt hinges

5/16-in. × 5/16-in. stops hold tin in door frame.

Detail of Door Stiles and Rails

10-10 To check a frame for square, I measure diagonally, from corner to corner. If the frame is square, the measurements will be exactly the same. If one diagonal is longer than the other, I loosen the clamps and tap the frame into square.

10-11 I use a utility knife to cut the tin for the panels. Guiding the blade against a framing square, I make 6 or 7 passes to score the tin.

10-12 After scoring the tin, I bend the sheet back and forth until the metal fatigues and shears on the score line.

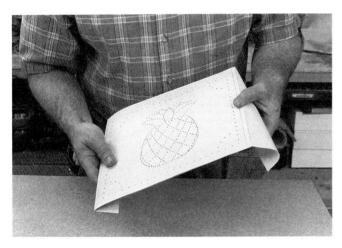

10-13 Each tin panel requires a fresh paper pattern. I make 11-in. by 17-in. photocopies of the pineapple pattern and fold the ends back over the tin to hold the pattern in place.

10-14 On my workbench, I set up a station to punch the tin. It's a sheet of particleboard to protect the benchtop. I clamp the tin panel and the pattern down tight with some angle irons screwed to the particleboard. Pieces of wood would also work fine.

ing the knife against the edge of a framing square and making 6 or 7 passes (*photo 10-11*). Then I bend the tin back and forth until it shears along the score line (*photo 10-12*). I get a clean, straight cut.

Now for the pattern. When I read up on pie safes, I learned that the tin-panel designs on old pie safes were often based on quilt patterns or butter-mold patterns. I thumbed through some quilt books for ideas, then sketched out a pineapple design that had the right look (*drawing 10-G*). I guess you could call it an "Abram Original." You might want to come up with a design of your own. I sat down at my drawing board and made a full-size drawing of the pineapple and border. Then I took a felt-tip pen and put a dot everywhere I wanted a punch mark. Then I made six full-size photocopies of the pattern on a copying machine that handles 11-in. by 17-in. paper. Because I punch right through the pattern, I need a separate paper pattern for each panel. (The pineapple pattern in drawing 10-G is 60 percent of the original size. Take the pattern to a local copy shop and ask them to enlarge the drawing to 10¾ in. by 11⅞ in. to make a full-size pattern.)

On my workbench, I set up a station to punch the panels. It's just a piece of particleboard to protect the bench top from the punch. Hardboard or void-free plywood would also work fine. I fold the ends of the pattern around the back of a panel to hold it in place (*photo 10-13*) and then clamp the panel and pattern down tight with a couple of pieces of angle iron screwed to the particleboard (*photo 10-14*). Pieces of wood would work just a well.

The punching tool couldn't be simpler — it's just a scratch awl that I hit with a hammer (*photo 10-15*). It's a good idea to practice punching on a scrap piece of tin because the diameter of the hole depends on how hard you strike the awl. I shoot for a hole diameter of about 1/16 in. Punching the holes takes a lot of time, but it sure is fun. When the holes are all punched, I unscrew the angle irons and remove the panel from the work station. Punching makes the panel curl slightly and I flatten it out by gently rolling it back into shape with my hands (*photo 10-16*). Five more panels to go . . . I better keep punching.

10-15   The punching tool is just a scratch awl that I strike with a hammer. The force of the strike determines the hole diameter. I try for a 1/16-in.-diameter hole. I make a punch on each dot in the pattern — 450 holes for each panel!

10-16   Punching tends to curl the tin. I straighten the panel by gently rolling it back into shape with my hands.

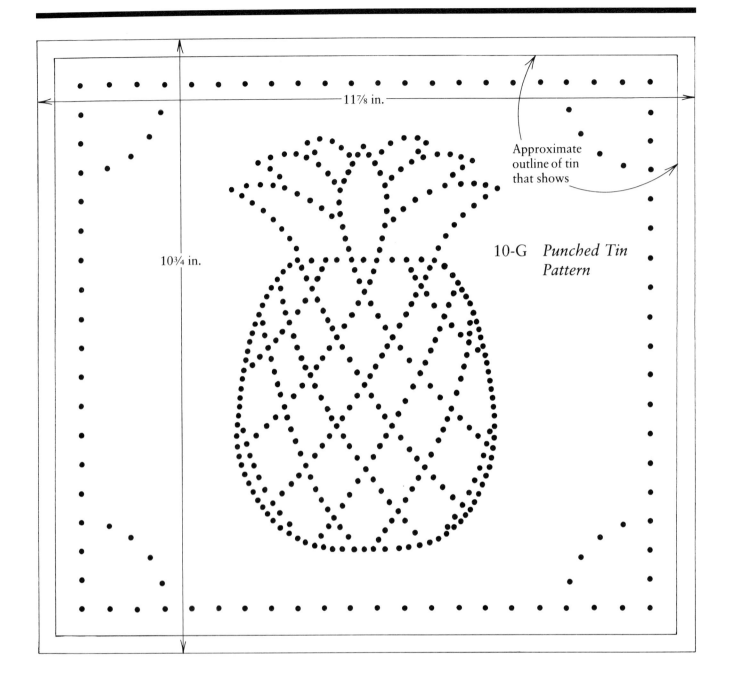

11⅞ in.

10¾ in.

Approximate
outline of tin
that shows

10-G *Punched Tin
Pattern*

With the panels completed, it's back to the woodworking. By now, the frames are all dry so I remove all the clamps, scrape off the excess glue with my paint scraper, and sand all the frames smooth with my random orbit sander.

Completing the Side Panels and Horizontal Frames

The top frame and the lower-drawer frame fit into 3/4-in.-wide dadoes milled in the sides of the carcass (*drawing 10-H*). I mill these dadoes on my table saw with a stack dado head set for a 3/4-in.-wide cut. I adjust the height to cut a dado that's 1/4 in. deep.

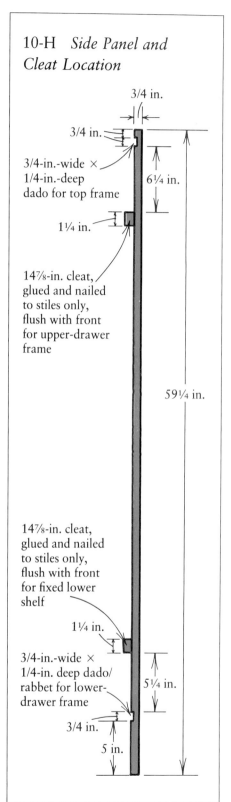

10-H *Side Panel and Cleat Location*

3/4 in.

3/4 in.

3/4-in.-wide ×
1/4-in.-deep
dado for top frame

6¼ in.

1¼ in.

14⅞-in. cleat,
glued and nailed
to stiles only,
flush with front
for upper-drawer
frame

59¼ in.

14⅞-in. cleat,
glued and nailed
to stiles only,
flush with front
for fixed lower
shelf

1¼ in.

3/4-in.-wide ×
1/4-in. deep dado/
rabbet for lower-
drawer frame

3/4 in.

5 in.

5¼ in.

10-17 The lower-drawer frame fits into dadoes in the sides of the pie safe. I mill these dadoes on the table saw, guiding the bottom of the side against the fence.

10-18 The upper-drawer frame and the fixed, plywood shelf are supported on 3/4-in. by 1¼-in. cleats glued and nailed to the insides of the pie-safe stiles. I hold the front ends of the cleats flush with the front ends of the sides.

I cut the dado for the top frame first. I position the rip fence 3/4 in. from the cutter and mill a dado on the inside face of both sides, keeping the top of the side against the rip fence. Then I reposition the rip fence 5 in. from the cutter to mill the dado for the lower-drawer support. This time I guide the bottom of each side against the rip fence (*photo 10-17*).

There's one more milling operation to perform on the sides. I have to mill a 3/8-in. by 3/8-in. rabbet along the inside back edges for the 1/4-in. plywood back of the pie safe (*drawing 10-B*). With the wooden fence attached to my rip fence, I position the fence to cover up all but 3/8 in. of the dado head. Then I adjust the height of the cutter to 3/8 in. and mill a sample to check the setting. Finally, I mill a rabbet along the back edges, making sure that I cut them on the inside of each panel.

Next, I install the 3/4-in. by 1¼-in. by 14⅞-in. cleats that support the upper-drawer frame and the fixed shelf (*drawing 10-H*). I mark off the locations for these cleats on the inside of the carcass sides. I hold the front ends of the cleats flush with the front edge of the sides and then glue and nail them to the inside of the side-frame stiles only (*photo 10-18*).

10-19 I glue and nail drawer guides to the drawer-support frames. The upper-drawer frame (shown here) gets 4 of these guides. Once the guides are in place, I glue and nail 1/2-in. by 3/4-in. drawer stops in between the side guides at the back edge of the frame.

There are a few more parts to go on the upper- and lower-drawer frames before I'm ready to put the carcass together. I glue and nail two 3/4-in. by 1¼-in. by 14⅞-in. side guides to the lower-drawer frame, setting the guides in 7/8 in. from the ends of the frame and holding the back ends of the guides flush with the back edge of the frame (See Project Planner and *drawing 10-E*). The upper-drawer frame gets four of these guides. I set the two outer guides in 5/8 in. from the ends of the frame, holding the back ends flush with the back edge just as I did with the lower-drawer frame (*drawing 10-D*). The inner guides are positioned 13⁵/₁₆ in. from the 2 outer guides, as shown in the drawing.

Once the side guides are in place, I glue and nail a 1/2-in. by 3/4-in. by 30¾-in. drawer stop in between the 2 guides on the lower-drawer frame (*drawing 10-E*). On the upper-drawer frame, I glue and nail two 1/2-in. by 3/4-in. by 13⁵/₁₆-in. drawer stops in between the side guides (*drawing 10-D and photo 10-19*). That completes the drawer frames.

Making the Shelves

The shelves are all cut from 3/4-in. birch-veneer plywood (see Project Planner and *drawing 10-I*). I do this on my table saw with a panel cutter to ensure that the cuts will be square. The fixed shelf blank (without the edging) measures 14½ in. wide by 34½ in. long. The 2 adjustable shelf blanks are 14 in. wide and 33⅝ in. long.

With the shelves cut to size, I install a strip of pine edging on the front of each shelf to cover the edge of the plywood (see Project Planner). The 2 adjustable shelves get a 3/4-in. by 1-in. strip. I glue these strips to the edges, holding the top edge flush with the top of the shelf, and fasten them with some 4d finish nails (*drawing 10-I*,

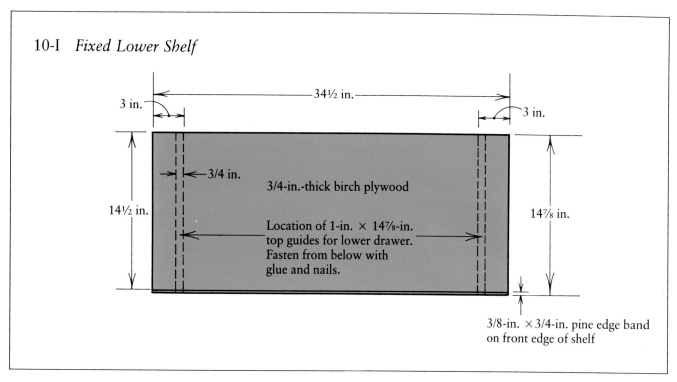

10-I *Fixed Lower Shelf*

34½ in.

3 in.   3 in.

3/4 in.

3/4-in.-thick birch plywood

14½ in.

14⅞ in.

Location of 1-in. × 14⅞-in. top guides for lower drawer. Fasten from below with glue and nails.

3/8-in. × 3/4-in. pine edge band on front edge of shelf

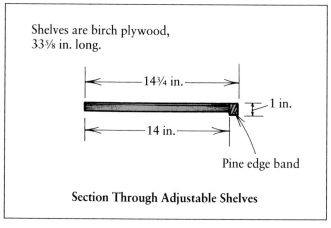

Shelves are birch plywood, 33⅝ in. long.

14¾ in.

1 in.

14 in.

Pine edge band

Section Through Adjustable Shelves

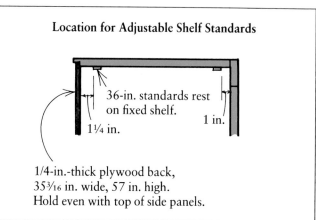

Location for Adjustable Shelf Standards

36-in. standards rest on fixed shelf.

1¼ in.   1 in.

1/4-in.-thick plywood back, 35³⁄₁₆ in. wide, 57 in. high. Hold even with top of side panels.

detail). The fixed, bottom shelf gets a 3/8-in. by 3/4-in. strip glued and nailed to the front edge with 1-in. brads (*drawing 10-I*). With the strips nailed in place, I finish sand the shelves with my random orbit sander.

There's one more thing to do to the bottom shelf before I assemble the carcass. I install two 3/4-in. by 1-in. by 14½-in. top guides to the underside of the shelf, to keep the lower drawer from tipping when it's pulled out (*drawing 10-I*). These guides are glued and nailed to the underside of the shelf, 3 in. in from each end.

Assembling the Carcass

Now I'm ready to assemble the carcass. I place one of the carcass sides on my workbench with the inside facing up. First, I install the upper-drawer frame to the cleat. I brush glue along the top edge of

10-20 I assemble the carcass on my bench, gluing the frames in one by one. I slide the end of the side far enough off the workbench for me to get underneath it to nail through the dado and into the frame. I used the same procedure to nail the top frame in its dado.

the cleat and the corresponding edge of the drawer frame and put the frame in place, making sure that the drawer stops on the frame are facing the back stile (the one with the rabbet). I hold the back edge of the frame flush with the rabbet in the stile (the front edge will project beyond the front of the stile). With a large spring clamp, I hold the frame tight against the cleat while I screw it in place with some 1⅝-in. bugle-head screws, screwing through the frame and into the cleat.

The top frame comes next. I brush glue in the dado and one end of the frame. I place the frame in the dado, align the back edge with the rabbet in the stile, and nail it in place with some 4d finish nails. I slide the end of the pie-safe side far enough off the workbench that I can nail into the top frame from underneath.

Now for the fixed bottom shelf. This one gets glued to the cleat near the bottom and nailed in place with 4d finish nails. Here, too, I align the back edge with the rabbet in the back edge of the stile.

The lower-drawer frame goes in last. I put glue in the dado — a little more on the rail end — and align the back edge of the frame with the rabbet. Then I nail it in place by sliding the end of the side off the bench just enough to get under it. The front of this frame will protrude beyond the front edge of the stile just as the upper-drawer frame did (*photo 10-20*).

Now I'm ready to put on the other side of the pie safe. I glue and screw the upper-drawer frame to the cleat and glue and nail the top frame, lower-drawer frame, and fixed shelf in place.

The 1/4-in. plywood back goes on next. In the planning stages of this project, I cut the back to its final dimensions (35³/₁₆ in. by 57 in.) on my table saw (see Project Planner and *drawing 10-I*). Now I turn the carcass facedown on my bench and measure across the rabbets to make sure that the panel will fit — in this case, I'm right on the money.

I brush glue on the back edges of the shelf and the frames and along the rabbets in the back edges of the stiles. Then I put the back panel in place. Holding the top edge flush with the top ends of the stiles, I tack it in place with some 1-in. brads, nailing into the rabbets and the back edges of the shelf and the frames.

Face Frame

I turn the carcass over so the front is facing up on the bench in order to install the face frame on the front of the pie safe. There are several things I need to do first.

In the planning stages of the project, I cut the face-frame parts from 1 × 6 pine and then ripped and jointed the 2⅝-in.-wide stiles and 1½-in.-wide rails to width (see Project Planner). Now I square up one end on my miter box and cut the face-frame parts to length — 59¼ in. for the stiles (*drawing 10-J*). I also cut to length the center stile that fits between the 2 upper drawers. This 4⅛-in.-wide stile is 5½ in. long (*drawing 10-J*). Before I cut the 2 rails to length, I measure across the front of the carcass to make sure that it's exactly 36 in. across the front. If it's slightly more or less, I make the rails a little longer or shorter as needed to fit between the stiles.

I lay all these parts out so I can mark where the rails join the stiles and also mark the locations of the biscuit slots (*drawing 10-J*). Then, with my biscuit joiner, I cut slots in the face-frame stiles, the ends of the 2 rails, the ends of the stile between the drawers (2 biscuits in each end), and the underside of the top rail where the middle stile joins. The bottom end of this middle stile joins the top of the upper-drawer frame (*drawing 10-A*). I also cut 2 biscuit slots in the upper-drawer frame where the stile will join.

It's easier to cut the mortises for the door hinges now, before the face frame's installed. As I've done several times in other projects in this book, I rout the mortises with a mortising jig and a guide collar in my router. The mortising jig is just a piece of 3/4-in. plywood with a rectangular cutout in one edge that's 1/16 in. larger all around

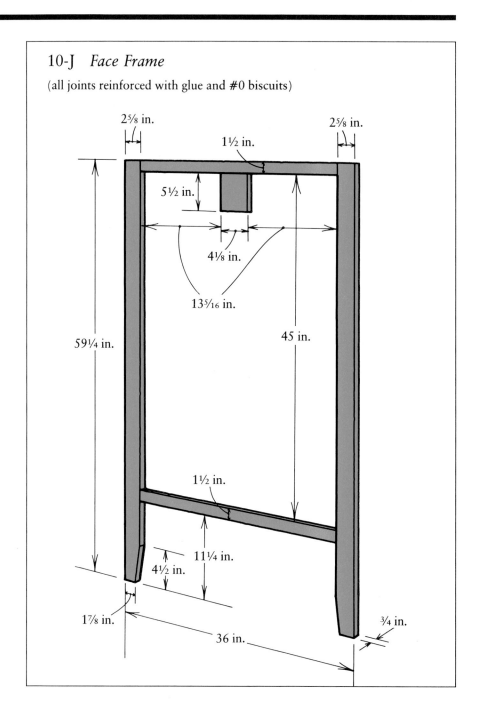

10-J *Face Frame*

(all joints reinforced with glue and #0 biscuits)

2⁵⁄₈ in.

2⁵⁄₈ in.

1½ in.

5½ in.

4⅛ in.

13⁵⁄₁₆ in.

59¼ in.

45 in.

1½ in.

11¼ in.

4½ in.

1⅞ in.

36 in.

¾ in.

than the mortise I want to cut. Wooden strips tacked to this edge of the jig act as an edge guide to align the jig with the edge of the stock.

To use the jig, I clamp the stile in my vise and lay out a centerline for all 3 hinges (*drawing 10-F*). Then I slide the jig up against the front face of the stile, line up the centerline on the jig's cutout with my layout mark, and clamp the jig in place. I set up my router with a 5/8-in. O.D. guide collar and a 1/2-in.-diameter straight bit and set the depth of cut to the thickness of the hinge leaf. Then I rout the hinge mortise, guiding the collar around the inside of the cutout. Then I square up the corners with a chisel. When I've finished the first stile, I rout the mortises in the other face-frame stile.

The bottom ends of the face-frame stiles are tapered to match the side stiles (*drawings 10-A and 10-J*). I lay out and cut these tapers just as I did for the side stiles, making the cuts with a handsaw and planing to the layout line with a block plane.

Before I can install the face frame on the carcass, I have to notch the corners of the upper- and lower-drawer frames for the face-frame stiles (*drawings 10-D and 10-E*). With a square and a pencil, I mark off a 3/4-in. by 2⅝-in. notch (measuring from the outside of the pie-safe side) and cut out these notches with a small backsaw (*photo 10-21*).

At last I'm ready to install the face frame. The left-hand stile goes on first. I spread glue on the front edge of the side stile and in the notches I cut in the drawer frames. I put the stile in position and nail it in place with some 4d finish nails (*photo 10-22*).

Next, I install the lower face-frame rail. I spread glue along the bottom, front edge of the fixed shelf and glue a biscuit in the stile.

10-22 I assemble the face frame one piece at a time. First, I glue and nail the left-hand stile to the front of the carcass.

10-23 Next, I put glue and a biscuit in the stile, spread some glue on the lower edge of the fixed shelf, and put the lower rail in place. I hold the top edge 1/4 in. below the top of the shelf and nail it to the shelf. The shelf edge acts as a stop for the doors.

10-24 I put glue and 2 biscuits in the top of the upper-drawer frame and slip on the center stile that goes between the upper drawers. Two more biscuits in the top end of the stile and I slip the upper rail in place over the center stile. I've also put glue and a biscuit in the stile to join the end of the upper rail.

Then I put a little glue on the rail end and slip the end over the biscuit. I hold the top edge 1/4 in. below the top edge of the shelf (*photo 10-23*). The edge of the shelf will act as a stop when the pie-safe doors are closed. Then I nail the rail to the edge of the shelf with 4d finish nails. I clean out the glue that squeezes out into the reveal area right away.

The center stile between the upper drawers goes on next. I glue 2 biscuits in the slots in the upper-drawer frame, spread some glue on the rail, and slip the lower end of the rail on the biscuits. The top rail goes on next, with glue and 2 biscuits to join it to the short center stile and a biscuit at the end to connect the end to the face-frame stile (*photo 10-24*). I nail this top rail to the edge of the top frame with 4d finish nails and clamp the short center stile in place.

When all these pieces are glued and nailed, I slip on the other face-frame stile with glue and biscuits in place. Finally, I nail this stile to the edge of the side stile with 4d finish nails.

After the glue is dry, I finish sand the face frame and sides with my random orbit sander. That about does it for the carcass. The only thing left is to put on the top.

Completing the Doors

After removing the clamps and scraping the dried glue off the doors, I rout hinge mortises in the edges of the stiles. So that the mortises line up with the ones in the face-frame stiles, I put the doors in position on the carcass and transfer the centermarks from the face-frame mortises to the edges of the doors.

I rout the door mortises just as I did the ones in the face-frame stiles. I clamp the door on edge in my vise, line up the centerline of the mortising jig with the centerline for the mortise, and clamp the jig in place. I repeat the procedure to rout 3 mortises in each door. Then I square up the rounded corners of the mortises with a chisel.

The next thing to do is to rout rabbets in the back of the door for the tin panels (*drawing 10-F, detail*). I set up my router with a 3/8-in. rabbeting bit and rout a 3/8-in. by 3/8-in. rabbet around the inside of the frame openings (*photo 10-25*). The bit leaves rounded corners and I square these up with a chisel (*photo 10-26*). Now I finish sand the doors, install the hinges, and hang the doors on the carcass. I'll install the tin panels after I finish the doors.

Installing the Top

The top is made of 1 × 6 pine, edge glued with biscuits (see Project Planner). After scraping off the glue and belt-sanding the panel smooth and flat, I joint one long edge and rip the other edge 17⅜ in. "strong." A pass on my jointer takes off the extra 1/32 in. of wood and gives me a final width of exactly 17⅜ in. Next, on my table saw, I use a panel cutter to square up one end of the top. Then I measure off 38¾ in. and cut the other end to length.

The top of the pie safe is screwed to the top frame. I drill 6 screw

10-25 The tin panels fit into 3/8-in. by 3/8-in. rabbets in the door frames. After scraping excess glue off the frames, I rout these rabbets with a 3/8-in. rabbeting bit.

10-26 The rabbeting bit leaves rounded corners on the door rabbets. I square these up with a chisel.

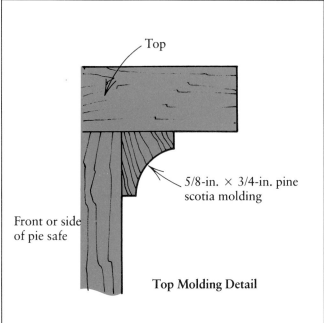

Top

5/8-in. × 3/4-in. pine
scotia molding

Front or side
of pie safe

Top Molding Detail

10-27 To dress up the top, I install
some pine scotia molding on the front
and the sides. I use my pneumatic nailer
to tack the molding in place with some
1-in. brads.

holes: one at each corner of the top frame and 2 on center, front and
back. I elongate these holes by rocking the drill back and forth parallel to the sides of the pie safe. These slotted holes allow the screws to
move so the top's free to expand and contract across the grain.

The top hangs over the sides and front of the carcass by about
1⅜ in. I position the top where I want it and screw it in place with
2-in. screws. I'm working in tight quarters inside the carcass, so I
have to install the screws with a stubby screwdriver.

To dress up the top, I install some pine scotia molding around the
underside of the top. I put on one sidepiece first, mitering the corner
on my power miter box. I tack the molding in place with some 1-in.
brads. The front piece goes on next, then the last sidepiece. I put a
little glue on the ends so the miters won't open up (*photo 10-27*).

Now I can finish sand the top with my random orbit sander. That
about does it for the pie-safe carcass.

Building the Drawers

The drawers of the pie safe are very simple to build. All 3 drawers
are constructed the same way. For this project, I thought I'd use an
alternative drawer-construction technique. The drawer fronts are
joined to the sides of the drawer with biscuits (*drawing 10-K*). The
drawers have an applied front that's screwed to the drawer box from
the inside of the drawer.

In the planning stages of this project, I cut out the drawer parts
from 1 × 6 pine and ripped and jointed them to a width of 5⅜ in.
(see Project Planner). Now I square up one end of each piece on my

10-K *Drawer Construction*

(all drawer stock 3/4 in. thick)

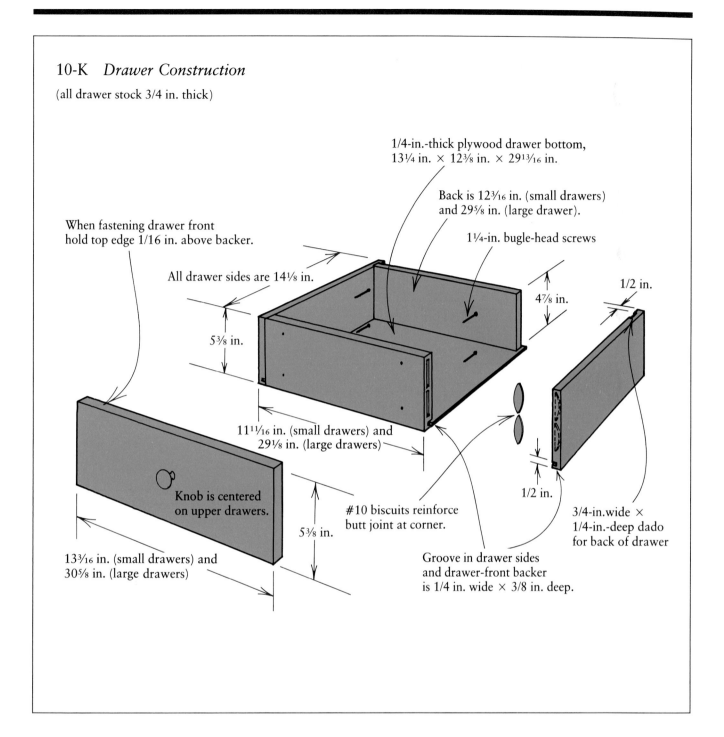

1/4-in.-thick plywood drawer bottom, 13¼ in. × 12⅜ in. × 29¹³⁄₁₆ in.

Back is 12³⁄₁₆ in. (small drawers) and 29⅝ in. (large drawer).

1¼-in. bugle-head screws

When fastening drawer front hold top edge 1/16 in. above backer.

All drawer sides are 14⅛ in.

5⅜ in.

4⅞ in.

1/2 in.

Knob is centered on upper drawers.

5⅜ in.

11¹¹⁄₁₆ in. (small drawers) and 29⅛ in. (large drawers)

1/2 in.

13³⁄₁₆ in. (small drawers) and 30⅝ in. (large drawers)

#10 biscuits reinforce butt joint at corner.

Groove in drawer sides and drawer-front backer is 1/4 in. wide × 3/8 in. deep.

3/4-in.wide × 1/4-in.-deep dado for back of drawer

miter box. Then I cut each piece to the finished length shown in drawing 10-K.

The 1/4-in. plywood bottoms fit into grooves in the drawer fronts and sides (*drawing 10-K*). I mill a 1/4-in.-wide by 3/8-in.-deep groove in the sides and fronts. I do this on my table saw with a dado head set for a 1/4-in. width. I raise the cutter 3/8 in. above the table and position the rip fence 1/4 in. from the cutter. Then I mill a groove on the inside of all 3 drawer-front backers and all 6 drawer sides.

10-28 Nothing fancy for the pie-safe drawers. Biscuits join the sides to the front. The 1/4-in. plywood bottom fits into grooves in the front and the sides. I use 4d finish nails to reinforce all the joints

10-29 After gluing up the drawer box, I clamp the applied drawer front in place and screw it to the drawer box from the inside.

The backs of the drawers fit into 3/4-in.-wide by 1/4-in.-deep dadoes in the drawer sides (*drawing 10-K*). I cut these dadoes with a stack dado head set for a 3/4-in.-wide cut.

So that all the drawer sides are exactly the same, I clamp a gauge block to my rip fence to locate the dadoes. The gauge block is just a piece of wood clamped to the table saw rip fence slightly forward of the blade (that is, toward the operator). I place a drawer side against the miter-gauge head and slide it to my right until the end stops against the gauge block. Then I move the miter gauge forward toward the blade to cut the dado. Moving the rip fence toward or away from the blade will change the location of the dado. When the wood contacts the cutter, the end should no longer be touching the gauge block. I position the fence and gauge block so the dado is 1/2 in. from the back end of the drawer side.

With the dadoes completed, I mark the locations of the biscuit slots in the drawer sides and drawer fronts. Each joint gets two #10 biscuits (*drawing 10-K*). I cut the slots with my biscuit joiner.

In the planning stages of the pie safe, I squared up the plywood drawer bottoms on my table saw (see Project Planner and *drawing 10-K*). The bottoms for the small drawers measure 12⅜ in. by 13¼ in. The bottom for the large, lower drawer measures 13¼ in. by 29¹³⁄₁₆ in. I like to orient the drawer bottoms so the grain of the plywood's face veneer runs across the width of the drawer.

With all the pieces ready to go, I sand them all smooth with my random orbit sander before I assemble the drawers. The procedure is the same for all 3 drawers. Working on one drawer at a time, I start by gluing biscuits in the slots and gluing the sides to the drawer front (*photo 10-28*). Then I spread glue in the dadoes and on the ends of the drawer back and put the back in place. I clamp the drawer together while I nail all the joints with some 4d finish nails. Then I take off the clamps, slide the plywood bottom in place (no glue) and tack it to the bottom edge of the drawer back with some 1-in. brads.

Finally, I screw the applied drawer fronts to the fronts of the drawer boxes with 1¼-in. bugle-head screws, installing the screws from inside the drawer (*photo 10-29*). I hold each drawer front in place with a clamp while I install the screws. The small drawers get 4 screws and the large drawer gets 6. I hold the top edge of each drawer front 1/16 in. above the top edge of the drawer box.

The drawer knobs come next. I drill 1/2-in.-diameter by 1/2-in.-deep holes in the drawer fronts and glue in the knobs. The tin and the rest of the hardware will go on later after I put on the finish. Before I move the pie safe into the finishing area, I go over it one more time with some 180- or 220-grit sandpaper and I'm ready to start staining.

Staining and Finishing

Staining pine can be tricky because of the grain. It tends to look blotchy with a dark stain and doesn't always look very good. I get good results on pine when I use a water-based stain and the following procedure.

I apply the stain with a brush, laying it on heavy, kind of like paint. I let the stain penetrate for a while and then wipe it with a rag that's been dampened with some stain. I dip the rag in some stain and rub the wood with the grain, evening out the stain by rubbing.

For the pie safe, I apply an "American Walnut" stain to all surfaces, inside and out, including the adjustable shelves that I'll install inside later. I also stain the knobs for the drawers and the 5/16-in.-square pine stop that will hold the tin panels in place (see Project Planner). I let the stain dry thoroughly and then brush on a coat of water-based satin-finish polyurethane, inside and out. When the polyurethane is dry, I sand lightly with 220-grit paper and apply a second coat.

When the finish is dry, I install the tin panels, holding them in place with the 5/16-in.-square pine stops. I butt joint the stop at the corners and fasten it to the door frames with 1-in. brads.

Then I install the magnetic catch on center beneath the upper-drawer frame. On the inside of the pie safe, I nail the 4 metal shelf standards to the sides (*drawing 10-A and drawing 10-I, detail*). The rear standards are located 1¼ in. from the back of the pie safe. The front standards are located 1 in. from the inside edges of the stiles. Next, I put the adjustable shelf clips where I want them and install the 2 adjustable shelves.

Now all I have to do is take my pie safe home from the shop and persuade someone to fill it full of pies. I think I know just who to talk to.

Index